207

pg. 1-8   194-207
92-104
109-116
122-134
155-182
135-190

THE COLOSSAL
P. T. BARNUM READER

THE COLOSSAL

P.T.Barnum
READER

NOTHING ELSE LIKE IT
IN THE UNIVERSE

PHINEAS T.
BARNUM

EDITED BY

James W. Cook

UNIVERSITY OF ILLINOIS PRESS

URBANA, CHICAGO & SPRINGFIELD

Library of Congress Cataloging-in-Publication Data
Barnum, P. T. (Phineas Taylor), 1810–1891.
The colossal P. T. Barnum reader :
nothing else like it in the universe /
Phineas T. Barnum ; edited by James W. Cook.
p.   cm.
Includes bibliographical references and index.
ISBN 978-0-252-03054-3 (cloth : alk. paper)
ISBN 978-0-252-07295-6 (paper : alk. paper)
1. Barnum, P. T. (Phineas Taylor), 1810–1891.
I. Cook, James W., 1966–   . II. Title.
GV1811.B3B37   2005
791.3'092–dc22 [B]   2005006666

Contents

Acknowledgments

The impetus for this reader was a series of conversations in 1998 with a fellow Barnum scholar, Terence Whalen, and Willis Regier, director of the University of Illinois Press. At the time, Whalen was finishing work on the first modern reprint edition of P. T. Barnum's 1855 autobiography for the Press and wanted suggestions of texts that might serve as useful supplements. These conversations led to the conclusion that the showman's six-decade career was simply too large, diverse, and interesting to fit into a short set of appendixes. Soon thereafter, I agreed to edit a full companion volume that would explore Barnum's multifaceted career beyond the autobiographies.

The project took somewhat longer to complete than I had anticipated, in part because the surviving sources are scattered in dozens of libraries, rare-book collections, and archives across the country, often in a chaotic jumble of uncataloged boxes and folders. The sheer travel time necessary for gathering a representative sample of documents was considerable.

In retrospect, though, the arduous process of tracking down and transcribing fugitive materials has been highly rewarding. Working on this book has taught me a great deal, for example, about how to conceptualize the rise of the modern culture industry (one of those academic catch phrases frequently invoked but rarely historicized). This project has also been beneficial for my teaching of U.S. cultural history. Despite the growing number of secondary studies on nineteenth-century popular culture, there are still very few primary document collections available. My hope is that this volume will help spark a new wave of edited collections and expose future generations of students to the rich diversity of the early "show trade."

✳

My first thanks go to the many libraries and archives that have preserved Barnum's extensive paper trail. These institutions include the New-York Historical Society, Museum of the City of New York, New York Public Library, Library of Congress, Bridgeport Public Library, Barnum Museum, American Antiquarian Society, Library Company of Philadelphia, Historical Society of Pennsylvania, Boston Athenaeum, Harvard Theatre Collection, Hertzberg Circus Collection, Parkinson Library and Research Center at the Circus World Museum, Shelburne Museum, Newberry Library, University of Minnesota Library Special Collections, Syracuse University Rare Books Division, British Library, William Clements Library at the University of Michigan, and University of Michigan Special Collections.

I owe an extra debt of gratitude to a pair of extraordinary reference librarians. David Smith of the New York Public Library helped me track down Barnum's *Adventures of an Adventurer,* one of the most elusive sources. His considerable skill and willingness to hunt for materials long designated as "lost" made the toughest research challenges genuinely exciting. John Barneson at the University of Minnesota Library kindly scanned large stacks of nineteenth-century newspapers.

For fellowship support, I am grateful to the American Antiquarian Society, Library Company of Philadelphia, Newberry Library, Gilder Lehrman Institute of U.S. History, and University of Michigan. The Office of the Vice President for Research at the University of Michigan also provided a publication subvention that helped defray some of the production and marketing costs.

Janet Davis, Martha Burns, Bluford Adams, Joshua Brown, and J. Stan Barrett generously shared photocopies from their own Barnum research. Their assistance made a "colossal" archival project more manageable. During this same period I served as a consultant for Josh's remarkable *Lost Museum* project (http://www.lostmuseum.cuny. edu). My thanks to Ann Fabian, Michael O'Malley, Roy Rosenzweig, Peter Buckley, Neil Harris, Ben Reiss, and the rest of the talented *Lost Museum* staff for stimulating discussions about Barnum's career.

My University of Michigan students in History 396, "The Emergence of U.S. Mass Culture," deserve a special word of thanks. Their clever insights and contagious excitement helped make this a better book. John Kasson and Janet Davis read the entire manuscript and offered many helpful suggestions. Willis G. Regier has been a terrific editor through the entire process. I am grateful for his invitation to serve as editor of this collection, as well as for his patience, enthusiasm, and good humor as the volume came to fruition. Carol Betts's exceptional copyediting improved the manuscript in numerous ways.

Finally, big thanks to Rita Chin and my parents for just about everything else.

The Architect of the Modern Culture Industry

James W. Cook

During his last British tour with the circus, Phineas Taylor Barnum (1810–91) liked to brag about the enormity of his own celebrity. Back home, he boasted, it was now unnecessary to put his name on the posters. The mere sight of his face was all the information the public needed. Barnum offered similar boasts about his impact on ticket sales: "I do not travel with the Show, but visit it a few times each season. Whenever my manager advertises that I am to be present, he estimates the increase in the receipts to be £ 200 per day." The showman's most intriguing anecdote involved a conversation with Ulysses S. Grant. It began with Barnum's speculation that the former president and Civil War hero must be "the best known American living." But Grant quickly corrected him: "You beat me sky-high, for wherever I went, in China, Japan, the Indies, &c., the constant inquiry was, 'Do you know Barnum?' I think, Barnum, you are the best known man in the world."[1]

These tales of celebrity from 1890 marked a turning point in the modern history of commercial entertainment. On one level, they documented a new type of fame–American made, mass produced, and globally distributed. Yet they also served as powerful evidence of what Barnum had accomplished over the previous six decades, when he created the first reserved seats; the first matinee shows; the first celebrity marketing campaigns; the first venues with national audiences; the first three-ring spectacles; and the first corporate models. It was Barnum, in other words, who built much of what scholars now call the "culture industry."[2] And by the end of the nineteenth century, this industry had grown to such a scale that one of its architects could boast of being the most famous man on earth.

Barnum was hardly alone, of course, in assembling the juggernaut. Even before he was born, Charles Willson Peale and Johann Maelzel offered popular curiosities for ambivalent republicans just learn-

FIGURE I

The man who modernized the show trade, Phineas Taylor Barnum,
shown during the middle portion of his career, 1855–65 (Library of
Congress, Prints and Photographs Division, reproduction number
LC-DIG-cwpbh-02176).

ing to let go of their theatrical prejudices.
T. D. Rice, George Catlin, and Isaac Van
Amburgh all made it to Europe faster. William Niblo and Moses Kimball catered to
new middle-class tastes with fewer mis-
steps. William F. Cody better understood
the power of spectacle to shape ideology.
Benjamin Keith and Edward Albee distributed variety shows to greater numbers of local markets.[3] Yet none of these
innovators really came close to matching

the Great Yankee Showman's durability,
range of products, or cumulative impact.
More than any other nineteenth-century
impresario, Barnum was the driving force
who transformed the show trade from a
set of vernacular traditions and local markets into a global industry.[4]

Readers interested in this remarkable
career have generally turned to one primary text: the showman's own autobiography.[5] First published in 1855 as *The Life of*

P. T. Barnum and then substantially revised in 1869 as *Struggles and Triumphs,* these volumes were among the era's best-selling memoirs. During the last two decades of his life, Barnum continued to revise their contents, adding new appendixes and issuing longer editions, one of which ran to well over eight hundred pages. The result was much more than a fascinating rags-to-riches tale. In telling the story of his own professional ascendancy, Barnum provided the nineteenth-century culture industry's most detailed record of capitalist expansion.

Yet the autobiographies are but one important piece of a much larger historical puzzle. Despite their considerable length, none of the editions is comprehensive.[6] *The Life of P. T. Barnum* ends a full decade and a half before the three-ring circus begins. And *Struggles and Triumphs* offers a remarkably sanitized version of events, often omitting or revising many of the showman's most embarrassing youthful transgressions. The most conspicuous example involves his professional debut—the 1835 Joice Heth exhibition—in which Barnum promoted an elderly African American woman as the 161-year-old former nursemaid to George Washington. During the early 1840s, the showman proudly claimed the hoax as his own, celebrating it as "one of the richest jokes ever played upon the public." By the mid-1860s, however, Barnum was one of the wealthiest businessmen in the United States and planning to run for national office. He therefore chose to dispense quickly with the "Heth Humbug" in *Struggles and Triumphs,* calling it "the least deserving of all my efforts." He even suggested that the scheme itself was "in no way of my devising."[7]

Such audacious revisionism demonstrates the necessity of reading Barnum comparatively, and with a keen sense of his larger marketing goals. To one degree or another, everything he ever published was a form of spin, an attempt to re-present himself and his products in ways that would appeal to his latest public. And this moving target traversed one of the era's broadest demographic spectrums: from rowdy mechanics and rural tourists to respectable merchants and foreign dignitaries. In some cases, heterogeneity in the exhibition hall required agile centrism on the page. Many of Barnum's writings, that is, aimed for and helped to define the cultural mainstream at a particular moment—its common tastes, curiosities, and prejudices. Yet the sheer volume and diversity of his cultural productions simultaneously created the need for a wide range of promotional strategies. As he knew from long experience, Bowery butchers and British royals required very different "puffs."[8]

What follows here is an anthology designed to track Barnum's shifting personas, representational choices, and publics across the nineteenth century. It is divided into five "galleries." The first highlights his serialized writings for two weekly newspapers: the *New York Atlas* and the *New York Mercury.* These writings include a semiautobiographical novella based on his exhibition debut (1841); his travelogues for the first European tour with Tom Thumb (1844–46); and his fascinating essays on promotional fraud (1864–65). The second gallery offers promotional materials for all of Barnum's most important exhibitions—from Joice Heth to Jumbo. The third gallery demonstrates his two-decade collaboration with Currier and Ives, the prominent New York lithographers. The central theme here is "wonders" (both human and animal), although the images say a great deal, too, about those standing in the audience. The fourth gallery provides an assortment of contemporary reviews designed to situate Barnum's exhibitions within the shifting tides of public opinion. The volume concludes with obituary commentary on the showman's historical legacy. In all of these selections, I have retained the original–and sometimes erratic–spelling and punctuation.

Collectively, these materials suggest a more complex Barnum than we have seen before: a moral reformer as well as a habitual hoaxer; an insightful critic as well as a savvy impresario; a master of images as well as an engaging writer; a relentless provocateur as well as a maker of family values. The documents also help clarify Barnum's relationship to what we now call mass culture. As Michael Kammen has argued, it is somewhat misleading to use this label for commercial forms produced before 1950, the pivotal moment when corporate chains, national markets, and simultaneous distribution became common features of the modern culture industry.[9] Yet, as Kammen himself acknowledges, the basic components of "massification" were beginning to take shape during Barnum's lifetime.[10]

Consider the question of distribution. For most of his career, Barnum worked at a particular site, the American Museum on lower Broadway or his circus offices in Bridgeport, Connecticut. Many of the products launched from these sites, however, circulated through much broader commercial geographies. They moved back and forth between contractual partnerships and interconnected networks of exhibition halls (as in the case of Tom Thumb). Or they traveled up and down the Eastern Seaboard on multicity tours (as in the case of Jenny Lind, the Swedish opera star). Or they followed the expansion of the transcontinental railroad and international shipping lines (as in the case of the three-ring circuses). Barnum's customers traveled, too, whether as part of doing business or to patronize entertainments that were themselves becoming tourist destinations.[11] And while the showman's career preceded newspapers of truly na-

tional scope, the press coverage for his shows was never merely local. As Barnum himself noted in *Struggles and Triumphs*, "newspapers throughout the country" began to copy his New York press releases during the early 1840s: "Thus was the fame of the Museum . . . wafted from one end of the land to the other. I was careful to keep up the excitement, for I knew that every dollar sown in advertising would return in tens, and perhaps hundreds, in a future harvest."[12]

The showman's role in transforming cultural consumption was similarly complex. Conventional scholarly wisdom suggests that Barnum engineered two basic modes of viewership: the early hoaxes, which fostered interactive decipherment and debate, and the later circuses, which dazzled increasingly passive, awestruck audiences.[13] This framework is useful, but there are a number of important wrinkles. Barnum's Feejee Mermaid exhibition of 1842, for example, would not have become the stuff of show business legend had it relied entirely on face-to-face debate. Part of what made the half-monkey/half-fish concoction different from many earlier amphibians on display was the mass-mediated character of the reception. While many viewers used the exhibition room as their primary site for assessing the mermaid's dubious authenticity, a much larger, secondary public participated from afar, analyzing conflicting reports through expanding networks of cheap periodicals that were themselves an innovation of the mid-1830s. In this way, the Feejee Mermaid helped to create both a new kind of audience (bound together by print sources) and a new mode of popular curiosity (perpetually excited, yet never fully satisfied).[14]

During the early 1870s, Barnum's circuses transformed cultural consumption once again, initiating what critics would

FIGURE 2

Lower Broadway viewed from Park Row, by Derpy after an 1850 drawing by August Kollner
(© Collection of the New-York Historical Society, neg. #61975). The American Museum
appears on the left; the Astor House, St. Paul's Church, and Mathew Brady's
Daguerreotype Gallery are on the right.

soon decry as "spectatoritis."[15] But even
the showman's largest three-ring extrav-
aganzas did not entirely supplant verbal
interaction with pure spectacle. More accurately, these vast entertainments offered
different modes of participation in adjoining spaces. While the big top inaugurated
a brave new world of anonymous crowds,
perceptual overload, and corporate sur-
plus, the sideshow maintained much older
carnivalesque rituals, such as the carney's
pitch and the intimate fascinations of the
anomalous body.[16]

Barnum, in short, never achieved mass
entertainment on the model we think of today: our Hollywood blockbusters that "open
everywhere."[17] But he did help to create these
cultural conditions. His was a public similar to those we now inhabit: multiregional,
heterosocial, and open to all ages; increasingly occularcentric yet never fully silent;
constructed by and through discourse; and
bound together by taste and habit as much
as profession or income. Somewhat paradoxically, the showman's quest for audience
expansion was often achieved reciprocally,

in relation to those who were left out of the socioeconomic amalgam. Barnum was a kind of innovator here, too. Although he priced his exhibitions low enough to attract many artisans and new immigrants, people at the bottom of the urban market economy generally could not afford twenty-five cents for an American Museum ticket, let alone three dollars to see Jenny Lind (worth about $5.50 and $70, respectively, in 2003 U.S. dollars).[18]

There were other gaps between the showman's egalitarian rhetoric and his desire to consolidate a respectable "family audience." In his more magnanimous moments, he liked to describe his public as just about everyone: the Universal Yankee Nation.[19] But in actual practice, Barnum's imagined community of happy consumers had clear limits and mechanisms of exclusion. During the late 1840s, for example, his widely advertised managerial reforms required patrons to give up their rougher consumption habits (such as drinking, smoking, and gambling) as a precondition of entry. He even hired a private security staff to enforce the new policies, bringing modern surveillance techniques into the traditionally volatile realm of popular amusement.[20]

Barnum's racial restrictions were still narrower. Before the Civil War, African Americans were admitted to the American Museum only at specially designated times. We know this because Barnum publicly advertised his racial rules in 1849, offering a one-day, five-hour window: "NOTICE TO PERSONS OF COLOR—In order to afford respectable colored persons an opportunity to witness the extraordinary attractions at present exhibited at the Museum, the Manager has determined to admit this class of people on Thursday morning next, March 1, from 8 A.M. till 1 P.M. Special performances in the Lecture Room at 11 o'clock." It is not entirely clear whether this notice represented an isolated event or the beginnings of a broader shift in the showman's policies. His newspaper ads during the 1850s made no mention of minority patronage, yet we know that Barnum encouraged segregated, off-site counterparts to some of his most successful exhibitions (e.g., the Grand National Baby Show). By the 1860s, one begins to find accounts of small numbers of African American patrons in the American Museum during normal operating hours.[21]

More certain is the fact that Barnum himself embodied many of the racial tensions and contradictions of his era. Although a strident critic of abolitionism during the 1830s and 1840s, he became increasingly sympathetic to antislavery in the years leading up to the Civil War. In 1865, he even ran for office as a Republican and proposed a universal manhood suffrage amendment to the Connecticut Constitution. Yet this dramatic political transformation seems to have had relatively little effect on Barnum's marketing choices. Even at the height of radical Reconstruction, he continued to promote brutally dehumanizing images of people of color on stage.

Barnum's relationship to the truth was similarly ambiguous. Popular legend suggests, of course, that Barnum was the progenitor of all show business tricksters. The materials in this volume will only bolster that reputation. A promotional pamphlet for the Joice Heth exhibition claims that she was the first person to "put clothes on the infant George Washington." The Feejee Mermaid pamphlet includes a bogus certificate of authenticity from "an eminent Professor of Natural History." And the pamphlet for one of Barnum's Circassian girls, Zobeide Luti, suggests she was saved from "the atrocities of a harem" by an American Museum employee.

None of these claims was even remotely true. But part of the reason we know this is because Barnum announced his own fraudulence with equal gusto. A month into his tour with Heth he took out anonymous press notices claiming she was a "machine made of India rubber," and to maintain public interest in the Feejee Mermaid, he secretly hired a rival showman to denounce it as a hoax. By the time Zobeide Luti made her debut in the late 1860s, such promotional tricks were largely unnecessary. As Barnum noted with growing annoyance, many patrons now regarded his most expensive and hard-to-find wonders as obvious fakes—even when they were fully genuine.[22] This was a way of doing business that produced cynics as well as suckers.[23]

Barnum's most dramatic impact, however, involved the expanding scope of his cultural production. Today, we often assume that the globalization of American entertainment began with twentieth-century cultural forms such as recorded music, film, and television. The documents in this collection suggest, however, that Barnum was thinking about overseas markets right from the start. We learn, for example, that he intended to take his very first exhibition to Europe in 1836, a plan that seems to have failed only because Heth died six months into the U.S. tour. In 1844, he tried again with Tom Thumb, launching a three-year campaign that covered much of the Continent. During the early 1870s, Barnum had acts in Cuba, Egypt, Hawaii, Australia, New Zealand, Malaysia, Japan, China, and the East Indies. By the 1880s, his circus agents sent back animals, peoples, and artifacts from virtually every corner of the globe.[24]

Barnum's career thus helps to clarify the intricate relationship between culture industry development and capitalist expansion. During the late 1830s, Barnum was an itinerant hawker hardly distinguishable

from his preindustrial forebears, often traveling by horse-drawn wagon. Less than a decade later, he had amassed enough capital in New York's burgeoning amusement markets to launch extended foreign tours (which in turn became purchasing sprees for his domestic venues). By the time of his death in 1891, Barnum's enterprises included a staff of thousands; separate publicity, advertising, and acquisitions departments; corporate mergers every few years; and brand recognition on four continents.[25] Historians have often noted that the United States' dominance in manufacturing preceded its military and political hegemony. Much the same, it turns out, can be said of the American show trade.

Not surprisingly, the most incisive critiques of such expansion came from foreign journalists. Some described Barnum as a new breed of imperialist, gobbling up national treasures with little regard for the concerns of local populations. Others complained that he lacked any semblance of taste or decorum, hawking his curiosities before royalty to increase their market value. Still others lamented that the shows themselves were beginning to resemble industrial production sites. As one English reviewer of the Barnum and Bailey Circus noted in 1889, "the spectator feels himself oppressed by the variety of efforts made for his entertainment. . . . He will perhaps be constrained to imagine himself in some vast factory, with its endless spindles and revolving shafts and pulleys."[26]

Even Barnum's toughest critics, however, usually acknowledged that commercial entertainment would never be the same. This uneasy mixture of scorn and respect is especially striking in the showman's 1891 obituary from the *Times* of London. For years, *Times* editors had complained loudly and often about the boorish Yankee from the land of wooden nutmegs. But looking back on it all, they could only conclude that Barnum represented one of modernity's defining features: "The chariot races and the monstrosities we can get anywhere, but the octogenarian showman was unique. His death removes a noteworthy figure from this amusing and crowded panorama of the nineteenth century; an almost classical figure, indeed, and a typical representative of the age of transparent puffing through which modern democracies are passing."[27]

Barnum's Serialized Writings

Most modern readers tend to think of Barnum's literary career as a minor sideline to his work as showman. Even those familiar with the autobiographies generally assume that they constituted the extent of his literary output. But in fact, Barnum published dozens of texts in a variety of genres. Some of these grew out of a new religious commitment or moral crusade (e.g., *Why I am a Universalist*). Others were attempts to repackage his entrepreneurial expertise as advice literature (e.g., *The Art of Money Getting*). The most important of Barnum's shorter writings appeared in two weekly newspapers, the *New York Atlas* and the *New York Mercury*. This body of work included a semiautobiographical novella, *The Adventures of an Adventurer* (1841); the travel letters known as the *European Correspondence* (1844–46); and a collection of essays entitled *Ancient and Modern Humbugs of the World* (1864–65).

Each of these series provides important new perspectives on the evolution of the modern culture industry. *Adventures* is the showman's earliest self-representation and the only one written before he was a star. The *European Correspondence* provides a week-by-week chronicle of his first international tour. *Ancient and Modern Humbugs of the World* addresses a basic question of nineteenth-century show business: how far could/should a promoter go in "puffing" his products? These texts are also distinguished by their mode of production. Because they were written as newspaper columns with regular weekly deadlines, many of the installments feel less carefully choreographed than the showman's books. There may be no such thing as an uncalculated public statement from the Prince of Humbug. Yet the serials enable us to see more of his day-to-day joys, frustrations, and gut reactions. Beyond the small numbers of surviving letters, this is about as close as one can get to Barnum unrehearsed.[1]

Gaining access to the serials, however, has proven enormously difficult in the past.

The tangled history of *Adventures* is a case in point. Barnum first published the novella in the *New York Atlas* between April 11 and July 4, 1841. The text then disappeared from view until 1989, when A. H. Saxon, a leading Barnum biographer, announced its rediscovery.[2] Subsequent studies offered deeper analyses of the novella's form and content but also pointed to an apparent impasse.[3] According to the best library records, there appeared to be no surviving issues of the *Atlas* from May 30 through August 15, 1841, which meant that scholars were left guessing about the novella's conclusion. The reappearance of the missing chapters in this volume owes to the correction of an old cataloging mistake.[4] During the 1920s, someone at the New York Public Library apparently mislabeled the *Atlas* and sent the key issues to storage, where they remained, forgotten and invisible, for almost a century.

This story points to one of the central challenges facing historians of the early culture industry. In their own day, periodicals such as the *Atlas* and *Mercury* were not hard to find. During the early 1840s, the *Atlas* boasted a circulation as large as that of any of the "Sunday sheets," with close to one hundred fifty purchase locations in Lower Manhattan alone.[5] The *Mercury* of the mid-1860s was even more ubiquitous, with a masthead claim of the largest weekly circulation in America.[6] Both papers, moreover, published some of the era's best-known authors. Barnum's writings for the *Atlas* appeared alongside urban sketches by Walt Whitman and Thomas Low Nichols. The *Mercury* likewise featured a large cast of pulp luminaries, including Ned Buntline (Edward Z. C. Judson), Pierce Egan, and Q. K. Philander Doesticks (Mortimer Neal Thompson). Why, then, have these urban weeklies become so scarce in modern library collections?

The answer probably begins with their content. The editors of the *Atlas* happily ignored moral reform causes such as temperance, sabbatarianism, and abolitionism—except, occasionally, to mock them. They devoted the bulk of their pages to serialized fiction understood as trashy even in its own day. And they offered extensive coverage of lowbrow amusements (e.g., blackface minstrelsy) typically shunned or ridiculed by more respectable papers. Gauging the readership for an antebellum periodical is a complex process, but there are some useful clues here. The *Atlas*'s list of purchase locations suggests an urban landscape of white-collar consumption that extended well beyond the boundaries of middle-class respectability—from Broadway concert halls and Bowery taverns to Chatham Street boardinghouses and Catherine Slip saloons. One suspects that early generations of archivists perceived the *Atlas* more as a chronicle of masculine misbehavior than as a worthy candidate for the accession list.

The *Mercury* of the mid-1860s was somewhat less rough and tumble. About half of the writers on the paper's "regular contributor force" were women, and the range of stories they generated points to an equally heterosocial readership. This was a periodical that covered ornamental gardening as well as fire department news, children's stories as well as murder trials. The *Mercury* thus provided an apt venue for a showman who had spent much of the previous decade reinventing himself as the nation's champion of "family amusement." Whereas Barnum made the amusement industry "innocent" enough to attract middle-class women and children, the editors of the *Mercury* offered formerly suspect activities such as blackface and boxing in a periodical marketed for "the morning breakfast table."[7]

In the end, though, these subtle distinctions of taste and decorum seem to have made little difference in the collections departments of twentieth-century libraries. More important, perhaps, was the fact that both the *Atlas* and the *Mercury* focused on local events and offered few illustrations (which probably made them less of a storage priority than competitors such as *Harper's Weekly* and *Frank Leslie's Newspaper*). And in retrospect, at least, the authorial rosters of the *Atlas* and *Mercury* share a common characteristic. With the exception of Whitman, no early contributor to either paper found his or her way into a twentieth-century literary canon.[8] By 1927, when Winifred Gregory's first edition of the *Union List of Serials* was published, both titles had largely disappeared from the shelves of American libraries. Only a very small number of incomplete runs survive today.[9]

SELECTIONS FROM
The Adventures Of An Adventurer: Being Some Passages In The Life Of Barnaby Diddleum (1841)

On June 14, 1840, the *New York Atlas* offered a brief notice about a coming attraction: "We shall shortly give a curious exposé of the Joyce Heth Humbug, one of the richest jokes ever played upon the public." A week later, the editors provided a more detailed explanation:

> We are now in possession of all the facts, documents, &c. connected with the origin, progress and termination of the exhibition of Joyce Heth, who was palmed upon the public with perfect success, as the nurse of Gen. Washington, aged 161 years! The truth is, she was not eighty years of age when she died, in 1836! The extra-ordinary developments and amusing, side-breaking anecdotes connected with this exhibition, illustrates the potent power of HUMBUG and the gullibility of mankind in a most eminent degree. We have the facts from the most authentic source and shall commence the publication in a week or two.[10]

This promise proved to be premature. At the very same moment, Barnum (the "authentic source" mentioned in the ad) was appointed director of amusement for New York's Vauxhall Gardens, a position that kept him busy for the rest of the summer. By early September, Barnum was out on the road, promoting a small troupe of dancers, musicians, and comics, from Buffalo to New Orleans. One imagines the young showman hauling his *Atlas* notes across the country, eager to deliver the exposé but unable to find much time to write. The inside story on the "Heth Humbug" remained his most valuable piece of literary capital. The question was how to cash it in.[11]

Barnum's answer finally arrived on April 11, 1841. It came in the form of a semi-autobiographical novella, *The Adventures of an Adventurer: Being Some Passages in the Life of Barnaby Diddleum*, which ran in the *Atlas* over the next twelve weeks. This somewhat crude attempt at picaresque fiction provides our clearest glimpse of the young showman as hunger artist. During the 1850s and 60s, Barnum wrote extensively about his early struggles, but he did so from a position of middle-aged confidence and affluence. *Adventures,* by contrast, is raw, scattered, and wickedly sarcastic. It is the work of an undercapitalized entrepreneur whose fledgling schemes had run into nothing but trouble over the previous four years.

Barnum's difficulties began with the Great Panic of 1837, a major recession that wiped out much of the New York amusement market.[12] Then Proler, his partner in a Bowery shoe-blacking business, fled to Europe, leaving him with little capital and a mountain of debt. Things picked up briefly when he tried his hand at one of Gotham's few recession-proof industries: blackface minstrelsy. But even this ultimately proved disappointing. As Barnum later explained, his most bankable talent of the early 1840s—an Irish American dance prodigy named John Diamond—had a distressing habit of "absconding" for better opportunities.

The few surviving documents from the period suggest a young impresario on the verge of collapse. Stuck in Mobile, Alabama, following one of Diamond's many disappearances, Barnum lashed out with a "circular letter" threatening lawsuits.[13] The breaking point seems to have come in March 1841, when he discovered one of his former employees successfully impersonating Diamond in Pittsburgh. Barnum quickly shut down this "trespass" on his livelihood with an onslaught of accusations in the papers. But the war of words cost him a day in the local jail.[14]

It is likely that Barnum began writing *Adventures* at just this moment, as he traveled home to New York from Pittsburgh on an Ohio River steamboat.[15] Significantly, Barnum's alter ego in *Adventures*, Barnaby Diddleum, conceives of the "Heth Humbug" in the very same setting. This chronology would also help to explain Barnaby's often rapacious approach to humbuggery. Following his failed western tour, Barnum was at rock bottom. He was mad at Diamond; mad at his competitors; mad at the dumb

luck of going into show business on the eve of a major recession. In the fictional world of literary satire, however, he could imagine alternative scenarios and outcomes. One can still hear the fits of sardonic laughter in some of Barnaby's monologues:

> Crown me with fame—erect a monument to my memory—decree me a Roman triumph—I deserve all—I stand alone—I have no equal, no rival—I am the king of Humbug—the king among princes. O, it is great, it is glorious—I chuckle now at the might of my sovereignty, the extent of my works, and laugh in ecstasy! . . . The enlightened, the ignorant, the lawyer, the student, the divine—young, old, virtuous, vicious—the good, the bad, and the indifferent, and over and above all, those immaculate men who sit in judgment over the world, the oracles of the press—the organs of the people, have been gulled by Barnaby Diddleum. Like the immortal Caesar I can say of the places I visited—*Veni vidi vici—ha! ha! ha!*[16]

It is important, though, not to push this compensatory reading too far. That Barnum never intended his swindling to be taken literally becomes clear in the opening lines of the story. His nom de plume, for example, is an obvious play on the word "diddle" (an antebellum slang term meaning "to fool" or "cheat").[17] In the pages that follow, Barnum returns again and again to an explicitly picaresque mode of address, invoking a wide range of conventional trickster tropes, such as the "cute Yankees" of northeastern folklore and the "half-horse/half-alligator" heroes of frontier fiction. Contemporary readers probably got the message. *Adventures* was close enough to real events to be billed as a "show business exposé." But it was also an explicitly tall tale full of audacious boasts and stretched truths. In Barnaby's terms, it was a humbug *about* humbug.

Recent scholarship has insightfully connected this picaresque voice to the values, tastes, and prejudices of the Jacksonian

PORTRAITS OF THE PEOPLE------NO. 62.

BARNABY DIDDLEUM.

FIGURE 3
_____

P. T. Barnum in the guise of "Barnaby Diddleum." This engraved portrait appeared in the *New York Atlas* alongside his serialized novella, *Adventures of an Adventurer* (1841).

Democracy. The abolitionists in Barnum's story appear as self-righteous dupes. The slaves shirk their labors and feign illness. The moral reformers are routinely hoodwinked or demonized. *Adventures,* in other words, was a satire specifically targeted for the Democratic milieu that populated the East Side taverns, dance halls, and boardinghouses where the *New York Atlas* was sold. More often than not, Barnaby's jokes come at the expense of northern Whigs and the moral crusades they championed.

Less well appreciated is the novella's deeply ambiguous portrayal of antebellum market relations. Much like the animal tricksters of folk tradition, Barnaby is an elusive shape-shifter who skirts a wide range of social and ethical boundaries.[18] His specific mode of transgression, however, continually reflects the poor market conditions and moral anxieties of the Panic years. Wholly indifferent to the welfare of his rivals and customers, Barnaby is at once a hero and antihero of early capitalism. He exemplifies the proudest achievements of the new market society (the proverbial "cunning" of northeastern entrepreneurs), even as he confirms its deepest fears (entrepreneurship taken to the point of megalomania and criminality).[19]

Adventures, then, was always about something much larger than one man's professional "struggles." By re-presenting his show business debut as a "rich joke" of predatory capitalism, Barnum left us a dark and deeply revealing report from the front lines of the American market revolution.

✳

The few editorial deletions from the following piece have been restricted to anecdotes with little bearing on Barnum's work as showman.

Chapter I

"Put money I' the purse."
–Shakespeare.

"John! Get money; honestly, if you can, but at all events get money."
–Old Man's Advice.

I was early impressed with the value of money, and the necessity of getting it. When a lad, I was considered extraordinarily smart, even for a Yankee, which is saying not a little. My friends, in consequence, I suppose, advised me to become editor and proprietor of the Northern Trust Banner.[20] I was doubtless urged to accept of the post, which is one of some distinction in a country place, where an editor is a "Sir Oracle" with all around, if not a little god, by a spice of vanity which is somehow or other mixed up in all natures, and which had well nigh kicked down my pail before I had milked my cow. I soon found that fame was all that I was likely to get, and that money, for which I thirsted from youth upwards, might walk out of my purse if I continued my avocation, but would by no possible means walk into it. My paper was founded on a system now nearly exploded–that of credit. If I looked into my books, I was unquestionably a rich man; if I felt in my pockets, they gave my books the lie direct. There was no agreement between them. My subscribers were numerous–they thought me a paragon. They gave me plenty of praise, but they gave me nothing else. They thought, perhaps, it was enough. I thought differently. So I sent fame to the winds, and my subscribers to the devil, and resolved to get into some new line of business.

In turning over my thoughts, I was something like the cat in the tripe shop, puzzled by which tempting morsel that presented itself to take. By the bye, the anecdote of Grimalkin is told of her disparagingly. It is thought by many that she was but a fool of a cat, and ought to have fallen to at once, and pounced upon the first mouthful that presented itself. I differ–I think the cat was perfectly right–she ought to be praised for her wisdom, rather than censored for her folly. She was doubtless considering which was the very best morsel in the room, and making up her mind accordingly. She might have thought one piece too fat, another too lean; one piece rather stale, and another somewhat tainted. I hold it to be a most admirable maxim, that all animals, whether men or cats, when they are "monarchs of all they survey," and have the power of choosing, should pause and deliberate, and select that which is likely to prove the most advantageous. Many money making schemes presented themselves to my view, dancing before my mind's eye like an air drawn dagger, and tempting me to clutch them. I thought of the great fortunes that had been made out of the head science, phrenology—of the still more splendid and Utopian science of animal magnetism, which, but for the difficulty of greasing the machinery, and making it run slick, would have turned the world topsy turvy, and I thought some good novel humbug, that smacked of the marvelous, that appealed to the imagination, that made faith, and plenty of it, a *sine qua non*, and that was spiced with science, or based upon it—for of all the humbugs with which the world has been humbugged since the serpent humbugged Eve, and Eve humbugged Adam, and all their sons and daughters have since humbugged each other, there is none so glorious, so radiant, as scientific humbug. The truly scientific are few, and a portion of these, in their remarkable thirst for discoveries, are apt to be led away by a plausible theory, and, by their approval, to give the base metal a current stamp. A still greater portion of those who pretend to be scientific, but who are asses in lions' skins, are sure to back anything which their wisdom cannot gainsay; and the mass who know nothing of science, and receive from the initiated, whether F.R.S.'s or A. double S.'s., matters in their peculiar line as gospel, are sure to fall into the trap, and approve most loudly—just as a man is sure to laugh more heartily than any body else at a joke which is pronounced to be devilishly good, but which is past his comprehension.[21]

Several schemes of the caliber of perpetual motion, and the discovery of the longitude, presented themselves to my imagination, but the fate of the Boston discoverer of go-it-iveness, and the unbelief that is attached to a self-believing to-be, discoverer of the longitude, somewhat deterred me. I was always impressed with the magnificent innovations of Sir Roswell Saltonstall, and the manner in which he snuffed out the Newtonian system. Fortunately for Newton, he died before this Daniel came to judgment. I liked his tomahawk cutting and slashing at the old science, and the beautiful simplicity of his orthography, and the mystification in which his discoveries were worked. But I detected that while this great man promised millions to those who would aid him, he could barely borrow half a dollar to purchase him a dinner, and that he was afterwards made the cruel sport and mockery of fellows who, in vulgar parlance, did not know beans, and so I thought I would not touch the Newtonian system. I finally gave up the idea for a time of starting a grand new scientific humbug. I have engendered in my brain a sort of nebulae which, when resolved into systems, will shine forth and astonish the natives. Those who don't understand my astronomical lingo, must suppose that I have a thousand little particles of scientific humbug in my cranium, which now form a chaotic matter, but which, in the course of time, will form themselves into something distinct and perfect. Think of me when some new and magnificent scientific theory is advanced.

A thousand sublunary schemes presented themselves to my imagination. Among the rest the ever memorable speculation then getting into ruinously fashionable vogue, the town and city lot speculation. I planned upon the top of the Rocky Mountains a magnificent city. I brought verdure out of the barren rock. I took a railroad up the side of the perpendicular mountain, and down the other side I carried a canal, navigable for ships of war. I raised loads of churches in this city, and fifty missionary depots for humanizing, civilizing, and christianizing the Indians. Judging from the manner in which such other speculations went off, I should have made a princely fortune out of the mercenary or pious gulls who would have been sure to have taken, but, I confess the soft impeachment, I was a young beginner in humbug, and this did appear to me to be such downright and damnable swindling, that hang me if I didn't turn away from it in right down earnest disgust. I know that there are a great many great men and great merchants in the city of New York who have thought differently, but those were my opinions at the time, and I was not remarkably squeamish either.

At last, I turned my thoughts to the stage. There was one person who pitched his or her voice one note higher than the majority of singers, and he or she coined money like dirt. Another woman could stand upon her toe, or elevate her wholly displayed leg as high as her head until scurrile jests were uttered upon her indelicately exposed person, and lo and behold she was run after by persons boasting of sense and refinement, and actually possessing wealth, who poured that wealth into her lap, while she made a pirouette, and doubtless, placing her finger to her nose, vanished, rejoicing in the capital which would shame the inheritance of many a principality in Europe, amassed here by the display of the anatomy of her person, which, if published as actually presented to every person in the pit of a theater, and to a portion of the boxes, would have caused the District Attorney to have indicted the publisher of such print as an indecent fellow; yet, to this display, virtuous women, by force of fashion, which I hope is an outrage upon their feelings, were taught to applaud. The humbug of exhibitions to please the *public taste* flashed fully upon me. This was the El Dorado of my hopes. I saw a Mexican mine of gold in it. I resolved to dig it. I immediately went to work, like a good general, whether male or female, who always should have two strings to the bow. I engaged an old superannuated negro woman, decrepit and infirm, and a very curious monkey,[22] and confiding the former to the care of a relative, set out with the latter on my adventures. I must reserve a description of the wench and of the monkey for the next chapter, when I shall commence giving passages from my journal,[23] for I kept a distinct record of each day's event. So "season your admiration for a while."

Chapter II

The negro wench, upon which I built my principle hopes of fortune, was a remarkably old looking animal, having been bed ridden for twelve years, and so wrinkled and shriveled and drawn up by disease, that her appearance indicated great longevity; but I made her look a great deal older. I extracted her teeth,[24] which caused her cheeks to sink in, and then I stated that she was the nurse of the immortal

George Washington and had for more than a century been a slave in the household of the Washington family–that the patriot had petted her, &c. I thought that the fame of such distinction would herald old Joyce above all negro wenches ever exhibited, and I was right, as will be seen in the sequel, wherein the manner in which I humbugged parsons, doctors, and even editors will be seen–but I must not anticipate.

My monkey was a smart monkey. The chief humbug I used with him was to state boldly that there never had been, there would be, and there never could be, such another extraordinary monkey in creation. If the public, in reading the bills had taken one monkey for the other, that is to say, me for the monkey, it would have been gospel truth.

In giving my adventures with the monkey, I may state generally that he was very successful, and brought me a great deal of money. I shall state some means that I adopted to make him draw, but shall give more particularly some adventures that occurred to myself in my travels.

JANUARY 3, 1836.–Every thing settled to start with the monkey in the morning. Went to church, but not with the monkey. Heard a sermon. The minister said that all sins committed were so done under the influence of partialism, and that no real Universalist who put *implicit faith* in the doctrine *could* commit crime. Why? Because all persons when sinning hope to escape, and believe they will derive more pleasure than pain in committing the deed. Universalism teaches absolute, unequivocal, and adequate punishment for every sin. Consequently, no perfect Universalist could sin. Now, I don't like to say much against such a comfortable faith as this; but, apart from what I conceive to be the *moral* tendency of the doctrine if there ever was in the flesh such a thing as a real perfect Universalist, I'll give up, that's all.

There is nothing remarkable in my journal for some days. I traveled *en route* for Washington. I got left by my conveyance twenty-five miles this side of Philadelphia, and made a triumphal entry into Camden on a pork wagon. On the 14th January, arrived in Washington–was much delighted with the appearance of the capitol. Mr. Barton, late Charge d'Affaires to France, came from New York to Washington at the same time that I did. His arrival was announced in the papers. Mine was not. No matter. The monkey's was.

Jan. 16.–The monkey's first appearance in Washington. Good house, though the snow fell to the depth of four inches. The ladies delighted with the dear fellow; thought him smarter than most of the senators and members of Congress. . . .[25]

Chapter III

It was very evident that in such a place as Washington, I must do something "wery pekooliar," to "put money I' the purse." If my monkey had been of the softer sex, and could have figured in short petticoats as a great dancer, there could be no count of my success, and that the members of Congress would have flocked to the perfor-mance, but unfortunately my monkey was not of the tender nature, and if it had been, its understandings would have sent it to perdition in the minds of those gentlemen who crave to see the display of a beautiful leg, and who pay more homage to such *exposes* as a pirouette in scant garments will produce, than to the greatest effort of genius that can be conceived. It is a mighty fine thing to elevate genius and to decry passion–but a manager who wants to stuff his breeches pockets must make the lat-ter a primary object. He can only live upon what the public will patronize, and if a number of cats can be drilled to dance a cotillion with grace, and such performance will attract a full, enlightened audience, and draw from them thunders of applause, the manager is an ass who does not bring the grimalkins forward.

There was nothing to be done but to get out a glorious bill, which I did–and great as has been the humbug of theatrical bills, I flatter myself that I have gone ahead of all others and introduced a system of puffing that has been most extensively copied.

I headed a bill, "For this night only." That line always tells. Let the public con-ceive that a performance announced for one night can never be played again, and it is a sure attraction. In the next line was emblazoned "The monkey's benefit." Then came some twenty lines describing the monkey in as many features. The monkey in serious pantomime–the monkey in comic pantomime–the monkey on his head–the monkey on his heels–the monkey in ballet–the monkey in the boxes, pit, and gal-lery, &c., ending in gigantic letters with the announcement that the monkey was the greatest monkey of two hemispheres. I pride myself on this humbug, which has been extensively copied and is thought *celestial*. . . .

[O]n going to Philadelphia I concocted one of the greatest plans of humbugging that ever helped to fill the pockets of an ingenious and enterprising artist. I had had only $75 one night in the theater with the magnificent announcement of four genuine real anacondas, "all alive, &c." together with a full description of the manner in which these "serpents" take down men, women, and children, oxen, and other cattle, and then lie down gorged, bloated, and stupefied, so that a new born baby may go up the monster and kill him in a twinkling. The humbug of which I am about to speak, I conceived in consequence of another man who had another monkey, boasting that his monkey was a better monkey than mine. Now I knew that my monkey was im-mensely superior to his, but this circumstance would have made no difference in regard to my project. I trailed upon him, and agreed with him for twenty-five dollars to come out before the public on a grand trial of skill between the two monkeys, for a sum of one thousand dollars. He, in consequence, inserted a card in two morning papers, challenging my monkey in the aforesaid sum, and I the next day published a card in the same papers accepting the challenge. The dear gullible public swallowed the bait, and believed it genuine. The night, the glorious night came on–the theater was crammed to suffocation. Men swore, children screamed, and women fainted.

The uproar was excessive–the calls for the music were incessant. The musicians acted with the utmost coolness–they looked round upon the excited and bellowing audience, and seemed to say to the demands for their performance, "don't you wish you may get it one single moment before the regular time," then . . . they took their seats–turned over the music–blew their noses–loosened their bows–screwed up their catgut–produced sundry horribly excruciating sounds, which are the effects of tuning instruments, and commenced playing.[26] To make a small digression, it is really a pity that in places of public entertainment, the nuisance of tuning instruments should be inflicted upon an audience. If I were the manager of a theater, I should make it a *sine qua non* with the gentlemen of the orchestra, that their catgut should be screwed up under the stage, and that the first note sounded in the orchestra should be the announcement of the overture.

The contest was a grand one. The two monkeys had practiced the afternoon previously, and it was agreed that my monkey should do his easiest tricks, in order to prolong the contest. It lasted about five minutes to the great and breathless interest of the audience, whose very souls were engrossed in the sum that was to be won by one of the monkeys. At length my monkey balanced himself upon his tail, a trick which the other monkey could not do. My rival then came forward, and acknowledged his monkey dead beat. His friends did not like the idea of his giving in, and shouted to him not to "give up the ship, to let his monkey try again," &c. Finally the curtain dropped upon one of the most delighted and essentially gulled audiences ever present at any exhibition whatever.

The next day I wrote a card for my rival, and left it at the office of the Pennsylvanian and the Inquirer. I made him acknowledge his defeat, and charge it to a weakness in his monkey's tail, caused by taking a dose of medicine the day previously, (false of course) adding that he would soon be recovered, and do all my monkey's tricks. The fact is, this was a virgin field of humbugging, and would bear digging over more than once.

In consequence of this plan, in due course of time, humbug the second was hatched–my rival published a card, stating that his tail was fully convalescent, and that he, the monkey not the man, would perform more tricks than mine, for $500 forfeit. As arranged between us, I accepted the wager on behalf of my monkey–my arrangement with the treasurer was to receive one half the receipts, after deducting $125 expenses, and to give my rival one-eighth over $300. The bill was headed, "Great trial of skill at the American Theater–The Champion in the field–Trial of skill for $500 a side," &c., &c. Notwithstanding a short announcement and capital sleighing, there was a capital house, and I vowed most fervently, as I counted the gains, to devote myself hereafter to the utmost to that most glorious of all sciences, the science of humbug.

Of my travels and adventures with this inimitable monkey, of the repetition of the Philadelphia trick in New York, by which the Gothamites can by no means laugh at the credulity of the Philamakinks–of the fifty thousand dollars I made out of the animal, and of the forty thousand I lost in handling the gambling game of *poker,* together with anecdotes of theatricals, and other persons, I may speak hereafter. I am now on the eve of narrating the greatest humbug ever perpetrated in the annals of the world. Before entering upon it, as I have mentioned gambling, I may as well state one rather curious circumstance. I was always to the world at large of a religious bearing, partly because it assisted my grand schemes, and partly because I had the gift of eloquence to a considerable extent, and was devilishly proud of it. This led me to become a preacher, and in all places where it would be advantageous to me, I figured as the *Reverend* Barnaby Diddleum. Upon the particular occasion to which I allude, I was in a small town on the northern border, and promised on the ensuing Sabbath to deliver a discourse.[27] I was at the time somewhat indifferently clad for a Reverend, who is nothing without his sables. I did not wish to purchase any clothes, as my funds were rather low; but I resolved to have a suit. So I took a trip over to Canada, and feeling pretty sure that a Yankee can beat a Canadian at almost anything excepting in loyalty to what, I believe Old Glory, (Sir Francis Burdett) called "the shadow of a king," I got into playing several games of chance with some former acquaintances. I won my clothes–brought them over in triumph, and on the ensuing Sunday preached an admired sermon on the fatal effects of gambling, which I have since learnt, totally reformed one habitual player.

Chapter IV

Crown me with fame–erect a monument to my memory–decree me a Roman triumph–I deserve all–I stand alone–I have no equal, no rival–I am the king of Humbug–the king among princes. O, it is great, it is glorious–I chuckle now at the might of my sovereignty, the extent of my works, and laugh in ecstasy! Other poor pitiful humbugs, of whom I am as heartily ashamed as Falstaff of his ragged regiment, have been content to gull a portion of the public mass–the unthinking, with their nostrums, promising them eternal health; others have promised eternal bloom, others have promised eternal happiness, and sold out sin licenses and security from damnation–all for a price. Others have made science subservient to their desires, and nicely dovetailing truth with falsehood, consistency with inconsistency, have taken in a few wise men whose learning has made them mad–all have done it for a price; but the success of these paltry, miserable humbugs has been comparatively small. A portion only of the public has worshipped the new lights, believed in them as an oracle, or idolized them as divinity. I have triumphed over all–I have marched a conqueror from city to city. The enlightened, the ignorant, the lawyer, the student, the divine–young, old, virtuous, vicious–the good, the bad, and the indifferent, and over and above all, those immaculate men who sit in judgment upon the world, the oracles of the press—the organs of the people, have been gulled by Barnaby Diddleum. Like the immortal Caesar I can say of the places I visited—*Veni vidi vici—ha! ha! ha!*

To give an account of this wonderful affair, I must make a retrograde movement, which, if you will accompany me, will take us both from the ancient city of the Knickerbockers, and place us in the state of men, half horse half alligator.[28]

It was on a beautiful spring day that I arrived at Paris, Bourbon county, Kentucky. By the bye, what a curious race we are in our passion for names. The idea of christening one town Paris, another Utica, another Rome—what high sounding names—and what queer and unpleasant associations it must give those persons who are well read in the classics—for my own part, I am not. My study is man, which a great Pope says, is the proper study of mankind. I study him deeply and closely on all occasions, for the general, but not often confessed purpose of getting as much out of him as possible. With the change of a single word, I say with the man in the play, "Now, then the world is my oyster, which I with *humbug* will open." Humbug is a much keener weapon than the sword now-a-days, and the man who is armed with it can do more than the most valiant Dick Turpin who ever cried stand, to a traveler. . . . .

Now to return to Paris, Bourbon county, Kentucky. I arrived there on a beautiful Spring morning. I was not long there before I found an old acquaintance, whom I had met in my travels. I looked upon this discovery as a God-send, and immediately questioned my friends as to the lions of the place. "There are none here," he replied, "none, unless you will rank as a curiosity old aunt Joyce." "And who the devil's old aunt Joyce?" I asked. "Oh a remarkably old negro woman that I am cursed with; she is about as old as Methuselah I believe—she has been bed-ridden for twelve years, during which time she has had a capital appetite, and seems no more inclined to join the black spirits of her departed brethren, then she did twelve years ago. She bears a charmed life, I fancy[,] and lives on for the sole purpose of picking my pockets by remaining, while I live, on the pension list."

I felt a great curiosity to see the woman who was thus swindling my friend by her disgusting pertinacity to cling to life at his expense, and accordingly went with him over to his plantation where at length I was introduced, without much form or ceremony, into the apartment of the venerable Joyce. She was very comfortably lodged, and seemed to be exceedingly happy. She was exempt from all work—the horror of a negro. She enjoyed the elysium of her race—idleness, to its fullest extent, and she was evidently determined to hold onto the good things of this life as long as possible; nor did she desire to forsake the bed-ridden comforts of the flesh for the uncertainties of an afterlife.[29] I was struck with this at once—but I was struck more with her extraordinary appearance of age. She looked like a galvanized mummy. It was enough to make a man's hair turn gray to count her years.

I thought this woman a great curiosity, and that she might be turned to some account by being exhibited. "You want to get rid of aunt Joice?" said I. "I do." "I'll do it. What will you give me?" "Oh!" said he laughingly, "she must die a natural death." "To be sure," said I, "and be as well or better taken care of than now. I have a crotchet in my head by which I may probably make something out of her. At all events, I'll take her off your hands if you'll give me something handsome." "Well, what do you want?" "Why, you say she is likely to live a dozen years yet. I think so too. Calculate what she costs you per annum, and I'll take her for the expenses of a year."

A bargain was immediately struck and aunt Joice became the property of Barnaby Diddleum, and, as will be seen in the sequel, contributed very extensively to the principal adventurers of an adventurer.[30]

Chapter V

My black beauty, after resting for twelve years on a bed where it seemed to be long destined she should die, now at an indefinite age, which I put down at one hundred and nineteen years, was raised from her lethargy, and commanded at my sovereign will and pleasure, to arise and commence her travels and adventures.

It is rather a curious thing to think of a woman, wrinkled, shriveled, dried up, diseased, and bed ridden, to begin her romance of life at the reputed age of nearly a century and a quarter, but over whose woolly head some eighty years had marched in regular workmanship style, performing their seasonable evolutions with all the regularity of clockwork, circus vaulters, or regular soldiers on parade. It is still more curious to look back and reflect a little on eighty defunct years which our time hath known. How each of these fine fellows were born in the heart of icy winters, fostered in the smiling spring, matured in the glowing summer, crowned in the imperial autumn, and withered in the embrace of winter, which has been to one and all a cradle and a grave, preaching a sort of dust to dust lecture to all the unbegotton years. I'm getting into the sentimental line here, but it ain't just in my way, so I'll get out of it as fast as I can, for I can hardly feel the bottom, and shall get out of my depth if I venture any further. I'll just say at last what I've been thinking of all the time. What a most curious thing it is to think how many fortunes have been made by humbugging in that time, and how man, like the seasons, performs his humbugs regularly, and will, till the crack of doom.–The world is fairly inoculated with the system, and can't get out of it no way you can fix it.

The first place that I and old aunt Joyce stopped at, was Louisville in Kentucky.[31] I did not exhibit her immediately, for the old girl was rather cantankerous. She had led an easy life of it. She had enjoyed a sinecure situation with her former master, and she by no means relished the idea of having her old bones trotted about the country, as she foresaw they would be, from one extremity to the other, without much of rest or ceremony. So leaving the old girl to rip out oaths by the volley, an accomplishment she was remarkably proficient in, I began to look about me for amusement.

I here fell into company with as fine a fellow as ever lived–a tragic actor, of considerable reputation, who, had his physical power been equal to his mental capacity, with a little of my divine art, would have been a paragon. We were seated one evening smoking a choice Havana, and discussing each a fine glass of whiskey punch, which we mixed up with Shakespeare, Kemble, Keane, Talma, and my monkey, when he said–"How is it Diddleum that your monkey's proceedings are recorded in all the principal of the chief cities of the union, while I play whole engagements that are not noticed at all?" "What! don't you understand that?" said I, in real astonishment.

"No," said he, "for though the unthinking may crowd thickly to see your monkey's feats and fall into ecstasies with its unintellectual performances–yet those gentlemen who wield the pen, who are of the press–to many of whom Shakespeare is a household god, as dearly worshipped as by myself–they at least should not neglect all his personators for the sake of monkey dancers and buffoons, however popular they may be." "Your simplicity almost makes me laugh. But I will put you in the way of being noticed in all the papers of all the principal cities, go wherever you will." "How?"

"In starring it in country towns and places you are sure of a long notice and a good one. You see editors in such parts don't get theatrical amusements too often in the first place, and they are pretty glad, where items of news don't run wild and are to be had for the trouble of catching as in New York–to get something to write about. By and by, it wouldn't be a bad plan on entering a town where you play to call on the principal paper or papers, if there are two, and say you will want a card for your benefit published, and this you must be sure to pay for in advance. Editors are plaguey shy of actors, and well they may be for they have lost a precious sight of money by some of them. I don't mean to say that the dollar or so you give for your card will affect a criticism–in some cases I know it won't, for I've tried it on–but human nature is human nature, and where a man's interests are concerned he is not always too stiff backed in his principles. At all events the card business can do no harm, and may do much good. I would as soon travel through the country without grease to the wheels of my wagon as to neglect it. Well, having got this notice you must take a dozen or twenty papers." "As a sort of grateful feeling, I suppose." "Pshaw! With a feeling of self-interest with which you must always be guided, if you wish to go ahead like a steamboat. One, of course, you'll reserve for your scrap book for your own amusement in showing it to your friends. The others you will send, of course, to the editors, or the principal editors in the chief cities, especially where you are likely to perform. You must mark the paragraph round with ink, and write on the margin 'please notice.'"

"I don't approve the plan."

"It does not always answer. The lazy fellows sometimes cut up a flaming criticism of some half a column into a mere notice of a line or two. There is a better plan—that of writing letters. It always takes. As you travel pick up all the theatrical items you can, send the intelligence in a letter, with an account of your own success. The last will be published for the sake of the first. This keeps your name constantly before the public.—Managers look to you and give you engagements, and the public are more disposed from hearing so much of you to do you justice." "Is this much practiced?" "It soon will be. At present I and a friend of mine at Baltimore, are the only persons who practice the plan to any extent. I have a copy of a letter now in my pocket, which I sent from New York to Washington. Here it is:

> Dear H: The monkey closed last night the most brilliant engagement known here for twenty years. It was his benefit, and despite the snow storm which raged all day and night, the house was the fullest and most fashionable of the season. The foreign ministers, the president's family, the fashionable members of Congress, &c. filled the boxes and parquette. At the conclusion of the performances the monkey was called out and literally covered with bouquets. A valuable present was thrown on the stage. It was a gold chain, attached at one end to a wreath of flowers, at the other to a silver ring. The monkey very gracefully placed the flowers on his head, and the ring on his tail. In consequence of a very general desire the monkey will perform for three nights more. Ward, the manager, a very worthy man, says he has lost money by all the stars except the monkey, and when its legitimate performances are concluded he shall turn the parquette into an arena for horse spectacles, which is a pity.

There now, you see my style, and you must see how advantageous it is to be thus before the eyes of the public. Don't mention this idea. It's between three or four of us, we may as well make the most of it."

"I will neither mention it nor use it—nor can I look with any other feelings than that of disgust—no offence to you—upon a system which, practiced extensively, will thrust brass upon the public for precious gold, and keep the sterling metal hid in obscurity." Saying this, he bade me good night. It's all very well to have fine principle, but it may be carried to excess. Here's a man now, a real genius, a fine fellow, who will never be worth a cent because he won't take the necessary means to push himself before the face of a community which have made up its mind to see no one who is ready to stare it out of countenance. He won't humbug and he's poor—I will and I'm rich.

I soon got Joyce into training, and from a devil of a termagant, converted into a most docile creature, as willing to do my bidding as the slave of the lamp was to obey Aladdin. I discovered her weak point. It was discovered in seven letters—W-H-I-S-K-E-Y. Her old master, of course, would indulge an old bed-ridden creature in no such luxury, and for a drop of it, I found I could mould her to anything. I accordingly tried the Museum and exhibited her. She took tolerably well. Visitors would lift up their eyes and exclaim–"Dear me," "Gracious," "Well I never," and some of the pious people asked whether she was prepared for a change, to which she replied altogether irreverently, much to my chagrin at the time, though I was glad of it afterwards, as it enabled me to provide against so important a difficulty for the future.

We packed up and set off from Louisville to Cincinnati, which was the second place of exhibition of this unfledged wonder. "Joyce," said I, *en route,* "I want you to grow older before you get to Cincinnati." "What, again, Massa?" "Yes Joyce, they love you the more the older you grow. You must be twenty-four years older. Remember now." "Give me some whiskey then," said Joyce, ripping out more oaths than a man-of-war could utter. "You must give over swearing too." She swore she'd be d–d if she could or would. But upon promising her nightly a good stiff glass of the nectar, that warmed her old heart, she said she'd continue to keep dark with the dames before company, but she'd be d–d if she wouldn't make up for it when they were gone.

At Cincinnati matters went on very well. A great number of the people and none of the pigs came to see the prodigy, and went away wondering. I found Joyce far more manageable than I expected, and in consequence my ideas began to expand in regard to the value I could make of her, and in my next place I matured the great scheme which is unparalleled in the history of the world.

Chapter VI

A steam boat is a great place for reflection. When the body is unemployed, the mind works more intensely. Not that a person need be at any loss for amusement or preoccupation on board one of these vessels; he may always find sufficient of both in the study of character. A capital place for that is a steamboat. We meet a great many queer and comical persons in every day life–but our own occupation perhaps prevents our studying them, and perhaps their occupation gives a sort of interest to them which takes from their strange appearance, so that they depart without any comment. Not so on board a steamboat. It is almost impossible to step on the deck of one of these exquisite go a headers without feeling perfectly astonished at some of the strange specimens of humanity that meet the eye.

What with reflection and study, I had a very pleasant time of it in my passage from Cincinnati, a distance of 250 miles. Seated alone, on deck, I saw as many and more images of the future in the waters, lashed into a milky foam by the monster wheels of the vessel, as Macbeth did in the boiling cauldron. First of all, and all along, lay Joyce Heth, black as midnight, and blacker for the whiteness of the foam in which my mind's eye saw her. My good genius hovered over her, and showed countless wealth to be made out of her. But how? Her great age was a great thing, but after all, an old woman, how old soever she may be, is but an old woman, and very few persons care to behold a parcel of dried bones, covered with shriveled skin, which living anatomy has no reminiscences. Reminiscence, ah! That's the word—that's the idea. It is associations that draw in the gaping and admiring crowd, and cause them to pour their cash into the longing hands of Barnaby Diddleum. If I could only make her the mother of Pharaoh, and get up a little reminiscence of her grief when her son with her hosts were drowned in the Red Sea. How long was it since Pharaoh lived? Some—pshaw—the public won't swallow that—besides the Pharaohs were copper colored, not black? How if I style her the Queen of the greatest of African nations—the Humbugaboos—who was torn from the embraces of her doting and affectionate husband, and two helpless babies, that were taking the precious nutrient from her ebony breasts.[32] Trash! The public here would care but little if she were the mother of all her subjects. It must be here that she must wield a fairy wand. It must be *here* that airy fancy must cast a spell round her rotten old bones. It must be of the glorious revolution that her reminiscences shall speak. She must be the attendant of some great character—must have known him from a boy—must invest him with a precociousness that shall make men stare and wonder. Who shall it be? What great statesman or warrior, whose name is immortal, whose fame has been trumpeted, whose memory is beloved by his countrymen, shall I attach to her?

From the white foam, as if in answer to my thoughts, rose a bright galaxy of stars "whose lives, whose fortunes, and whose sacred honors," were in the cause. Each countenance was radiant with light, and each temple was bound with undying laurel. But there was one who rose towering above them all—a sun whose radiance eclipsed even the brightness which it is immortal glory to obtain. He held the position of a king, but was not called by that name. He stood before me by the prouder title of the Father of his People. I made up my mind at once, and my good genius smiled upon me while her treasures which increased in bulk amazingly, seemed to be within my clutch. From that moment, it was a thing fixed and immovable as the law of the Medes and Persians, that Joyce should be no other than the nurse of the glorious George Washington. . . .

At Pittsburgh, the golden drama commenced. I taught Joyce, by the aid of her great delight, whiskey, and the occasional indulgence of a pipe, a few anecdotes of Washington when a boy—how he would never tell a lie, and some other amiable traits, which Joyce became quite perfect in, after some good drilling. She had an excellent memory, and had wit enough when asked questions she could not answer, to speak of lost memory, fatigue, &c. Pittsburgh was astonished at the nurse of Washington, who in traveling from Cincinnati had reached the enormous age of one hundred and sixty one years! Three weeks we staid at Pittsburgh, taking in money all the time. Editors, physicians, clergymen, ladies, loafers—all came tumbling in, and all went wondering out.

I felt, on leaving the place, that there was a great deal yet to be done. What I did, I will record in the next chapter.

Chapter VII

The mighty scheme for the bold game I have played, was matured in my journey from Pittsburgh to Philadelphia. I was so full of it that I cared not to exhibit my wonder until I arrived in the latter city. I was, however, prevailed upon by "numerous families of distinction," in the little village of Greenburgh to exhibit Joyce. They saw her, they forked out the needful, and thanked god they had lived to see the nurse of the father of his country.

Before entering Philadelphia I manufactured a number of witnesses, whose testimony should leave no doubt of my statement of Joyce's age, or the fact of her being Washington's nurse. You must take little more trouble with persons in large cities than you do with persons in country places—The latter are so unsuspecting, and would not dream of doubting your word; but the former are so dreadfully smart—they know everything, and are not to be done. O! no! They must be satisfied. Certainly. Take the trouble to give them satisfaction, in other words do your work like a master spirit, not like an apprentice. Give honor to the noble art of Humbug, and you may lead them by the nose like asses. My witnesses were documents. The principal of which was a *bill of sale*, purporting to be made by Mrs. Atwood, sister-in-law to Augustin Washington, to William Bolen, the father of the Kentuckian of whom I took her. This document, to give it a good mummy-like, antique look, was baptized in tobacco juice, and dried in smoke, until it looked ancient enough to have been the last will and testament of King Cheops, or a *billet doux* from that amorous lady, Mrs. Potaphor. The document was dated 1727, at which time it stated Joyce to be 54 years of age. It made the year of her birth the anno domini, which was known to mortals as Mr. 1694 [*sic*]. With this I felt pretty comfortable—still it was not enough. Joyce had learned a number of anecdotes, as good as new, of her dear George. She had acquired the habit of speaking slowly and sanctimoniously, as became a religious person, and the only reason that she did not turn up her eyes like a duck in a thunder storm, was that she had no eyes to turn up. She was as blind as the infant offspring of a lady mouser, in the first week of their existence. Still this was not sufficient. She belonged to no church. The world don't care a fig for your religion, unless you are a sectarian. You are as Jack Falstaff, a most glorious humbug by the way, likened Dame Quickly to, an otter, neither fish nor flesh—there is no knowing where to have you. You must be a sectarian, to be respected as a religious man, and the reason is this, that if you belong to a sect, all the members think your addition great glory, and that you have taken the only true and legitimate railroad to Paradise—this gives them great pleasure; while other sects believing that you have got into the wrong box—denounce you and your creed, and endeavor by assuring you, you are going post to blazes—to save you from the great fire, and that gives them a pleasure, so that they are all pleased. A man who visits all sects, gets a great deal of good out of them; for they are all good in the main, and well meaning. His ideas become expanded. He looses the dross that covers sectarians. The constant friction with different sects rubs it off, and in heart and soul he is, perhaps, the most pure worshipper of "the one great cause" extant; but he will get no credit for it—while a man who joins a church, and makes up his mind to believe as it does, may become bigoted and prejudiced against his neighbor in religion, and possess no Christian charity—few sects do for one another—and yet be greatly respected—on the one side as a good and pious man, on the other as a good and pious, but wrong thinking individual.

My mind was made up—I baptized Joyce Heth on paper, and baptized the paper in tobacco juice. The deed was consummated, and all the world was to know that old Joyce had been a member of the Baptist church for 116 years—that she was the last member of those good people with whom she practiced her devotions—that they were all in glory, the pastor and his people—and that she was only waiting till the thread of life which held her, like a cow by the leg, to the earth was mapped, to join them in bright beatitude.

I was now armed at all points, and ready for the war, and thus certain of success, I entered Philadelphia—the city of brotherly love, and I suppose sisterly devotion. Philadelphia is one of the most quiet looking cities in the world. Its streets are kept so beautifully clean, that you are almost inclined to take off your boots, if they are dirty, for fear of soiling the pavement. There is no bustle and noise as in other cities of its size, and the people have generally a pious air—so that you feel at first as if you had to mind your P.s and Q.s, and you practice before a glass for some time to give your face a properly elongated appearance suitable to the gravity of all around you; but you haven't been long in Philadelphia before you begin to understand the way of making clean the outside of the platter, and leaving the within dirty. Your sanctity won't kill you there. If there isn't more systematic though quiet indulgences to be found constantly practiced there than in New York, or any other place, I am not the King of Humbugs—Such a place is always favorable for an exhibition.

My first operation after taking the Masonic Hall for a show room, was to visit the various newspaper offices and pay for an advertisement for a week. I also invited all the editors to an interview with old Joyce before the public were admitted. They were a curious set of fellows, the Philadelphia editors, in those times. They seemed to belong by right to the city of brotherly love, for they were quite united. If one expressed a favorable opinion, you were pretty certain of having a favorable opinion from all. There was no having too much of a good thing there. If you took in six papers, and found on Monday a choice article in one of them, it would take you till Saturday to get rid of it, as the matter used to be carried, not unfrequently, from office to office, until it had gone the rounds. The editors came in. They saw the documents—they saw the woman—they were unanimous. They would as soon have doubted their existence as the statements we put before them. Joyce behaved uncommonly well. She did not swear. She was pious with the Inquirer, and poetical with the Gazette. All were delighted with her. They retired—I rubbed my hands with delight—Joyce had an extra quantity of whiskey, and swore *ad libitum*. She began to take a great delight in the humbug, which was a profitable one to her. On the following morning the whole press came out in full blast. The nurse of George Washington—the venerable nurse—was to be seen at Masonic Hall. The whole city was excited—Joyce was the lion, and the people were stuffed. . . . .

Chapter VIII

On arriving in New York, I found that our fame had preceded us. Joyce was heralded in all the papers, and Victoria herself would hardly have made a greater sensation. Still there was a caution in all the announcements that betokened the editors had an idea Joyce was a humbug.

I looked out for the finest exhibition place in the city, and found it at Niblo's Gardens. These gardens are very beautiful. It is astonishing how much has been done in a little space. It shows what the genius of an individual may effect; but it takes a downright smart fellow like Barnaby Diddleum, and a few others to make a mouse an elephant. Wm. Niblo, the proprietor of these gardens is the king of good fellows, and beloved by all who know him. Joyce was delighted with his whiskey, which she swore to be the best she ever tasted. Independently of the beauty and the convenience of the place, there was another reason that I hired it. It was to draw in the saints. Niblo's is the only place of amusement where the shining lights of righteousness will be seen. You may give them there the same entertainment that you have in a theater, and they will see no offence in it, although they denounce theatrical performances in good set terms, and swear that Old Nick is the proprietor of all theaters extant—that managers are his lessees—actors his servants—"His Majesty's servants," as they say at the Drury Lane when the garter is worn on the leg, not the arm; and that the audience that visits such abomination is on the high road to damnation.[33]

I was settled, and according to custom, paid my respects to the Press, without whose aid and influence I could do nothing. Talking of the press, reminds me of a singular circumstance. There was a quack doctor living in New York, who advertised extensively, and might be said almost to have coined money. He had the curiosity at one time to save up all his advertising bills. At the end of the year he counted the cost, and found he had expended over five thousand dollars. He was quite frightened, and believed he should be ruined. He left off advertising immediately. At the end of another year he came to the conviction that he was a great fool; and that he had made, by advertising, at least five hundred percent premium. He went back to first principles–the principles by which he was made. Another quack doctor, however, in the mean time had taken the field and gained the ascendancy, which by constant advertising he kept up. In all the newspapers I advertised, and for my advertisements I paid in advance. I invited all the editors also, to a private exhibition. They came and were satisfied–they could not be otherwise. Joyce had improved most wonderfully in piety. She went ahead at the hymns like a steamboat. Her great improvement was owing in some measure to the exertions of a smart, shrewd man, a Yankee of course, to whom, for the purpose of exhibitions and my own personal convenience, I sold a small share in my black beauty.[34] He gave her the true conventional tone, that distinguishes at once the righteous from the wicked. The sanctified nasal twang drawled out *ad libitum,* and which stamps them all like a flock of sheep that are branded. He taught the nature of experience–how to get up a bit of prayer for set occasions, and to speak by the card in relation to the church of which I had determined she belonged.

All persons now crowded to see her. The scientific–the physicians, among whom was Dr. Rogers, who was taken in most deliciously, as I shall afterwards show. It may be a curiosity, now that I am giving the whole humbug, to insert one of my handbills. The first I published for New York was the following.

> NIBLO'S GARDENS.–The greatest curiosity in the world, and the most interesting particularly to Americans, is now exhibiting (for six days only.) At the Saloon fronting on Broadway, in the building recently erected for the dioramic view. Joyce Heth, nurse to Gen. George Washington (the father of our country,) who has arrived at the astonishing age of 161 years, as authentic documents will prove, and in full view of her mental faculties. She is cheerful and healthy, although she weighs but forty-nine pounds, she relates many anecdotes of her young master, she speaks also of the red coats, during the Revolutionary War, but does not appear to hold them in high estimation.
>
> During the short exhibition in Philadelphia, she has been visited by crowds of ladies and gentlemen, among whom were many clergymen and physicians, who have pronounced her the most ancient specimen of mortality, the oldest of them has ever seen or heard of, and consider her a very great curiosity.
>
> She has been a member of the Baptist church for upwards of one hundred years, and seems to take great satisfaction in the conversation of ministers who visit her. She frequently sings and repeats parts of hymns and psalms.
>
> As she remains in this city but for a few days on her way to Boston she can be seen from 9 A.M. to 10 P.M.
>
> P.S. A more interesting account of this extraordinary woman will be given hereafter.
>
> Admittance 25 cents. Hours of exhibition from 9 A.M. to 1,–and from 6 to 10 P.M.

This was good, but in my second bill, which announced the old woman for six nights longer, I gave something better. Here it is:

> Joyce Heth is unquestionably the most astonishing and interesting curiosity in the world. She was the slave of Augustine Washington (the father of George Washington,) and was the first person *who put clothes on the unconscious infant,* who was destined in after days to lead our heroic fathers to glory, to victory, to freedom. To use her own language when speaking of her young master George Washington–"she raised him."

The sentiment of putting clothes on the unconscious infant sold well, and many fine ladies in their national enthusiasm, envied the black paws of old Joyce, for the office they had performed.

I was now quite a lion myself, and invited out here, there and everywhere. I was all things to all people. Studying character, and playing upon the folly and credulity of mankind. I have always made it a point to see how far humbug can possibly be carried, and I have been a little astonished sometimes at my own success. In all the parties that I have visited, I have been questioned like the Moor of Venice, as to my travels and adventures, and I have given them in parcels, which I am bound to forgive any Iago for calling fantastical lies. I have humbugged the good people of New York pretty extensively in private practices, as I call them; but the country is the place. There you have open mouthed, goggled eyed wonder, astonishment and faith to an unprecedented degree. . . . To return to Joyce. We were in the height of our glory–making money as fast as could be, when one day we made a discovery that frightened us out of our lives. What that was, I'll tell in another chapter.

Chapter IX

The fright of which I spoke, was occasioned by my finding accidentally that I had called, in my bill of sale, Virginia a state, in the year 1727, when in fact it was only a colony. How this could have escaped the notice of the learned persons who had witnessed my humbug in Philadelphia and in this city, I am at a loss to conceive. It was my luck. I certainly deserved to be blown to the personage, "who carries his tail as a gentleman carries his cane," for my egregious folly. I immediately withdrew the bill of sale that contained this most startling, but as yet undiscovered error, and taking it to a copyist, asked him to transcribe it. He readily agreed, and I read to him the paper, simply changing the word "State," as written in the original, to the word "Colony" of Virginia, as it ought to have been. When we had got through I read the matter over to him, and asked if all was right. He religiously believed that it was. I said you must go before the Recorder, and swear to the fact of the faithfulness of this copy, as I have to send the original to Virginia. He did so. He went before double-X Recorder Riker, an amiable man, who treated every convict like a gentleman, and made a sort of apology to every rogue or thief he sentenced, saying that the crime they had committed was practiced to a great extent in the community, and they must suffer some. The Recorder administered the oath, and took his fee. The copy was exhibited, and was as good as the original paper, and much more safe. I now felt clear of all difficulties, and enjoyed my good fortune.

The New York editors aided me beautifully at that time, but there was no New York Atlas then. O! it was a glory almost equal to the glory of taking in money, to take in the editors of the emporium city. Ha! ha! I laugh at them whenever I think of the subject. I will give a few specimens of their wisdom:[35]

JOYCE HETH—The arrival at Niblo's Gardens of this renowned relic of the olden time, has created quite a sensation among the lovers of the curious and the marvelous, and a greater object of marvel and curiosity has never presented itself for their gratification. From the length of her limbs and size of her bones, it is probable that she was a large, stout woman, in her day; but now she comes up exactly to one's idea of an animated mummy. Her weight is said to be less than fifty pounds. Her feet have shrunk to mere skin and bone, and her long attenuated fingers more resemble the claws of a bird of prey than human appendages. The presumed date of her birth is 1674—which would make her age, at the present time, upwards of 161. Notwithstanding her burden of years and infirmities, she is lively, and seems to retain all her senses wonderfully. Her hearing is almost as acute as that of any person of middle age.—*N.Y. Sun*

The "old one" has arrived, and crowds of ladies and gentlemen have visited her at Niblo's. She is lively, and answers every question cheerfully. From the bill of sale of this old lady from Gen. Washington's father, we can have no doubt that she is 160 years of age. Her appearance is very much like an Egyptian mummy just escaped from its sarcophagus.—*N.Y. Evening Star*

JOYCE HETH—This living mummy, on whose head 161 winters have sprinkled their snows, is now exhibiting at Niblo's Garden. She was born in the year 1674 during the reign of Charles the 2d of England, and Louis the 14th of France, and independently of her great age, she is an object of curiosity and interest to the American public, as having been the nurse of the great Washington.—*N.Y. Sunday M. News*

ANTEDILUVIANS—We venture to state, that since the flood, a like circumstance has not been witnessed equal to the one which is about to happen this week. Old Joyce Heth, whom we mentioned on Friday holds a drawing room at Niblo's this day, which is to be continued till Saturday. Ancient or modern times furnish no parallel to the great age of this woman. Methuselah was 969 years old when he died, but nothing is said of the age of his wife. Adam attained nearly the age of his antiquated descendant. It is not unlikely that the sex in the olden time were like the daughters at the present day—unwilling to tell their age. Joice Heth is an exception; she comes out boldly, and says she's rising 160.—*N.Y. Daily Advertiser*

This old creature is said to be 163 years of age, and we see no reason to doubt it. Nobody indeed would dispute it if she claimed to be five centuries, for she and the Egyptian mummy at the American Museum appear to be about of an age.—*N.Y. Courier & Enquirer*

JOYCE HETH–The dear old lady after carrying on a desperate flirtation with Death, has finally jilted him. In the future editions, we shall expect to see her represented as the impersonation of Time in the Primer, Old Time having given her a season ticket for life. The Wandering Jew and herself are the only two people we know of that have been put on the free list of this world for the season of eternity.–*N.Y. Spirit of the Times*

Was not this beautiful–was it not glorious? The firm faith in the reputed age of the old girl–the great stupidity of all, in not discovering the palpable fraud published before their eyes, in calling Virginia a state, when it was only a colony! Joyce now became more pious than ever. The whiskey, never stinted after a good day's performances, did the business, and she balanced accounts with her conscience in proportion to her hymning it in the day. Sometimes, indeed, the effects of her potations were carried into the hours of the exhibition, and not a few persons have seen her positively fuddled. None, however, suspected the cause, or dreamt that Joyce could have swallowed Jonah's whale, if it had been converted into Monongahola. They looked upon her inebriety as a weakness of nature in consequence of her extreme old age, and said: "Poor creature, she is overcome!" They were right, she was *overcome!*

But the greatest glory for Joyce was an event that occurred about this time. In consequence of her great piety, several sisters of the church to which they wished her to belong, were exceedingly anxious that she should take the sacrament. Joyce, who had become an excellent actress, and knew that an extraordinary performance invariably insured her an extra proportion of grog, expressed the blessed satisfaction and comfort it would give her. Accordingly on the following day, an elder of the church and the sisters waited upon her, and administered the sacrament. They talked of holy things and heavenly comfort, and Joyce assented to all they said, and now and then echoed one of their speeches, or edged in one of her own. They went away delighted with her piety. I took good care that the affair should be noised abroad. It was published in all the papers. From that time the religious old women came down in crowds, and some of the abolitionists piously believed that the virtue and goodness of Washington might have been, and doubtless was, strengthened by the exemplary piety of this wonderful woman.

I had great leisure, now that my companion attended to the old woman, and I employed it in various ways to my own advantage. In particular, I took good care to mix in society as I could, and raise the curiosity of my hearers in regard to Joyce, by little anecdotes, which I knew, would be repeated every where. When I was cornered for an explicit statement of some affair, concocted on the moment, and not sufficiently digested to satisfy the too credulous, I had to resort to mystification. . . .

Chapter X

There was an old gentleman who was mightily delighted with Joyce on account of her *penchant* for smoking. This was no other than the illustrious Laurie [*sic*] Todd.[36] Every man has his hobby–his *penchant*. Laurie Todd, known better to the unlettered as Grant Thorburn, had his little bit of comfort–his "peculiar wanity," as Samivel Veller might say. It was tobacco. Now at that time, as in all times since the introduction of the plant, there were a number of persons who would rail in good set terms against the use of a pipe, and declared it to be calculated to smoke the soul out of the body, if not to prepare it for the devil's great meerschaum, in which his Satanic Majesty is to smoke the wicked. The fact of Joyce Heth having smoked for twice the usual period of many lives, was an argument in favor of Laurie's favorite custom, that he could by no means forego. Accordingly an article under old Grant's proper signature and dated at "Hallet's Cove," appeared in the Evening Star, from which we extract as follows,–"*Important Discovery,* which it's presumed, will set forever at rest the long and learned dispute about smoking tobacco being poisonous. I have been to see Joyce Heth today. I find that with all her other rare qualities, she is a *profound smoker.* Her attendants are obliged to abridge this luxury, else the pipe (as they say) would never be out of her mouth. I asked her how long she had used the pipe; she answered one hundred and twenty years. So, if smoking be a poison, it is, in her care at least, a very slow one. Now, you intemperate mortals, who make smoking a church felony, there is not one among all your *anti pipe* association that will live to see one hundred and twenty years, though you were to stand on the top of the Andes mountains, and not a pipe within one thousand miles of you."

Commenting on this, the Transcript wrote as follows: "*Long Life to Smoke*– Laurie Todd has made a discovery, which very much tickles his propensity for smoking. He has discovered that Joyce Heth, the hundred and sixty one years old woman[,] has been a profound smoker for the last hundred and twenty years. He therefore concludes that if smoking be a poison, it must, at least in her case, be a slow one. Laurie generally has a pipe in his mouth; and now that he has made this discovery, we suppose he will never be without one; and the next century, we will read in the Knickerbocker (vol. 175) an essay from his pen, on the 'Preservation of Human Flesh' by the use of tobacco smoke, as exemplified in his own case." The Sun also said: "*A practical vindication* of the character of our long standing, calumniated, much injured *tobacco*–is afforded in the person of that venerable relic of antiquity, Joyce Heth. She is a profound smoker! And has been one *hundred and twenty years!* What will the alarmists, who have been sounding anathemas of 'learned length and thundering sound' against this genuine American institution, now say, to sustain their unholy crusade against 'the weed.' Verily, if tobacco is a poison, it is a monstrous *slow poison*."

To make the exhibition more interesting, I now published her life, giving a full and particular account of all those things which might have happened to her, and which was as good as if it had been gospel truth, instead of a pleasing romance from beginning to end.[37] This work brought more grist to the mill. . . . I now left New York—beautiful New York which had in its returns to my coffers, exceeded my utmost expectations. I now feared nothing. If the Gothamites could not discover my weakness—if they could not wound me, even in the heel, I felt myself encased in armor impervious to all the world and his wife. I now set forth with a light heart for Providence, where some very singular adventures befell me, as strange as true; all of which I shall faithfully record for the benefit of a most essentially humbugged world.

I embarked upon a steamboat, and in due time was in Providence. It was a great manufacturing place. Cotton factories are there in their glory, and a great number of pretty girls, God bless them, and all men love them, are to be found there. The girls in all manufacturing towns are fine creatures for exhibitions. Their sedentary lives, and their many privations, render anything in the shape of amusement a glory to them, and the satisfaction they receive upon all and every occasion, especially when they are escorted by their beaux, and what pretty girl is without them, renders their company as profitable to the exhibition, as it is pleasant to themselves.

The papers came out in grand style on my behalf. There is no half way business as there is in New York. They go the whole figure, and d—n the odds. Take for example: "To say we are astonished would be but a feeble expression of our feelings. We look on this extraordinary specimen of humanity, with something bordering on awe and venera-tion, and when we heard her converse on subjects or circumstances which must have occurred more than a century since, and especially those connected with the birth—the infancy, and the childhood of the immortal Washington—the mind was carried away by an intensity of interest, which no other object of curiosity has ever created in our breast. Before having seen this woman, a person may be inclined to be incredulous as to the story of her very great age. He may think of demanding documentary evidence in proof. But the first glance at the original before him will banish all skepticism on the subject, and on examination, he will find evidence stamped upon it by the hand of nature, too plain and forceful to require corroboration."—*Providence Herald*.

This was, as the old song says, "A sample of all the rest." I was doing a good busi-ness here when suddenly I found a difficulty which I had not foreseen, and which threatened to turn all my milk sour. In my pamphlet of the life of the illustrious Joyce, I had stated that she had been a slave, and that her family were slaves. This was a great point for the priests. They had not had an original subject for a long time. They preached most fervently against the abomination of citizens giving their money to a creature whose family were slaves. My attendance fell off. The priest-ridden people, under the anathemas of the clergy, came no more. Curiosity itself was damped. The pastors triumphed; but they little knew Barnaby Diddleum, the King of Humbugs. I smiled so complacently as I said to myself, "Well, I know how to fix 'em." I resolved to turn the tables upon them, and I did it. I told one and all, that though it was true the family of Joyce were in bondage–yea, verily in slavish bondage, such as the Israelites suffered under the slavery of the Egyptians–yet the object of the exhibition was to enfranchise them–that all the money collected by the exhibition of Joyce, went to this glorious purpose. A sudden revolution followed. The ministers then repented in sackcloth and ashes. More fervently than they had preached against the exhibition they now preached in favor of it. They exhorted their congregations to go–to contribute their mites in behalf of the glorious cause, and how many quarts of oil they promised them for the single drop, which they gave now, is more than I can say. Enough to say, a reaction took place. My exhibition room was crowded. Emancipation and blarney carried all before them, and I pocketed the rhino. "Vive la Humbug!" . . . .

Chapter XI

From Providence I proceeded to Boston. The papers at once took up the cause, *Ecce signium.*

> The certificates which were shown us, from respectable and worthy men, and the bill of sale, we think establish her extreme age beyond doubt.
> *Boston Traveler.*

> Wonderful as it may seem, there can be little doubt but that she is as old as she is represented; the abundant testimonials, together with a thousand circumstances, go to prove that she has lived in this bustling world 161 years.
> *Boston Chronicle.*

> Joyce Heth has a continual throng of visitors at her rooms in Concert Hall. She presents every mark of extreme old age; she is a perfect mummy, and the only difference between her appearance and those relics of antiquity is, that she breaths and moves; in every other respect she exactly resembles a mummy.
> *Boston Daily Advocate.*

> AN AGED BAPTIST. We are informed that at the special request of Joyce Heth, the 161 years old woman, religious services were performed at Concert Hall yesterday afternoon, by the Rev. Mr. Hague, pastor of the 1st Baptist Church in Boston. Joyce has been, (as the Church Record in Virginia proves) a member of the Baptist Church 116 years! She appeared to take a lively interest in the ceremonies, and during their performance she sung two antique hymns, and *lined* them, as she did, and as was the custom, more than century ago.
> *Boston Merc. Journal.*

I opened on a Wednesday at the Concert Hall, and had for three days the room crowded with visitors. On Monday, the attendance was very thin, I inquired the cause, and soon found that my old enemies in the clergy, had been preaching against Joyce. She was a slave. It was of course an abomination in Massachusetts. In New York and Philadelphia, every tub stands on its own bottom, but in Massachusetts piety and pickles rule the roast. In that State the outside of the platter is not merely washed, but scrubbed until you can see your countenance in it. Of course the reflection is beautiful. The worthies might have cowed ordinary men as they have by the thousand–but my deeds unbonneted, have shown that they had an extraordinary man to deal with in Barnaby Diddleum.

I immediately wrote to every clergyman in Boston, enclosing a ticket "free gratis for nothing," assuring them, as I had done in Providence, that Joyce was no slave; and inviting them to see her, fully satisfied, that "one trial would prove this fact."

"Now Joyce," said I, "you must mind your P's and Q's, the real legitimate Blue Skins will be down upon you, and you will be subject to a strict examination."

"Never mind Massa," said Joyce, "gib me plenty of whiskey, and I'll be as blue as de best ob em."

They came, Joyce assured one and all she was no slave, that she was freed, and that her exhibition had set at liberty already her grandchildren; that her children were all dead–but that her great grand children were still slaves, and that the money to be obtained from the friends to whom she looked for earthly comfort as well as for heavenly satisfaction, would set them all free, and make them independent niggers. She expressed a wish to take the sacrament, which was administered every Sunday afterwards. The clergy wondered, believed and prayed; and what was more to my purpose, preached. Again my room was crowded, and I rejoiced over the humbug I administered to the Blue Skins.

I was questioned particularly as to the great grand children of the nurse of Washington. I told the priests that there were five of them all slaves, that they were valued at $800 each, and that the sum total to be collected was $4,000. Never did the clergy preach or pray more fervently in any cause than that this sum might be poured into my coffers. The exemplary piety of Joyce carried conviction. It dispelled the shadow of a doubt. Her old age, her sightless orbs, her reminiscences, all cut and dried, and learned by rote, walked into their affections like a streak of lightning. It would have been treason to religion to have doubted, especially when in intense fear, in anticipation of a strong potation of the *erature,* she poured forth her querulous voice in a hymn. Joyce was always great in singing, and "possum up a gum tree" or a sacred effusion were equally relished by her. She took an actual pleasure in the thing. In one of the prayers that were poured forth at this time, the pious preacher said, "We pray not that a thousand persons may attend this exhibition; no, nor two thousand, nor three, nor four, nor five thousand; but that tens of thousands may flock to it, until the iron bonds of slavery are broken up, and scattered like chaff before the wind." The speaker saw an infinite wisdom in the preservation of the dry bones–and these bones above all other bones–the honored bones of the nurse of the father of the country, the man, the patriot, and the Christian. The mummy herself was out, and she knew it, and for what purpose? Why for the sacred, glorious, and blessed purpose of the withered skeleton's liberating her own posterity, or as poor Power might have said, of liberating her own ancestry, from the power of the cruel task masters, who, in the blackness of their hearts could not recognize in the blackness of the skins of the Africans, "a man and a brother";–men who presumed to think them lesser in creation's scale on account of their smell, as if all smells did not come from heaven. I thought to myself, if those smells belonged to Paradise, I would rather be excused from entering the Elysian Fields. . . .

To return to the clergy. One of the fraternity visited me and Joyce Heth on a Sunday, and said, "Mr. Diddleum it is well to do good even on the Sabbath day, have the kindness to appropriate this ten dollar bill to the benefit of the great grand children." I took the money, I could not do less without betraying myself, although all I expected or wanted of the black cloth, was to preach in my behalf. That night a few friends with myself spent it in champagne and oysters for our own benefit. As I was filling my glass with the sparkling liquid, I thought of Sheridan's scene in Duenna, where the money left by a deceased for the masses, is sent to the Abbot's wine merchant, and the priests remember the defunct in their glasses. That Sheridan knew something of human nature. Moreover, he was a great humbug–I like his memory for that, but I cannot forgive him for dying poor, with the many facilities he had for dying rich. He, by his wit, his talent, and above all, his humbug; ought to have made a splendid fortune, and not have suffered himself to be neglected and despised by those to whom he was a sun in the hey day of his life. A regular Yankee would not have been so improvident. . . .

We are all proud of the Magna Carta of our ancestors, which we believe we have carried out in our Independence; an Independence sealed by the sacred blood of our forefathers. We are proud of the Anglo Saxon blood flowing in our veins, and which is destined to infuse itself over the whole globe. The new world and old alike show it.

To return to Joyce, I am eternally digressing, but I am writing an impartial history of my movements, in which every thing curious is noted down. The Common Council charged me $40 for a license to exhibit. I told them it was too high, but that I would call in a few days, in the mean time I would consider it. In the mean time I had published my bills announcing the philanthropic object of the exhibition. I called, and was informed that under the emancipating circumstances, not a cent would be charged for the license.

After three weeks public curiosity slacked. The prayers came like angels visits, few and far between. I thought that there was something in "Boosting" yet, and on the principle of "Old Viginny never tire," I resolved to call it out. I prepared a communication for each Newspaper signed, "A Visitor," proclaiming the whole exhibition to be a most ingenious hoax. I stated that Joyce Heth was a wonderful piece of mechanism, worthy of Maelzel himself. That she was no more nor less than a machine made of India Rubber and whalebone, and that the responses to questions put, were made by a ventriloquist. Thousands flocked to see the automaton, and I made–I coined money out of this scheme.

Who shall now say that Barnaby Diddleum was not the King of Humbugs?

Chapter XII

While I was at Boston I heard that the Centennial anniversary of Hingham, a small place about thirty miles from Boston, was to be kept with great pomp, and I determined to take Joyce there.

Upon my arrival I had a number of bills printed with a wood cut of Joyce Heth.[38] A sharp looking boy came to me and asked if I wanted them distributed, I gave him a couple of shillings, and he promised to circulate them in every part of the town. As soon as the exhibition was opened a number of people flocked to it; and on being asked for the price of admission which was twenty-five cents, presented the bills which I had directed the boy to give away. The young rascal it appeared had sold all the bills at a cent a piece, saying that they would admit the bearer to the exhibition. The people were pretty mad at this and they looked foolish enough. However, their curiosity was too highly excited to keep them back, so they paid their admission and eased their hearts by sending portions of the boy's body and the whole of his spirit to a place where no thermometer ever ranges in the vicinity of zero. Before leaving the town, I had another intercourse with the young gentleman, it was in the street, the moment he saw me he took to his heels and ran as if for his life–my legs were rather the longest and I overtook him. He was terribly frightened at first, but not a little delighted at receiving half a dollar instead of a good thrashing which he deserved.

I completely took the shine out of the anniversary. A town one hundred years old was a great thing in the eyes of the country people, but a woman who was sixty one years of age before the town was born, was a much greater curiosity.

From Hingham I returned to Boston, and thence traveled to Lowell–Lowell is a great place. Its cloth factories are considerable of a sight. But its girls! Ten thousand of them as smart creatures, take them in the lump, as a man might ever dream of seeing in the world. Some of them are very handsome, and some of them are plain enough. But they all have a knowing air stamped upon their faces and in their speech, which seems to say, "do you see any thing green in me?" There are few fellows who are a match for them–as for your New York dandified-lady-killers, the Lowell girls would knock them into a cocked hat, and send them home so used up that their mother would not know them. The girls are too sensible and spirited to have any fancy for such miserable specimens of humanity. As for the rest, they are like girls all the world over, fond of being told of their beauty, and rarely disinclined for a flirtation. There is one thing to be observed, however, in conducting a flirtation with these girls. You must always carry a clothes brush in your pocket–that is, if you do not want all the world to know your affairs, and you go so far in your attachment as to steal a kiss. You see, these girl's dresses, from the nature of their employment are, literally speaking, covered with fine particles of cotton, which are not perceptible to the eye. Now, in stealing a kiss, there is always a little struggling, if only for form's sake, besides, in the opinions of many connoisseurs, it enhances the pleasure, and in this struggle these fine particles, as if ambitious of cutting a figure in the world, leave the light dresses where they are not seen, for the black coats where they are too apparent. I had a friend who stole a kiss of a very pretty factory girl as he was going to a large party. He got a box on the ears for which he cared but little, and was exposed by his coat before the whole party, for which he cared a great deal. Ever since that time he has carried a clothes brush in his pocket, and recommends, with unbounded philanthropy all young men who visit Lowell to follow his example.

I did a good thriving business in Lowell, and was well patronized by factory girls, who took a great pleasure in talking with Joyce, and asking her whether she wouldn't have a husband, to which the old girl expressed her ready assent. . . . I left Lowell when the attraction fell off and returned to Boston, from whence I proceeded to Worcester. There I had great sport. There was a great society there, called the Worcester Antiquarian Society. It is impossible for me to speak of all the good the very erudite and learned men have done. They have doubtless done deeds deserving of immortality, that a poor ignorant creature in conjunction with all the world, except the town of Worcester, is ignorant of. An Antiquarian Society is a great thing, and its members are great members. They are poets in their way, many of them; and like Lord Burleigh, see things that are not in sight. A common man gazing upon a piece of charred wood, (no pun) would put it down as "sich"; but an antiquarian–honor to his wisdom, the most peculiar of humbugs, a fellow who humbugs himself–will at once discover in it a thunderbolt which once and a long time ago ranged through heaven's high vault, leapt from a thunder cloud and fell upon *terra firma*, in order that he might show his wisdom and his might in making the discovery. A piece of potter's earth, manufactured in the year of our Lord one thousand eight hundred and forty, he can carry into far gone ages, and prove incontestably, to his own satisfaction and to the wonder and astonishment of the gaping ignorant, to be a part of a vessel manufactured by the Egyptians, from which circumstance he feels convinced that Christopher Columbus was a day after the fair in discovering the New World; and that the red skins are, to all intents and purposes, the descendent of that identical copper colored gentleman called Pharaoh, who was so improvident to cross the bed of the Red sea after the Israelites, and was drowned midway.

Well this Antiquarian Society pounced upon Joyce at once. I believe they were out of capital. That no potter's earth of some twenty or thirty years standing had been discovered in Worcester, or that no stones had been discovered which, by a convenient stretch of the imagination, could be converted into a Roman road–Joyce was an antiquity–in their eyes a glorious antiquity in a fine state of preservation. The members came down in a body, and they glorified exceedingly. They advised all the world and his wife to do the same, and I gloried exceedingly. But the greatest act of the Worcester Antiquarians, was a petition from the very learned and erudite body, requesting of me to grant them a precious boon, as a most special favor. It was no more nor less than a request for a lock of Joyce Heth's hair, that the memento of one hundred and sixty-one might be placed in their cabinet of antique curiosities. I condescended to grant the request, and a lock of her wool now adorns a niche in the sanctum sanctorum of the Worcester Antiquarian Society, unless the members, ashamed of their collective wisdom, have expunged their own resolutions and sent the inestimable lock to perdition.[39]

I may mention here something similar, which happened at Boston. While there, the President of the Plymouth Antiquary Society brought me a small piece of the old Plymouth rock as a great curiosity, in exchange for a lock of the wool of Washington's reputed nurse. As a great friend of the *antique* I gave it him.

My next place of destination was Springfield. On the way I stopped one Saturday evening at a small village. I had no idea of exhibiting Joyce, but her fame had made so great a sensation, that I was immediately waited upon with a request that I would be so kind and obliging as to take their money and favor them with a sight. It was impossible for me to stay in the place longer than that night. So it was agreed, that as soon as we could get Joyce into a spare room, the exhibition should take place.

I had in the first place to order the old woman up into the garret, where she was visited by the landlord and the members of the family. Among the last, there was a pretty and interesting young woman who was with Joyce and myself.

"You would not think," said I, determined upon having some fun in playing upon her credulity, "that this is no woman, but a mere automaton." "No, indeed," said she. "It is a fact." "Why, I'm sure it's a woman. I heard her speak." "Ventriloquism and machinery, nothing more. You need not laugh, I'll convince you. Now observe, when I touch a spring on the right side of her nose, she will say yes; when I touch a spring on the left side of her nose, she will say no."

Joyce, who was always ready for fun, and who entered into all sorts of humbugging, suffered a slight grin of pleasure to play for an instant round her old mouth, and then remained as quiet as one dead. "Joyce," said I, touching the right side of her nose, "are you an automaton?" "Yes," she answered. "Are you a living woman," touching the left side. "No." "You see now my dear, how it is done," I said to the pretty woman. "But she's warm," said the visitor, whom I put down for one of the servants of the establishment. "That is done," said I, "by the effect of artificial heat." "Well, I do presume to say," continued the young woman, "that there is not a person in this house who does not believe her to be alive."

Away she went to make the discovery to the whole household. Laughing heartily at the conceit, I went down into the bar and told the landlord how I had humbugged one of the servants, describing her. "That d–d fool," said the man, "I must stop this," and he rushed out of the bar. On his return, I asked him what the young woman said. "She feels herself quite unsettled," said he, looking as red as a turkey-cock's comb. The wonder then came out. It was his wife I had been gulling, mistaking her for a domestic. The business the landlord had that night, and my own liberality, not merely reconciled him, but put him into an exceedingly good humor. I took $43 in a few hours, and the following morning started for Springfield. . . . .

Chapter XIII

I did a great business at Springfield. The court was in session, and judges–good judges they were–came and pronounced Joyce a glorious case. Lawyers followed the example of the judges, and all the bar was taken in. . . .

I should state here that in all the eastern cities and towns, I made great capital out of the imaginary great grand children of the nurse of Washington. I made it understood wherever I went, that the proceeds of the exhibition, after deducting the expenses, were appropriated solely to the purchase of their freedom. The inquiries that were made were very pressing. The ministers, and regular abolitionists, as most of the people, to do them justice, are, always desired to know how much was wanted to complete the good work in which I was engaged. I soon found that by putting the sum at a low figure my attendance was increased. While there was a hope that the balance of the money could be raised in any place, the citizens strove most vigorously to put it in my hands. This was, curiously enough, exampled at a small village at which I exhibited Joyce Heth for one day only. On the following morning, as I was about to start, I was waited upon by a minister.

"How much is required, Mr. Diddleum," said he, "to set those poor slaves at liberty. My heart bleeds for them." "O, don't make your mind uneasy," said I, "only sixty-seven dollars is wanting, and that I shall raise at the next place I visit." "Only sixty-seven dollars! Stay here and exhibit, and I'll engage you receive the whole amount." "I should be very happy, but I am under an engagement to be elsewhere, and I cannot break my word." "O, if it could be done here! If we could have the glory of driving the last nail in the coffin of slavery, I should be content. Mr. Barnaby Diddleum, when must you go?" "Now!" "This instant?" "Yes." "If you could wait a couple hours only, I think I could raise the sum. We must have the proud satisfaction, and not the vain glory of driving the last nail in the coffin of slavery. Stay two hours." "Well, as you are so anxious, I will stay two hours. I am a poor man, and have only a small salary, but will contribute five dollars myself," and taking a V out of my pocket, and handing to him–"O, this is liberal–it is kind–it is generous–nay more, it is good, but you will be rewarded hereafter for it," he exclaimed enthusiastically, as he left the room. "In two hours," said I to myself, and I sat down quietly waiting his return.

Within the two hours he came back, his face radiant with smiles, and his eyes beaming with delight. "I have got it–I have got it," said he. "Here it is–sixty-seven dollars. The great grand children are free–their bonds are broken–their chains are unlocked–they own no master–they are as us–free, free, free! Heaven be praised." He went on in this strain for some time, and then handed me over the cash. There was one bad dollar bill in the amount, but I thought I would not tell him of it, as he had taken so much trouble. He told me moreover that he had contributed twenty dollars himself to make up the fund. This circumstance settled any qualms of conscience that might have arisen in my susceptible bosom in regard to taking the money. I have hated the priests for the most part with a Carthaginian hatred, and I have had good cause as you shall hear.

In the commencement of my adventures I stated that I was at one time the editor and proprietor of the Northern Trust Banner.[40] While thus employed, I took great deal of pains, with much pleasure, to expose the crimes of the clergy. There was plenty of room for it. Besides I was a very young man at the time, and had a Quixotic sort of an idea that I could regulate the moral machinery of the world wherever I was read, and make all the men, women, and little children, virtuous and moral by the force of my precepts. Of course this got me great ill will, and the clergy were determined to make me suffer for it. This was their opportunity.

In the town in which I resided, lived a miserable, miserly Presbyterian deacon, named S–y. He was one who tried to serve God and mammon most confoundedly. In the opinion of the faithful, he did the former to perfection, but the outside of the platter was the only thing he ever washed. He had, in his corrupt heart, an Augean stable that all the Herculeses in creation would fail to cleanse. He was a great temperance man, but recommended spirits to be taken as medicine, and as a medicine only. There was great policy in this. He kept a store and sold his peculiar kind of medicine. By this he saved paying a heavy license, and whipped the devil round the stump in more ways than one. The sanctified and the avowedly temperance men could go into his store with perfect propriety, when they would not on any consideration be seen to enter a hotel or a grog shop. The whole business was beautifully arranged. There was a wonderful deal of indisposition, and a great call for the medicine, which was purchased in large quantities, and generally carried off in an oil can or coffee pot, or some innocent domestic utensil, but never in a black bottle, for that would have betrayed the secret. But who would suspect an oil can of filling the lamp of a man's body with brandy, or a coffee pot bringing a Christian soul to his cups.

With this interesting virtue he had many others, but they were generally so cloaked, that though you could swear to the sound of the cloven foot, it was rarely that you could catch an actual glance of it. One beautiful virtue in which he had shone pre-eminently, was that of note shaving. There is no shaving broker in Wall Street who would act more remorselessly than he in the business.

A poor lame orphan boy who was subject to fits and at times could hardly be said to be *compos mentis,* received from his boss a note for $42 for work done in a comb factory. The boy wanted some money and was anxious to get the bill cashed. He went to the Presbyterian deacon who gave him $25 for it. The note was perfectly good, and if the boy had not been in every thing, except his trade[,] an idiot, he could not have been swindled so outrageously. The case was one of peculiar outrage, and burning then with virtuous indignation, I exposed the whole of the facts with such comments as I thought and hoped would harrow up his pernicious soul, and show it to the world, covered with rank leprosy.

He immediately commenced an action against me for libel. But even his great rage could not for a moment swallow up his greater cunning. He reflected that a criminal prosecution would be conducted at the expense of the State, and that a civil prosecution at the expense of his darling breeches pockets, so criminal was the word, and a most criminal business it was.

During the whole of the trial a number of clergymen sat at the bench with the judge for the purpose of influencing the jury by the weight of their cloth. At one time there were nine clergymen on the bench. I proved every thing I had stated, and my counsel was confident that I should be acquitted. The judge, a recent convert to religion, who looked upon the priests as they represented themselves, and thought it a sacrilege to write against the holy order, charged the jury strongly against me, and the jury, after a long consideration, brought me in guilty, believing, as some of them afterwards confessed to me, that sixpence damages would be rendered. The sentence was that I should be imprisoned for sixty days, and pay a fine of $100. The clergy shook hands in great glee, and I, for the most meritorious act of my life, for exposing a most worthless and abject scoundrel, was deprived of my liberty, and robbed of my money.

To render the case more peculiarly disgusting, to show the blackheartedness, the fiendish malice of my rascally persecutors, I was not sentenced, for telling the truth of a miscreant, until the last day of the term, when I was brought up with a murderer. A prayer was made in behalf of the two miscreants, and all the clergymen glorified. Now you see what reason I have to hate these men. I should state however, the bright, as well as the black side of the case. If any doubt remained on the minds of the jury at the time of the trial, it was all removed shortly afterwards. The people generally believed me to be an ill used man, and the deacon a friend of Diabolus. At the expiration of my term of bondage, I was escorted through the place by two thousand persons in procession, music playing, banners flying. A grand public dinner was given me, and I returned like a conquering hero from my two months incarceration. . . .

At Hartford I played the old game in regard to the grand children. As I left, when I got on the boat for New York to attend a grand Fair at Niblo's Garden, I found that there was at that place $240 waiting to complete the sum, and I said to my companion–"Well, these eastern people have been very generous in their desire to free the great grand children. I'll be generous too. There's $240 wanting to accomplish the object. I won't mind it. I'll let the great grand children go. So let it be considered from this time and forever, the great grand children are, and shall be free. We did not inform the towns that we had visited, how summarily the job was effected. My reason for becoming so generous was, that I knew the humbug would not go down in New York, and could only be turned to account among the red hot abolitionists.

Chapter XIV

I arrived with my dear darling, in time for the great fair of the American Institute. Joyce Heth was duly entered. She was not an American manufacture; but she was a great national curiosity. The good Gothamites, who had visited Joyce on her former sojourn in the city of the Knickerbockers, were much struck with a remarkable change in the appearance of her hair. When she was here previously, it was perfectly gray–now it was much darker. "A miracle!" they exclaimed. "This wonderful woman, so long and so miraculously preserved, is exempt in every way from the common ills of mortality." They commented upon the extraordinary circumstance, and deduced therefrom, that in a few years Joyce's hair would probably become raven black. They did not know that Barnaby Diddleum had created the miracle–that he had caused the old iron gray hairs to assume a brownish hue, and that the whole mystery of the thing, consisted in the application of some hair dye. I found that the faith in Joyce could not be shaken, and that any humbug I could administer, would be swallowed greedily. So I determined to lay it on with a trowel.

The new miracle took, and all those who had been to see the gray hairs, came to see the brown. The place was besieged, and numbers were turned away unable to get a sight during the hours of exhibition. The famous Dr. Rogers was a visitor, and took a lively interest in the concerns of my old woman. He asked my intention in regard to her. I told him I should exhibit her a short time longer in this country, and then take her to England–the El Dorado of my hopes. The Doctor extracted a promise of me, that if Joyce died in this country, he should have the postmortem examination of her bones. This exhibition was more profitable than the first.

While there in New York one of the circus people, whom I had met in my travels with the monkey, had an engagement at the Franklin Theater. He was considered a good singer in the country places; but the town did not affect him. He had a great deal of impudence in his composition, and did not care whether he was affected or not, so long as it did not interfere with his salary. On the night that he first appeared at the Franklin, he was hissed—he bore it with stoical indifference, and then advancing to the foot lights, stretched out his hand before the audience, and exclaimed: "Hiss, and be d—d! I'm used to it."

All circus people are curious characters, especially when they come in contact with regular actors, who view them much in the same light as sailors regard marines. Actors maintain a profound disgust for the sawdust, and the circus people have a supreme dislike to the legitimate business, which they regard with supreme contempt. Yet it is the ambition of the circus folks to play in a regular theater. When they do get the chance—when a manager in want of novelty tries whether quadrupeds will draw where bipeds have ceased to attract, the circus people are great folks. It is a remarkable fact that each of them grows a head taller upon such occasions.

There is a vast deal of difference in the standing of the professors of the two branches of entertainment, as there ought to be, and the manager of a circus is not, in the eyes of the world, unless he is one of those glorious, whole souled fellows, like Rufus Welsh, held in such estimation as the manager of a theater. But for all that, I had much rather be the manager of a circus than the manager of a theater. Fame is all very well; but money's better. Jack Falstaff was right in his notions of honor, uttered over the dead body of Hotspur. Honor! Poo—the *eagles!* I have known several proprietors of circuses, who have amassed large, and some of them princely fortunes; but I know of no manager of a theater, who has amassed a princely fortune. I know, however, of a long list of managers, who have been ruined. Hamblin is the only manager in the city who has not suspended. He has made a fortune in his time, and as he has breasted the worst of the theatrical storm, I hope he will once more have a fair wind and sail into the haven of prosperity.

A theater is a pretty difficult sort of place to manage. It all looks very nice in front; but if there is not a little h—l behind the scenes every now and then, why I know nothing of the matter. The jealousies between the women alone, are enough to keep a manager in hot water all the time. But that is only a part of his trouble. Every actor in his establishment seems to think that it is his province to resist the manager to the utmost, and that if the manager objects, it is to do him a moral injury. Every soup entertains the idea that he can play Richard as well as Kean—Coriolanus as well as Hamblin, or Spartacus as well as Forrest.[41] The consequence is, that they are dissatisfied with all the parts they get, and talk very loudly amongst themselves, of throwing up their parts, which they rarely do though. The men are as jealous as the women. Every Mr. A thinks he is wronged all the time that Mr. B plays the leading second business. Actors sometimes take whimsical methods of revenging themselves, for these supposed partialities. At one of the principal theaters in the city, there were two actors, Mr. H and Mr. B. Mr. H always imagined that he was wronged by Mr. B's sustaining some of his favorite parts, and on one occasion, he took down the regular call in the green room, and stuck up the following: "Tomorrow at eleven. The Castle Spectre, or the Humors of Young B–."

Managers have another evil to contend against. It is, that after the greatest pains have been taken to produce a piece in a style that will make it attractive, and recruit the treasury–one of the performers may become so inebriated as to be unable to play, and by this, the piece be altogether marred. An actor at the Bowery, on one occasion, in going to the treasury for his salary, was informed that he was forfeited the amount. "O, very well," said he, walking out. The following week he was fined a few shillings for breaking some regulations of the theater. "I expected it, I was fined last week for my whole salary." "You know what for? I suppose," said the stage manager. "No," said the actor, with the utmost nonchalance, "I did not think it worthwhile to inquire." To sum up, managers are crowded with evils, which circus people and exhibitors like myself, don't know. The horses are never jealous of each other, on account either of their beauty or their paces, and if one rider should become *non compos* you have only to clap another on the back of a horse, and the country people, God bless them, are ignorant of the exchange.

But I am making a long digression, and yet as it all comes under the head of exhibitions, for a theater is no more than an exhibition house, it is not altogether out of place. Joyce traveled from hence to Albany–from Albany to Troy. She then came back and proceeded to Newark. It would be useless to speak further of the number of adventures. Every fresh town was a counterpart of the last we visited in regard to the enthusiasm that prevailed in her behalf–to the desire of seeing her, and the glorifications and hallelujahs that were poured forth when she had been seen. Fanny Essler is now a great business. Her followers and admirers are multitudinous; but she never had the number that the immortal Joyce boasted, and then Joyce's followers were such good, moral people. They sang psalms and discoursed on heavenly things.

From Newark, through New York, Joyce proceeded to Connecticut. I stayed behind for the purpose of making arrangements for our projected trip to England. I often mused on the fortune I should make among the islanders, who boast "Slaves cannot breath in England, they touch our country and their shackles fall." In this they humbug themselves. There is no country in the world in which more miserable slavery exists. Compared with the poor creatures in the English factories, who die young, and yet too old for the accumulation of the suffering crowded into their brief career. Slavery, as it is known in the south, is Paradise to Hades. I almost counted my gains. John Bull is so easily humbugged. I felt that I should have quite easy sinecure of it. There would be no occasion for the exercise of my talent. I could lead him by the nose as asses are. Well, I contented myself with the reflection that I should pocket his sovereigns. I was always partial to sovereigns, they are such sterling fellows; but then I always want to keep them under my thumb. . . .

While I was building castles in the air, of the great wealth I and my heirs would inherit from my trans-atlantic trip, I received a letter that floored all my schemes, and put an end to all my day dreams. It informed me that Joyce Heth was dead–that the old woman had kicked the bucket–that I could humbug the world no longer–that death had taken the business out of my hands, and that the nurse of Washington, after being passionately attached to liquors all her life, had finally gone to the *land of spirits.* "She should have died hereafter," I exclaimed on reading the black intelligence of the death of the black. And she *should* have died hereafter if I had been with her. In other words she should not have died at all. She might have been seriously indisposed–so much so as to prevent her from being exhibited in this country probably, but she should not have died to the world. I would have buried her old bones, and with an old substitute, which I easily could have provided, embarked for England. One humbug would have answered just as well as another. I bitterly regretted that I had left the old woman at all.

Oh! John Bull, what a dear, delightful humbug you have lost. How the tale of your great grandchildren would have been swallowed by your good natured simplicity–your easy gullibility. I might have put down twenty at eight hundred dollars a piece, and have raised the sum twice told in London alone. It was, however, now, of no avail to moan over the past. I had only to consider how much I might make out of her remains.

Her body was at once sent on to me, and I immediately went to Dr. Rogers. He told me of my promise, and said that the dissection would aid the cause of science. There is no doubt but that it would aid his cause too, if matters had taken the turn he anticipated. I saw this at once, and determined to have a finger in the pie, and come in for my share. I told him that his religion might be science; but that mine was dollars and cents, and that I wanted to make something out of the affair.[42]

The doctor advised me to get a large room, and to charge fifty cents admission, to witness the dissection, which I did. He also wrote a letter to R. A. Locke, the editor of the Sun, for the sake of calling attention to the last exhibition of Joyce. The result of this last exhibition, in which Dr. Rogers served as the carver to the defunct, will appear in the next chapter.

Chapter XV

According to the directions of Dr. Rogers, I hired the City Saloon in Broadway, opposite St. Paul's, and erected seats to accommodate 1000 persons. Dr. Rogers gave me a note to his friend, Richard Adams Locke, esq., author of the moon hoax, then editor of the Sun, who, accordingly, recommended every friend of science to attend the post mortem examination of the old woman–as doubtless, new and important facts would be brought to light, which would greatly promote the cause of medical science. The Sun, and other papers, also contained an advertisement, announcing that Joyce Heth would be post mortemed by Dr. David L. Rogers.

The important hour arrived, and seven hundred people paid their half dollars, and quietly seated themselves in the City Saloon. This collection of persons was composed entirely of learned and scientific men, including surgeons, physicians, medical students, lawyers, and clergymen. Several of the last class tried, on the strength of their black coats, to get a free admission, but as this was the *last appearance* of Joyce *Heth,* I had no further favors to ask of the priests, so they couldn't come in–I made them plank the half dollar. If I had my will, many of those wolves in sheep's clothing should be sheared twice a year–but as it is, they shear their flock fifty two times a year, and milk the goats (beg from the world's people) as often as opportunity offers. However, as this portion of the community are *humbugs,* I suppose I ought not to find fault with them, for humbug is my hobby.

When the 700 persons were fairly seated, Dr. Rogers made his appearance, bearing in his hand eight or ten knives and other instruments. These the Dr laid upon the table, rolled back his sleeves, and rolled his eyes with an air of triumph upon the assemblage. The Dr looked, and doubtless felt, as if this was the proudest moment of his life, and he was so filled with the vast importance of his subject, that he could not do less than deliver a speech before commencing operations, which he did in nearly the following terms. "Gentlemen, you see before you the most important subject that ever graced a dissecting table. Never since the flood, have we heard of a person reaching the astonishing age which this woman undoubtedly has. We shall, unquestionably, in the course of this examination, make many important discoveries not laid down in our medical books. You are aware, gentleman, that ossification usually commences in the wrist of an ordinary person at about the age of fifty-five years, and gradually follows the arteries towards the heart. While traveling in Italy, several years since, I had the distinguished honor of being present at a post mortem examination of a woman who died at the age of 116 years. In that instance, we found the arteries ossified in the immediate region of the heart–and in the present instance, we shall unquestionably find the arteries in close connection with the heart, and probably some portion of that organ itself in a state of ossification."

With these remarks, Dr Rogers commenced cutting into the breast, and before having entered scarcely through the skin, he stopped and remarked, "Here, gentleman, are evident marks of extreme longevity–the appearance of the skin denotes the most advanced age, &c, &c." Thus the doctor went on, committing himself at every step–not, in fact, making any discoveries whatever, but feeling confident he should soon do so. Finally he opened the breast, and thrust his hand into the cavity of the chest–in this position he stood for a moment in silence–his countenance began to change–disappointment was stamped on every feature–presently he moved his hand around in every portion of the cavity, in the vain expectation of finding his anticipated "ossification," but alas! What did not exist could not be found–every artery was as soft as an infant's, (and why should this not have been? For the truth is, Joyce Heth never lived over seventy five years–all appearances to the contrary were induced by disease).[45] Mortification, and the most profound astonishment, was depicted on the learned doctor's countenance–he felt that he had been humbugged–he felt that the cause of science had been trifled with, and its disciples bamboozled, and he knew not what to say. He stood speechless for some minutes, the audience regarding him with breathless curiosity–at last the love of science triumphed in his mind–the agony was over, and he exclaimed, "Gentlemen, I am inclined to think there is some mistake here. The arteries, in connection with the woman's heart, are as soft as an infant's, and I can discover nothing which indicates that she has lived more than seventy-five or eighty years at the utmost!"

Now, there is no doubt, but Dr Rogers is as skillful a surgeon as this country contains, and although I feel some pride in numbering him among my victims to humbug, I confess, that in this decision, he was perfectly correct, and that the decision itself evinced his thorough knowledge of the science of surgery, and his determination to defend it, even at the hazard of exposing himself as one of the "deluded" believers in the "gammon" of Barnaby Diddleum. This announcement of the learned doctor's, threw the whole learned and scientific body into commotion and confusion. They were petrified with astonishment–they had great faith in Dr Rogers, and now they seemed to doubt their ears! They had fully believed that Joyce Heth was 161 years old, and now to hear Dr Rogers strike off eighty-six years at one swoop, was indeed astounding! For a few minutes not a word could be said–at last, an old gray physician arose and said: "Dr Rogers, we are all aware that ossification of the arteries is usually the attendant of old age–so are gray hairs, so is baldness–but there are exceptions–may this not be an exception?" "It may be," said Dr Rogers with an incredulous shake of the head, which as plainly as a shake of the head could say–"but I don't believe it."

The exhibition now hurried to a close, there being nothing more to say; and the examination, which was expected to last some three hours and result in the most stupendous discoveries, was fully concluded within twenty minutes from its commencement. As the audience of seven hundred passed out of the door at which I was standing, with a face as long as deacon Seth's, when he is planning how to rob a widow or orphan, many remarks were dropped, indicating the belief that Dr Rogers was mistaken; and that, in fact, Joyce was as old as represented. At last, all had left the room except Dr Rogers, his friend Richard Adams Locke, myself, and a legal Yankee friend who had traveled with me, and who alone was in the "grand secret."

"Gentlemen," says the doctor, addressing myself and my Yankee friend, "between you and me, and the gate post; that woman has never lived more than seventy-five or eighty years. Why, I calculated to have spoiled half a dozen knives in cutting the ossification from around her heart, and yet everything is soft as an infant's." "But," I replied, "Doctor she must have been 161 years old, for the documents fully prove it." "I care nothing about the documents sir, they must be forgeries, or apply to some other individual, probably long since dead. I have no doubt you are honest about it, and believed all you said, (I could hardly keep from bursting into a laugh,) but there is an egregious mistake somewhere."

My legal Yankee friend, who was always perfectly at home in any company, and who would never let a chance for a good joke pass unimproved, now stepped up to the doctor, brushed back his hair, and sticking his thumbs in the sleeves of his vest, exclaimed: "Doctor, why do you say you disbelieve in her great age?" "On account of the absence of ossification, and the soft state of her arteries and heart." "Oh! Doctor, that can all be accounted for on scientific principles." "On scientific principles? How so?" exclaimed the doctor with much energy, and evincing a great curiosity to hear anything on the subject of science. "Why," replied my legal friend, "you will recollect, Dr Rogers, that Joyce Heth was a member of the Baptist church one hundred and sixteen years, and of course she would have a very soft heart."

"The h–l she would!" exclaimed the doctor in a rage, the truth flashing upon him, that I and my friend were laughing in our sleeves, and that he was the subject of our joke–then running his arm through that of his friend Locke, off they started in a great passion. The cat was now in a very fair way to be let out of the bag–in fact, I cared not how soon this was done, for all the money that could be made out of the old woman. I had now only to bury her decently, and let the world make the most of the humbugging I had given them. From the abrupt manner in which Dr. Rogers and Mr. Locke left us, I was assured the whole humbug would be exposed in the next day's Sun–and such was the case.

I must here mention a very philanthropic act performed by Mr. Cowperthwaite, the undertaker, at the corner of Catherine street and East Broadway. As soon as I learned of the death of old Joyce, I determined that she should, after being post mortemed, be placed in as good a coffin as I could purchase, and be transported back for internment in my native village, Bethel, CT, where she died. I accordingly, called on Mr. Cowperthwaite, who has long been established as an honorable and gentlemanly undertaker, and asked him the price of his best mahogany coffins. He told me, and mentioned that I wanted a coffin for Joyce Heth. "Is it possible!" exclaimed the benevolent man–"is then the nurse of Washington dead at last?" I assured him this was the case, and he then, with a very correct and commendable eye to business, declared that if I would wait three days before moving the coffin, and thus allow him to exhibit the same with her name and age thereon, he would furnish it for $20 less than the price he had named, and which, he assured me, was much below cost. Wishing to do the good hearted man a favor, I consented to the arrangement, and the consequence was, a silver coffin plate was displayed at his door for three successive days, bearing the following inscription:

JOYCE HETH

AGED

161 YEARS

The body of Joyce was placed in due time in the splendid coffin, and buried in the church yard of Bethel, Fairfield county, Connecticut; and, ere long, I intend to do, what I have already too long deferred, place a monument to her memory. I have often laughed to myself, at thinking what some future Antiquarian Society may do, if they happen, while excavating the old graveyard to make room for the march of improvement, to discover the coffin plate announcing 161 years as the age of an individual. What sage speculations, such a discovery might give rise to! When Joyce was buried there, in the richest coffin ever placed in that burial ground, a stupid, straight-jacket, penurious, Yankee, named Seelye, remarked, that he was satisfied that Barnaby Diddleum intended to dig up the corpse before long–that the burial was only for *effect*–for he would never suffer so valuable a coffin to be wasted away in the earth! Now such an ass as that don't know how to appreciate the glory of spending money, as well as making it. But to return to Dr. Rogers and Richard Adams Locke. As I expected, from the temper in which Dr. Rogers and his friend Locke, left the dissecting room, the Sun came out in a long and flaming article, from which I make the following extracts, the balance of the article being a scientific account of the dissection, which would occupy more space than it is worth.

> *Dissection of Joice Heth–Precious Humbug Exposed*–The anatomical examination of the body of Joice Heth yesterday at the City Saloon, resulted in the exposure of one of the most precious humbugs that ever was imposed upon a credulous community. We were somewhat surprised that a public dissection of this kind should have been proposed, and were half inclined to question the propriety of the scientific curiosity which prompted it. We felt as though the person of poor old Joyce Heth should have been sacred from exposure and mutilation, not so much on account of her extreme old age, and the public curiosity which she had already gratified for the gain of others, as for the high honor with which she was endowed in being the nurse of the immortal Washington.

> From the evidence of these and numerous others in the whole pathological anatomy of the body, which our imperfect acquaintance with the science prevents our describing, it seemed to be the unanimous opinion of all the medical gentlemen present, that Joyce Heth could not have been more than *seventy five*, or at the utmost, *eighty years of age!* There is therefore a moral certainty that her pretensions to the extraordinary longevity of 161 years, all her stories about suckling George Washington, and about her fondness for "young master George," have been taught her in regular lessons, for the benefit of her exhibitors. We believe,

however, that the persons who exhibited her in this city inculpated in the deception, but that they took her at a high price, upon the warranty of others. Still it is probable that $10,000 have been made by this, the most precious humbug of modern times.[44]

The assertion of the Sun, that it was the unanimous opinion of all the medical men present, that Joyce Heth was not more than seventy five or eighty years of age, is incorrect–such *was not* the impression of half of that learned body. Several of the medical men present at the time, came out in the papers after the dissection, and defended Joyce Heth tooth and nail. In other portions of the article which appeared in the Sun, Mr. Locke tried to defend his friend, the Doctor, by saying, that he, the Doctor, had always believed it to be a hoax. Such a pretence might almost be excusable for a man who had not got his foot in it as deep as those men had–so I let that go. The fact is, all who were present at the dissection knew that Dr. Rogers believed Joyce to be as old as represented. But this announcement in the Sun, came like a clap of thunder in a cloudless sky upon some 30,000 persons in this city, who had visited Joyce and "believed." They were astonished beyond conception. But they did not, could not, believe the report of the Sun. Why, reasoned they, to say nothing about the absurdity of believing that any person would dare to originate and circulate a story of this kind, and manufacture certificates and bills of sale to prove it; every appearance of the woman gives the lie to the assertion of the Sun; for, certainly, we never saw a person look as old as she did, by eighty years.

Well, this was pretty fair reasoning, for really, if I possessed infinite power, I should not have known which way to go to work to make Joyce look older than she did. But as all signs fail in dry weather, so did the data on which the believers founded their faith. Joyce was not more than "seventy-five or eighty years of age." The above announcement appeared in the Sun of Feb. 26th, 1836. On that day, my legal Yankee friend and myself were walking down Nassau street, when who should we meet, but James Gordon Bennett of the Herald. "Well," says Bennett, "you are a pretty brace of rascals to be exhibiting an eighty years old nigger for 161!" "Never mind," says I, "Bennett, you will find who is humbugged one of these days." "Why so? What do you mean by that?" "Never mind what I mean, you will hear soon." "But stop Barnaby," says Bennett, "don't be in such a hurry, come in my office."

It struck me just then, that it would be well if I could get a good joke on Bennett, so we walked into his office. "Come," says Bennett, "tell me, you humbugging villain, what do you mean by your mysterious shrugs and hints." "Well," said I, "I'll tell *you,* but mind you don't say anything about it. Between ourselves, Joyce Heth is alive and doing well in Connecticut, and the person whom Dr. Rogers and the medical faculty have been dissecting, is an old woman who died out at Harlem the other day." "My God! Is it possible," exclaimed Bennett, "that's the best joke I ever heard in my life. I'll publish every word of it." "Oh no," says I, "you must not do that, I would not have it published on any account, for the longer people suppose she is dead, the better she will take when she comes back from Connecticut." "I can't keep it," says Bennett, "it is too good a joke to be kept dark a moment, and I always go in for giving the first news. Now, Barnaby, do you keep this from the other editors, and let me come out tomorrow morning with this *exclusive* news; and, my boy, when Joyce returns here, I'll puff her to the *skies*." Well, thinks I, there's some need of her being puffed in *that region* about these days, so I told Bennett, that seeing it was him, he should have the whole story; and that I would not tell it to another editor in this city till he had published it.

Bennett was, of course, delighted; and commenced immediately taking notes as I divulged this important secret, and from these notes, Bennett manufactured the following article, which appeared in his paper the next day—27th Feb.

> Another Hoax.
>
> Annexed is a long rigmarole account of the "Dissection of Joyce Heth," extracted from yesterday's Sun, which is nothing more or less than a complete hoax from beginning to end. *Joyce Heth is not dead.* On Wednesday last, as we learned from the best authority, she was living at Hebron, in Connecticut, where she then was. The object on which Doctor Rogers and the Medical Faculty of Barclay street have been exercising their knife and their ingenuity, is the remains of a respectable old negress called AUNT NELLY, who has lived many years in a small house by herself, in Harlem, belonging to Mr. Clarke. She is, as Dr. Rogers sagely discovers, and Doctor Locke his colleague accurately records, only eighty years of age. Aunt Nelly before death, complained of old age and infirmity. She was otherwise in good spirits. The recent winter, however, has been very severe, and so she gave up the ghost a few days ago.
>
> Some person in this city, we believe one of the advertising doctors who had been hoaxed by the Lunar Discoveries, in the manufacture of which it is now believed that Doctor Rogers had a principal hand along with Sir Richard A. Locke, resolved, as soon as he heard from a friend of the death of poor AUNT NELLY, to send her body into the city, and contrive to pass her off upon the Medical Faculty for the veritable Joyce Heth. The trick took. Several of the hoaxed went, looked, wondered, and held up their hands in astonishment. Her death was announced in the Sun, and a *post mortem* examination prepared. The public swallowed the pill. Aunt Nelly, neglected, unknown, unpitied when alive, became an object of deep science and deeper investigation when she died. She looked as old and ugly as Joyce herself, and in that respect answered the thing exactly.
>
> Such is the true version of the hoax, as given us by good authority, of the story told in the following piece of humbug, taken from yesterday's Sun.

Here follows the article from the Sun, to which Bennett adds the following remarks.

Thus far the Joyce Heth hoax, for the verity of which we have names and certificates in our possession. But before we conclude, we must now put a few plain questions to Doctor Rogers, who figures so conspicuously in the above report. Are you not, Sir, the real author of the Lunar Hoax? Did you not furnish Richard A. Locke with the most of that humbug? Did he not, at your request, undertake to pass for the author to the world? Is it not known to you that he is incapable of writing the scientific portion of the hoax? If Dr. Rogers will deny explicitly, under his own signature, what is conveyed in these queries, through the columns of the Sun, we shall then stir our stumps and see if we can't produce certificates of their truth.

The appearance of this article produced as great a sensation as that in the Sun the day previous, but it was much more satisfactory to the large portion of the population who had visited Joyce. "Ah, ha!" said they, "we knew it was not possible that Joyce Heth was as young as represented by Dr. Rogers—and the whole thing is easily accounted for now." But if this news was agreeable to the public, it was not so to Dr. Rogers nor Mr. Locke. They knew perfectly well that they had cut up the genuine Joyce, but they knew also that Bennett was cutting them up, and that however much Bennett was hoaxed, the public would put the boot on the other leg, and believe Bennett instead of them. The joke was considered a rich one, and scarce anything was talked of except the ingenious manner in which the "wrong passenger" had been slipped on to Dr. Rogers and the medical faculty. Rogers and Locke writhed under it, and the latter strenuously denied it in the Sun. But Bennett being sure he was right, was determined to "go ahead," so he laid it down heavier than before. Finally, Locke came out in the Sun, and charged me with deceiving Bennett—said I did it only for the sake of keeping the press in a broil, and if I did not stop it "he would make the city too hot to hold me." That threat had no effect except to make me almost suffocate with laughter, and so I kept the ball a rolling. One day I was in at Bennett's office, and says he, "Barnaby, you see those rascals still deny that they were hoaxed with 'Aunt Nelly'—now I'll tell you what to do. Do you go out to Harlem and get me a dozen good certificates of the death of Aunt Nelly, and add your affidavit of the manner in which she was passed off to Dr. Rogers for aunt Joyce. That will nail the gentlemen—and there will be no chance for them to stir again—they have been most cursedly hoaxed, and I am determined they shan't get out if it."

I promised all that was requested, and marched out, and of course I *kept out* for some time. In fact, I went to Washington that week, and was gone several months. A friend of mine, however, sent me the Herald regularly. I saw by that, which way the cat jumped. Bennett waited patiently a few weeks for my return with the certificates, but as no Barnaby Diddleum appeared, he began to think that he had been diddled. Every day strengthened his belief in the unpleasant conclusion to which he had arrived, and in the meantime Locke succeeded in turning the tables upon Bennett, and kept up a constant fire; showing how Bennett had been hoaxed with the "Aunt Nelly" story. Bennett, at last, becoming convinced that he had been done, made a desperate

effort to extricate himself, and succeeded pretty well. He came out with an article
something like the following:

> Dr. Rogers still denies, through his friend Locke, that he was humbugged with an
> *extra nigger* in the pretended Joyce Heth examination. Now we make Dr. Rogers
> the following offer. If he will come out in the Sun with his own name, we will bet
> him $350, being his half of the proceeds of the dissecting exhibition, that Joyce
> Heth is now in Connecticut. Now let the Dr. "down with his dust," or acknowledge
> he was hoaxed. In further evidence of the truth of our position, we publish the
> following certificates which were taken at Harlem yesterday.

Here followed half a dozen fictitious certificates stating that the persons certifying,
know "Aunt Nelly," that she died, was conveyed into the city, &c., according as Bennett had published—we have only room for the following, from among the certificates
above alluded to:

> Mr. Editor, the Sun has been egregiously hoaxed—or the doctors have hoaxed
> the Sun. Mr. Locke, the man-bat man, has only been passing off, I fear, another
> humbug on the public. I understand that the old black woman dissected by Dr.
> Rogers, is a poor old woman called Aunt Nelly, who lived in Harlem. I have been
> out and seen her often, I know a man did intend to exhibit her about the country,
> but the winter closed in, and she died too soon.
> Sullivan street, Feb. 27th. Peter McCarty.

> Harlem, Feb. 29th, 1836. Mr. Bennett, I have seen your account of the examina-
> tion of Joyce Heth. It is all hum—I know the woman passed off for Joyce Heth
> was a respectable negress who lived alone in a house near this place, and died
> recently. She was taken to the city, and passed off upon the doctors, to make an
> exhibition of. If you want further particulars, I will be in town soon and give you
> the particulars.
> John P. Thompson

Thus did Bennett get out of the scrape at last, and thus do I close that portion of
my adventures which relates to the illustrious nurse of Washington.

SELECTIONS FROM THE
European Correspondence (1844–46)

On March 17, 1844, Barnum returned to the pages of the *New York Atlas* with a series of travel letters designed to promote his first international tour. Known collectively as the *European Correspondence*, this was by far the largest of Barnum's writing projects beyond his published books. Over the next two years, he produced ninety-seven articles, many of which ran into multiple columns and thousands of words. Barnum used this front-page forum to comment on a wide range of contemporary topics: from the daily logistics of international touring to foreign debates over American slavery. The series came to a close on May 10, 1846, with a final installment written aboard the steamship *Great Western.*[45] Reflecting upon his long transatlantic adventure, Barnum now described himself as a true "cosmopolite." He had also become a very rich man and, quite probably, the most famous impresario in the world.

Barnum's second *Atlas* assignment thus served as the culmination of one of the era's more remarkable professional turnarounds. In the weeks immediately following the conclusion of *Adventures,* full-blown desperation had begun to set in: "Living in the city of New-York with nothing to do and a family to support, in a very short time exhausted my funds, and I became about as poor as I should ever wish to be. . . . I began to realize, seriously, that I was at the very bottom of fortune's ladder."[46] Yet, as Barnum scrambled to "keep the pot boiling at home," he also began to recognize one of the new market economy's more remarkable features. For the cold-blooded huckster, it was sometimes possible to generate profits with

little more than hollow promises and a few friends in the newspaper business.

The first step came in the fall of 1841, when Barnum finagled a loan for the American Museum using a worthless piece of Connecticut swampland (Ivy Island) as collateral. He then drove off a better-financed group of rival investors by publishing anonymous "squibs" (some of which appeared in the *Atlas*) to kill their stock offering. Six months later, he engineered a badly needed infusion of cash and press attention with a bogus wonder–the Feejee Mermaid–that had been defunct for almost two decades. The key ingredient was a marketing program that soon became a Barnum signature. If your product lacks a buzz, make one up. Invent expert testimonials. Pretend previous triumphs. And for the pièce de résistance, hire fake rivals to accuse you of doing so.[47]

Next came the most successful and enduring production of Barnum's entire career. This is how he described the "discovery" in November 1842: "I had heard of a remarkably small child in Bridgeport; and by my request my brother brought him to the hotel. He was the smallest child I ever saw that could walk alone. He was not two feet in height, and weighed less than sixteen pounds. He was a bright-eyed little fellow, with light hair and ruddy cheeks, was perfectly healthy, and as asymmetrical as an Apollo. He was exceedingly bashful, but after some coaxing he was induced to converse with me, and informed me that his name was CHARLES S. STRATTON."[48]

There was one major sticking point. Stratton, he learned, "was only five years old, and to exhibit a dwarf of that age might

FIGURE 4

An early daguerreotype of General Tom
Thumb (Charles Stratton) (Library of
Congress, Prints and Photographs Division,
reproduction number LC-USZ62-109908).
This image shows Stratton's appearance
during his first international tour (1844–46).

provoke the question, How do you know
that he *is* a dwarf?" Barnum's solution was
to construct an entirely new persona. He
inflated the boy's age to eleven. He ordered specially designed costumes and
a tiny horse-drawn carriage. He changed
the name on the playbills to "General Tom
Thumb." He even taught his "diminutive
prodigy" to smoke cigars, drink brandy,
tell risqué jokes, and sneak kisses from
female fans.[49]

Early installments of the *European
Correspondence* show us how this "man in
miniature" became one of the nineteenth-
century's first international celebrities.
Barnum's opening move was to scout the
London amusement trade by reading ev-

ery newspaper he could find. He then sent
off "letters of introduction" (we would call
them press releases) to leading editors and
theater managers. Meanwhile, Stratton and
entourage set up shop in one of the city's
toniest West End neighborhoods. This
choice of location reflected more than the
showman's improving financial situation.
It was also a calculated promotional ma-
neuver designed to raise the status of the
exhibition. As Barnum later noted, "dwarfs
were at a rather low figure in the fancy-
stocks of England."[50] But the West End address sent a very different message: the
general was no ordinary dwarf.

Such bold claims naturally depended
upon attracting the right sort of public. Barnum thus spent much of the first season
courting the "fancy stocks" of London–from
expatriate bankers to Queen Victoria herself. He also made elite patronage a central
promotional theme, dropping big names
from Stratton's "autograph book" and commenting upon the heavy traffic of carriages
along the curb. Barnaby Diddleum, one
imagines, would have ruthlessly mocked
such a fashionable crowd, or at least spiked
the punch at Buckingham Palace. The Barnum of the *European Correspondence,* by
contrast, chose a more refined form of
engagement. Clearly delighted with the
"blushing honors" thrust upon him, America's most notorious trickster now bowed
politely, accepted presents from the royal
family, and sent them home to the museum
as proof of his rapid ascension.

The broader implications of this strategy become clearer as the series progresses.
Consider the letters recounting Stratton's
performances for Queen Victoria.[51] Early
on, Barnum depicts himself as a kind of
provincial greenhorn. He gushes about
"the magnificent picture gallery" or the
thrill of putting his "hand on the throne."
Soon, though, a more impressive tale of
Yankee ingenuity begins to emerge. Bar-

num and Stratton routinely enter the palaces as bowing plebians. But they depart as conquering entrepreneurs. By the end of the cycle, even Victoria herself has been reduced to a fawning consumer.

The showman's discussion of the old English fairs follows a similar narrative arc.[52] As Barnum knew quite well, these ancient sites of carnivalesque revelry were the cultural seedbeds of his own industry. In the opening lines, he briefly acknowledges that the crowd before him was many times larger than any he had witnessed in New York City. Quickly, however, Barnum begins to shift from wide-eyed tourist to more confident critic. His condescending conclusion draws a kind of line in the historical sand. On one side is the "foul place" that European carnival has become. On the other is Barnum himself, now cast as the show trade's more respectable future.[53]

This is not to suggest that the *European Correspondence* failed to praise foreign achievements. Barnum introduces us to wax figures "more *life-like* than any I have seen," automatons that throw their American counterparts "far in the shade," and industrial expositions "more fine, curious, and wonderful than any thing ever seen at Niblo's." But the descriptions rarely end with expressions of deference or wonder.

Rather, when Barnum comes upon something truly remarkable, his standard response is to purchase the novelty and ship it home, thereby transforming his travel letters into advance promotions.

Barnum's closing installments mark the start of a much larger geocultural shift. Only a decade or two earlier, American performers were a rare sight on European stages. Yet, as Barnum surveyed London's entertainment districts during his final months of touring, he noticed the beginnings of a pattern that would become all too common over the next century: "The universal Yankee nation is pretty well represented here at present, so far as amusements are concerned. . . . [All] are successful, and will be able to pocket and carry back a few of the pounds which their brethren lavished on foreign talent."[54]

✳

Barnum often failed to put dates on his European letters. For the sake of consistency, I have therefore chosen to list the dates of their publication in the *Atlas*. Most of these letters were written about four to six weeks before publication. This delay reflected the exigencies of Barnum's touring schedule, as well as the time required to ship a letter across the Atlantic in the mid-1840s.

MARCH 17, 1844

Liverpool. Messrs. Editors—According to promise I hasten to give you notice of my "whereabouts" and "matters and things in general"; but as I have not been half an hour on shore, I trust that yourselves and your readers will make allowances for my present unfitness to indite even a tolerable epistle, which is all I am able to do under the most favorable circumstances. But I detest apologies—so here goes.

On Thursday, the 18th of January, at 11 o'clock, I stepped upon the new and splendid packet ship Yorkshire, Capt. D. G. Bailey, bound for Liverpool. My party was six in number, viz.: General Tom Thumb, his father and mother, Professor Guillaudeu, the French naturalist, Mr. Ciprico, the General's tutor, and myself.[55] At half past 11, the cables were cast off, the ship left the wharf, gallantly led down the bay by two steamboats for that purpose. The City Brass Band, attached to the Museum, kindly volunteered to escort us down to Sandy Hook, accompanied by many of our friends. I have traveled through every state in the Union, and over a considerable part of the Canadas, but I have always contrived to do so by stage, steamboat or railroad, and, therefore, all I saw on board our noble ship was entirely new to me. What with the depression of spirits I felt on leaving family, friends and home, and the dread of sea sickness, I was in what we Yankees call "a considerable of a stew." The deck was covered with ropes, blocks, and cables; sailors were running in all directions; the pilot, a gruff looking chap with a high florid complexion, was giving orders in language that was Greek to me; and such expressions as main-brace, mizen-topsail hilliards, main-topsail brace, and forty other (to me) equally unintelligible phrases, I became utterly confused. I was out of my element—I had got beyond my depth—I was, to use a homely expression, like a cat in a strange garret. . . .

At half past 1 o'clock, the bell of the steamer gave notice for our friends to leave the ship. That moment my usually high spirits fell below zero. As I successively grasped for the last time the hand of each friend as he passed to the steamboat, I could hardly restrain a tear; and here a little incident occurred that made me weep in spite of myself. One of my friends, in giving the parting palm, quietly slipped into my hand a keepsake, saying, "Accept this little trifle to remember when far from *home*." I could not utter one word in reply. I strove to check the tears, and essayed to speak, but the words stuck in my throat. The steamer cast off, and the excellent band struck up "Home, sweet home." The tears then flowed thick and fast.

The distance between the ship and steamboat is fast increasing—I stand on the quarter deck, waving my handkerchief to my friends—the music still floats sweetly and directly over the water. Hark! The band strikes up "Yankee Doodle"; we all give three hearty cheers, and wave our hats, in which even the sailors join, and I care not to acknowledge that I wept freely, overpowered as I was with mingled feelings of joy and regret. At 2 o'clock, P.M. the pilot left us, and thus was broken the last remaining link that bound us to the shore. . . .

MARCH 31, 1844

London. Messrs. Editors—The mails for Liverpool close in a few hours, and as this is the last chance to write, previous to the departure of the steamer for Boston, I embrace it. . . .

Every morning I find on my table the London Times, Morning Herald, and Advertiser; in the evening I take the Sun and Globe, and on Sunday I have several weekly papers. This you may think is rather extravagant, inasmuch as the papers cost ten cents each; but that is not the way business is done in London. I *hire* the reading of each daily paper for a shilling each week, and the weeklies for two pence! Carriers hire out their papers in this manner, at various prices, according to the lateness of the hour it is taken–and, indeed, they are hired at *reduced* prices, on the second and third day after publication, until, in fact, they are literally "used up!"

. . . There are but few streets here that I have yet seen that are wider and finer than our Broadway; but there are *so many* Broadways here, and such a host of Bowerys, or streets surpassing in every respect our Bowery, that a New Yorker soon begins to look upon Gotham as a little village. Of course there are several streets here that throw our Broadway altogether in the shade. Among these are Regent street, Oxford street, Piccadilly, High Holborn, Strand, Pall Mall, &c.; in fact, all of the West End is on a scale of magnificence worth traveling miles to behold.

My house is on Grafton street, close by Bond street, and in the very heart of fashion. Lord Brougham resides next door but one to me–half a dozen countesses are my nearest neighbors, and the house I occupy has been rented for several years by Lord Talbot. From this magnificent mansion, I have sent letters of invitation to the editors, and several of the nobility, who have called to see Gen. Tom Thumb, and have of course been delighted. Mr. Everett, the American minister, called last week, and was highly pleased with the little General. We dined with him the next day by invitation, and his family would not let the General off till they had loaded him with presents. Mr. Everett kindly promised to call at the palace today in person, with a view to having Gen. Tom Thumb introduced to the Queen, which will doubtless be done this week, unless the court mourning prevents.

Last night the Baroness Rothschild sent her carriage for us. We spent two hours in her mansion, which eclipses everything in the shape of luxury that I have ever seen. Some twenty lords and ladies were present, and on taking our leave, an elegant purse, containing twenty sovereigns, was quietly slipped in my hands–a good evidence of the high favor in which Tom Thumb stands in London among the nobility. . . .

You will see by all the London papers with what *éclat* Tom Thumb was received at the Princess's Theater. Our course is *onward!*

I have already engaged some great novelties for the American Museum. They will arrive in New York about the 5th of April. I am also negotiating for something new in the way of public exhibition, which will delight the citizens of the new world. I have just heard from my agent, whom I had dispatched through France and Germany. He has already secured some extraordinary curiosities for the Museum, natural and artificial, animate and inanimate.[56]

I have visited Drury Lane, Covent Garden, the Chinese Collection, Catlin's, Madame Toussard's wax works, Adelphi Theater, &c., but I must defer noticing these and all the *lions* till my next.[57] A ticket has been sent me to attend the great *bal masque* at Covent Garden to-night. I *guess* I shall go. It is to be an immense affair, although tickets are but half a guinea each. Many of the nobility will be there. The tickets were mostly taken ten days ago.

Guineas here go just about as far as dollars do in New York—very little further. However, I like that. A young man once asked his father where he should go to make money. "Where eggs are a dollar a dozen," replied the father. He was right. Go where everything is dear to *make* money, but go where things are cheap to spend it. Adieu.

APRIL 24, 1844

London. . . . On my return home, I found several carriages at the door, and upon entering was introduced to Lord Chesterfield, the celebrated Count D'Orsay, and a party of ladies who were waiting to see Gen. Tom Thumb. They were all delighted with the greatest *little* man the world has ever produced, and went away promising to call again with many of their friends. I have lying upon the table in my drawing room an album in which all the nobility who visit the General enter their names, so that I shall upon our return have a valuable book of *autographs* to exhibit to the visitors of the Museum. In company with those gentlemen was Henry Baring, Esq., one of the eminent bankers. I have already registered on my *diary* invitations for the General to several parties. One for next Monday night, is to the house of Mr. Drummond, the banker, who is to give 20 guineas ($100) for the company of the General and myself half an hour. . . .

MAY 5, 1844

London. Messrs. Editors—I had intended to have written you half a dozen letters by the steamer that sails tomorrow for London; but here I am within one hour of the closing of the mail, and only this much written. The fact is, I have had no time to look at the "lions" since I wrote you last. I jumped into an omnibus last week, to go and look at St. Paul's, the Tower, &c, and the only other passenger was a well dressed, intelligent-looking gentleman. I soon commenced a conversation with him; informed him that I was a stranger in London, and begged him to inform me what was most remarkable and best worth seeing in the city. "Well," he replied, "there are *many* wonders in London, which may occupy your time for weeks; but the most remarkable at present here, and indeed the whole town talk, is General Tom Thumb, the American dwarf." I preserved an *incognito,* but I took a hint, and felt it my duty, as a *public benefactor,* to *show* the *greatest* lion in town, rather than to be spending my time among the "cubs"; and this may be my excuse for deferring to speak of London's permanent wonders till my next letter.

Since I wrote you last, I have been twice with Tom Thumb before Queen Victoria, at Buckingham Palace–once before the Queen Dowager, at Marlborough House–have exhibited the General to the Queen of the Belgians, Prince Albert, the Duchess of Kent, the Prince of Wales, the young Princess Royal, the Duke of Wellington, and thousands of nobility–have attended two of the queen's levees at St. James' Palace–visited the first nobility at their residences–passed several hours on three separate days, in examining all the wonders and magnificence of St. James' Palace–have put my hand on the throne itself, and done many more marvelous things, which I will not mention at present; but I must say that if I was not a remarkably *modest* man, I should probably brag a little, and say that I had done what no American ever before had accomplished; but being "remarkably modest," I shall say *nothing,* but wait for an American to appear who has visited the queen at her palace *twice* within eight days, on each occasion been received with smiles, cordiality, sociability, and royal favor.

You will see by the papers (from the London Times down) that Tom Thumb has received a magnificent present from Queen Victoria, and that the Queen Dowager is having a watch made on purpose for him. You will see, indeed, that Gen. Tom Thumb is all the rage in London, and, as "the season" is only just commencing, you may imagine what a harvest of glory and pounds awaits us.

I have already seen and learned enough to fill a dozen volumes, and therefore shall not be much troubled to find matter for letters *weekly* for the Atlas, but you must this time excuse me. My "blushing honors" have been thrust so fast and thickly on me within the last ten days, that I can talk of nothing else. Perhaps, by the next ship, I may be able to *change the subject;* at least, for your sakes, as well as your readers', I will *try.* I send by this steamer, for exhibition in the Museum, various curiosities obtained in the palace, as well as little presents given Tom Thumb by the queen's own hand. I also send the queen's autograph, as well as the autographs of many of the first lords in the land. I have likewise shipped a large collection of natural curiosities, birds, quadrupeds, shells, &c., selected by Professor Guillaudeu, who is now in Paris, engaged in the same occupation, and will proceed to Germany and return to New York in June. Several performers of rare talent are also engaged for my lecture room. I have taken copious notes in my diary of all I saw in the palaces of my previous visits–of the armory room, the tapestry room, the great reception room, the throne room, &c., &c., as well as the description of the feathers, diamonds, India shawls, &c., displayed by the visitors at the queen's last drawing room–and as this is a treat seldom, if ever, enjoyed by an American, I shall not fail to give your readers the advantage of it, the first leisure moment I find. . . .

Messrs. Editors–Everybody nearly has heard of the English *Fairs*. What they were in olden times I don't know, but they are certainly now-a-days very *small affairs*. A fair was held the three first days in Easter week at Greenwich, a few miles from London. Being desirous of seeing what was going on, and at the same time having an eye to *business*, (for I supposed that probably some novelty might be exhibiting there, which would cut a dash in the American Museum,) I took a friend and proceeded to Greenwich with him one night at nine o'clock.[58] We took the cars, and in fifteen minutes were set down at Greenwich. We found the town thronged with people, and in *this* country "throngs" mean upwards of a considerable many. In New York, ten thousand persons make a pretty large company; in England, *fifty thousand* persons make but a small turn-out.

My friend led the way, and we soon found ourselves in the middle of the fair. It was held in an immense park filled with booths of all sorts, shapes, and sizes, and illuminated and decorated in the most fanciful manner. One booth was for the sale of ginger cake; another for *toys* of all kinds; then there was an exhibition of a learned pig, big snake, and dwarf woman, "all for a penny"; another was for the sale of ale, sandwiches, and other "refreshments"; another had *theatrical* performances, the actors and actresses, dressed for their various characters, to entrap a few were walking up and down on a large platform erected in front of the booth; then there was a dancing booth, and a rum shop, and a circus, a set of jugglers, more ginger cake shops, two giantesses and a white negro, then more cake shops, then another penny show of some description, another dancing booth, a professor of magic, the learned goats, a calf with two heads, more ale and sandwich shops, more dancing booths, more wonderful shows, more gingerbread stalls, and so on to the end of the chapter. Every booth had its crier and bell ringers, and its man with a big tin trumpet, through which he would make the most deafening, eloquent, and pathetic speeches, to induce the crowd to patronize his establishment. I visited all the shows, and found them literally "outside shows"; and after being squeezed nearly to death, and rendered deaf by the outrageous bedlam like screeches, ringing of bells and yelling through trumpets, we made our exit, being perfectly satisfied that an English "Fair" in these degenerate days is the most *foul* place a man could easily get into. On our return we found all the first and second class cars filled with passengers, so we were glad to get a chance in the *third* class, which consisted of an open box, the sides of which were about breast high, containing *no seats,* and into this we were crowded all *standing,* and packed at about the rate of two human beings to the square foot. I was at one time fearful of getting my pocket picked, but, on reflection, knew there was no danger, for we were packed so tight no person could move his arms or hands no more than if he was pinioned. What made our situation *doubly* interesting, was the fact that about half of our fellow passengers were *females,* so that we carried a portion of the "fair" with us, and quite as *near* to us as was at all comfortable.

I have several times visited the Royal Polytechnic Institution, in Regent street. It is a public exhibition, established for the advancement of the arts and practical science, especially as connected with machinery and manufactures. It contains many halls, lecture rooms, and other apartments, and is worth going to see. . . . One side of the large hall, under the gallery, contains various working models of machinery kept in constant motion, and this is the most interesting portion of the whole establishment. I have recently purchased all the working models of machinery belonging to the eminent Professor Partington, and shipped them to America, for the Museum. They are fully equal to those of the Polytechnic Institution. The galleries of the Polytechnic are filled with cases containing specimens of almost every description of manufacture in the kingdom. The building contains a large lecture room, in which lectures are given on most scientific subjects, and the experiments interspersed exhibitions of the powers of the microscope and beautiful dissolving views. For instruction and amusement, I know no place in London to be preferred before the Royal Polytechnic Institution. It is open day and evening, and lectures on various scientific subjects are given at one, four, and nine o'clock, P.M. I have made the acquaintance of the managers, and through their influence have negotiated for the hire of a set of dissolving views, surpassing in magnificence anything of the kind even in England. I cannot use them in America, however, till I have a larger lecture room, which I trust will be soon.

Madame Tassaud's exhibition of wax figures is also worth visiting. The figures are more *life-like* than any I have seen, and indeed nearly one half of them are arranged to move by internal machinery, so that a person scarcely knows which are wax figures and which are visitors. One old gentleman was sitting down with spectacles on his nose, quite absorbed in viewing a group of figures. I accidentally stepped on his toes; he looked up to me with a frown, and I begged his pardon as politely as I knew how; he made no answer, and a dozen of the visitors laughed at me! I found that I was speaking to a moving *wax figure* of Cobbett! I afterwards stood admiring the beautiful movements of a figure of a man, which was sitting with a number of pamphlets in its hand, and systematically moving its hand to and fro. I thought the movement beautiful and the figure quite natural. Presently it got up and marched into the private office, so that my "figure" proved to be flesh and blood, and was the man employed to sell the catalogs of the establishment. . . .

JUNE 9, 1844

London. Messrs. Editors—In one of my former letters, I promised to give an account of the reception of Gen. Tom Thumb and myself at Buckingham Palace. I will try to be as brief as possible. When the queen sent for us the first time, special instructions were given us, by her command, to let the General appear before her, as he would anywhere else, and not to be instructed to use any of the titles of royalty, as the queen desired to see him act *naturally* and without restraint. This was much the best plan, and enabled the General to appear to much more advantage. We arrived at the palace, and were conducted by the lord in waiting through a long corridor to a broad flight of marble stairs, which led to the queen's magnificent picture gallery, where the Queen and Prince Albert, the Duchess of Kent and twenty or thirty of the nobility were awaiting our arrival. They were standing at the further end of the room, when the doors were thrown open, and the General toddled in, looking like a wax doll gifted with the powers of locomotion. Surprise and pleasure were depicted on the countenances of the royal circle, at beholding this *mite* of humanity so much smaller than they had evidently expected to have found him.

The General advanced with a firm step, and he came within hailing distance[,] made a very graceful bow and exclaimed, "Good evening, *Ladies* and *Gentlemen.*" A burst of laughter followed this salutation. The queen then took him by the hand, led him about the gallery and asked him many questions, the answers to which kept her and all assembled in an uninterrupted strain of laughter. The General familiarly informed the queen that her picture gallery was "*first rate,*" and told her that he should like to see the Prince of Wales. The queen informed him that the prince had retired to rest, but that he should see him on some future occasion. The General then gave his songs, dances, imitations, &c., and after a conversation with Prince Albert and all present, which lasted an hour and a quarter, we left. As we approached the door, the queen's favorite poodle dog discovered the General, and gave a bark which quite startled him from his propriety. He however recovered immediately, and commenced an attack upon the poodle, and a funny fight ensued which caused a roar of laughter from the queen and her friends. The lord in waiting playfully remarked to me, that he hoped the General had sustained no *damage,* for in that case he much feared a declaration of *war* from the American government.

The queen was modestly attired in plain black, with no ornament whatever. Indeed, surrounded as she was by ladies dressed in the highest style of magnificence, their dresses sparkling with diamonds, a stranger would have selected her as the last person in the circle who could have been the Queen of England. She is of small stature, and not of the most beautiful form or countenance. Her appearance is extremely modest and unassuming. Her face is the picture of amiability, and her eyes, soft and full, seem to be the index of a good heart. She is withal very sociable and amiable in her manners, and one feels immediately at ease in her presence, and cannot realize that he is conversing with the greatest potentate in the world. I need not say that I was delighted at this total absence of formality, and could not forebear contrasting her kind and sociable manners with some of the New York aristocracy with which I have sometimes come into contact. It is a lamentable fact that a small portion of the *elite* (so called) of America in their attempts to *ape* the English aristocracy, entirely overdo the business, and instead of proving themselves worthy to be called the "best society," they show that they are only poor *imitators*–purse proud, haughty, and self conceited. By their actions they engender the detestation of the sensible portion of the community, instead of commanding their respect and esteem, as they could be a more affable and proper course of conduct. I need scarcely say that I do not allude to the great body of our most wealthy citizens, but of a certain *few* ignorant and vulgar persons, who by some sudden freak of fortune have amassed great wealth, by the influence of which they crawl into good society, and take the first opportunity of proving the old adage, "put a beggar on horseback," &c.

On our second visit to the queen, we were received in what is called the *yellow drawing room*, a magnificent apartment, surpassing in splendor and gorgeousness anything of the kind that I have ever seen. . . . We were ushered into the room before the queen and royal circle had left the dining room, and, as they approached, the General bowed respectfully, and remarked to the queen that "he saw her before," adding, "I think this is a prettier room than the picture gallery–that chandelier is very fine indeed!" The queen smilingly took him by the hand, and said she hoped he was very well. "Yes, ma'am," replied the General, "I am first rate." "General," said the queen, "this is the Prince of Wales," leading the prince up to the General. "How are you, Prince?" said the General, shaking him by the hand; and then standing beside the prince, he remarked–"the prince is taller than I, but I *feel* as big as anybody," upon which he strutted up and down the room as proud as a peacock, amid shouts of laughter from all present.

The queen then introduced the Princess Royal, and the General immediately led her to his elegant little sofa, which we took with us, and with much *nonchalance* sat himself down at her side. He went through his various performances as before, and the queen gave him an elegant and costly present, which had been made by her order expressly for him, and for which he told her "he was very much obliged, and would keep it as long as he lived." The Queen of the Belgians (daughter of Louis Philippe) was present on this occasion. She asked the General where he was going from here. "To Paris," he replied. "Who do you expect to see there?" asked the Belgian Queen. Of course all expected that he would answer, "the King of the French"; but the little fellow replied–"I shall see Monsieur Guillaudeu in Paris." The two queens looked inquiringly to me, and when I informed them that Monsieur Guillaudeu was my French naturalist, who had preceded us to Paris, they laughed immoderately.

On our *third* visit to the queen, Leopold, the King of the Belgians, was also present. He was highly pleased, and asked a multitude of questions. Queen Victoria desired the General to sing a song, and asked him what he preferred to sing. "Yankee Doodle," was the quick reply. A burst of laughter followed this reply, which was as unexpected to me as it was to all present, and the queen good humouredly remarked–*"That is a very pretty song, General*–sing it, if you please." After remaining an hour we left, and at parting the queen said–"Good by, General, I hope we shall see you again." . . .

JUNE 16, 1844

London. . . . I have this moment received letters from New York, conveying the painful and totally unexpected intelligence of the death of my youngest child. Such a calamity, at all times heart-rending, is much more painful under the peculiar circumstances in which I am placed. But a few months ago, I left her blithe and merry, blooming in health and happiness; and now, without a moment's warning, I learn that she is the tenant of the grave. But a few days ago I sent her presents, which I hoped would give her joy. Alas! before they have crossed the Atlantic, she is placed beyond the reach of either pain or pleasure, so far as this world is concerned. I had fondly hoped to meet her on my return, but a good and wise Providence has ordered otherwise; and painful as is the effort to the parental feelings, still the doctrines of Christianity, and a belief and confidence in the goodness of a Creator, whose attributes consist of infinite power, wisdom and *love,* enables men all humility to say, "not my will but *thine,* oh God, be done."

I can write no more to-day.

JUNE 23, 1844

London. . . . The observance of the Sabbath here is just about the same as in New York. By some mischance my steward neglected on Saturday fortnight to procure *bread* for the following day, so on Sunday at dinner time I sent him for a loaf. He returned without it; he could get none. I inquired the reason. "Oh," says he, "*mother church* rules in London, and her decree is that all *baker* shops be closed on Sunday, but if you should happen to want *rum, gin, or brandy,* you could get plenty; for tippling shops are open at every corner!" I thought that a very fair hit at "mother church."

Speaking of church reminds me of another anecdote. Nearly all the exhibitions in London employ a dozen or two men to go about the streets carrying their bill boards far above their heads, being attached to a pole which they carry on their shoulders. Thus you will meet these itinerant advertisers with their lofty placards, announcing the place and time of exhibiting the "Chinese Collection," "Ojibeway Indians," "Grand Diorama," "General Tom Thumb," "Panorama of Hong Kong," "Wilson's Scottish entertainments," and scores of other exhibitions. While taking my morning ride the other day, I discovered a *new* moving sign of this kind, many rods ahead of me. It had large *brass* letters of the highest polish, and they glistened in the sun like burnished gold, and therefore could be seen at a great distance. There! thinks I, here is another "*show*" arrived in town, and a formidable opposition it may prove, for really they are cutting a *splendid dash,* to begin with. As we approached the moving board, I began wondering what exhibition it could be–whether it was a cannibal, an ourang outang, a learned pig, or whether possibly the "striped pig" had arrived from Boston; but my doubts were soon solved, for we came so near that I could read the show bill, and what do you think it was? This was the whole inscription: Prepare to Meet Thy God–On the reverse side also the same–Prepare to Meet Thy God.

This *brass* bill contained not another word, and of course gave no clue to the names of the *brazen* faced projectors; but I felt quite anxious to learn what gentlemen had opened this new branch of "show business," and where they *exhibited* themselves. So I asked the "board man" what was the object of his brass mandate. He replied that "church meetings were held three times per day at present, at Exeter Hall, (the head quarters of priest craft in this country,) and that he was sent out for that establishment."

What blasphemy it is thus to make a "show" and merchandize of the Word of God! But there are some fanatics in the world, who would reduce the character of the Almighty to that of a Connecticut peddler. . . .

JULY 21, 1844

L ondon. . . . A lady, the other day, who came in her carriage to the exhibition of General Tom Thumb, hearing me say that the General was an American, pointed to Jocosot, an Indian chief who was in the room, and remarked–"They tell me that man is American also." "Yes," I replied, "he comes from America." "Are they *related?*" she asked, with perfect seriousness. Her idea of amalgamation would evidently well accord with those of the white ladies in Massachusetts who petitioned the legislature for the "privilege" of marrying negroes. . . .

Very few negroes are seen in London, and when seen at all they are generally walking arm in arm with a white person of the opposite sex.[59] A negro came into the General's exhibition the other night with a well dressed white woman on his arm. The darkey was dressed off in great style, with gold chains, rings, pins, &c., (niggers always like jewels,) and his lady love was apparently quite fond of him. I made General Tom Thumb sing all the "nigger songs" that he could think of, and dance Lucy Long and several "Wirginny breakdowns." I then asked the General what the negroes called him when he traveled south. "They called me little massa," replied the General, "and they always took their hats off, too." The amalgamating darkey did not like this allusion to his "brack bredren ob de south," nor did he relish the General's songs about Dandy Jim, who was "de finest nigger in de country, O," and who strapped his pantaloons down so fine when "to see Miss Dinah he did go." The General enjoyed the joke, and frequently pointed his finger at the negro, much to the discomfiture of "de colored gemman." . . .[60]

JULY 28, 1844

Paris. Messrs. Editors–When I wrote my last letter, I thought it doubtful whether I should be able, for the present, to visit the French metropolis; but, upon reflection, I determined to forego a press of business and numerous engagements, rather than to miss the "Grand Exposition" or great fair now open in Paris, and which is held only once in five years, and by the rules of which, *this* year, every nation and country is allowed to send in specimens of its manufactures, arts, inventions, &c. I certainly should have been beside myself if I had remained in London, and let this great concentration of the skill and ingenuity of the world pass away without my beholding it. So, concluding that I might combine business with pleasure, I engaged a French gentleman to accompany me, who has for many years been engaged in procuring curiosities in Paris for the nobility of England, and who will therefore, prove a great acquisition to me in exploring this great city in search of novelties for America; for I have brought along a few thousands, which I am determined shall be expended for the American Museum, if novelties of sufficient merit can be found in Paris, and I expect little trouble on that score, inasmuch as the "Exposition" must contain many wonderful things which have never before seen the light. But *nous verrons.* . . .

AUGUST 4, 1844

Paris. Messrs. Editors–I have now been five days in Paris, and as I have been on the move every moment when I was not asleep, I am getting partially acquainted with Parisian mysteries. I can assure you, I have seen many strange things not recorded by Eugene Sue.[61]

The first moment after our arrival, my friend and self bent our steps towards the "Grand Exposition," or great fair, opened in an immense building erected for the purpose in the *Champs Elysees.* We went there at 8 o'clock in the morning, and were readily admitted on showing our passports, although it is not open to the public till 12 o'clock. This gave us four hours to look about before the crowd arrived, but even then we had not a twentieth part of the mass of articles exhibited there. We ultimately spent three days in going over all the halls which are devoted to the purpose, and which, together make some five miles, which a person must travel over to see the whole. Only imagine that this great Exposition takes place but once in five years, and that it is open for persons of every art, trade and science in the world to exhibit their productions. I can give you no adequate idea of the immensity or magnificence of this array of the concentrated skill of the universe. Thousands of things not dreamt of in either your or my philosophy are here displayed, and nothing which I could think of or inquire after but was to be found here, and generally in some new or improved form.

Fancy five hundred American Institutes holding a fair at one place, and exhibiting articles five hundred times more fine, curious and wonderful than any thing ever seen at Niblo's, and you may get a fair conception of the display made at the "Exposition Publique des Produits de l'Industrie Francaise." The extent of the place can hardly be conceived, by hurrying through it, as some do, in six or eight hours; it is only by a calm examination of the whole that the immensity of the Exposition strikes you. It is folly to hurry through such a display heedlessly, when it is remembered that every article is a curiosity, every specimen a wonder, else it would not be there.

I took the cards of address of eighty-seven manufacturers of mechanical automatons, and other artists who have invented and manufactured curious articles, which I thought would be novelties of the American Museum; and I shall call personally on every one of these persons before I leave Paris. . . .

AUGUST 11, 1844

London. Messrs. Editors—I returned from Paris yesterday, having spent a fortnight in that delightful city, instead of three or four days, as I anticipated in leaving London; but my business and pleasure in that city was so happily combined, I could not tear myself away till I had, with an eye to the former, visited every artist whom I thought could contribute to my interests; and, with the other organ of vision directed to the latter, till I had beheld all the mighty works of grandeur and art for which Paris is so universally and so justly celebrated. The fact is, I saw so much that to me was new, grand, magnificent, and astonishing, that I should never be able to tell you *what* I saw, if I had not noted in my diary everything which struck me as worth giving more in detail hereafter. So I must apply to my notes, and give you my dish of hodge-podge and salmagundi helter-skelter, just as it happens; and a sorry dish I fear I shall make of it. . . .

Being attracted one night by some sweet strains of music which proceeded from a large saloon in the Palais Royal, I entered, and found it to proceed from an orchestra of eight musicians, all of whom were perfectly *blind*.[62] They played the clarinet, flute, cornet a piston, horne a piston, three violins, and a double bass, and they played with more effect than I ever heard from the same number of instruments. They played the overture to the "Bronze Horse," "Fra Diavalo," &c., very effectively. While listening to the music, I perceived opposite to me Dr. Jones, proprietor of the Royal Adelaide Gallery in London, and a particular friend of mine. I found on speaking with him that he had visited Paris with the same purpose which I had, viz.: to obtain novelties for the gratification of the public; that he had just arrived, and we at once agreed to "join teams" in our pursuit after the wonderful.

The next morning the doctor and myself commenced our researches, and in the course of three days we made ourselves acquainted with nearly all the most ingenious artisans in Paris. These extraordinary men usually have their work shops in the fourth or fifth story of a large house which stands back from the street, and which contains from sixteen to twenty different tenants engaged in as many different occupations. On the ground floor of these buildings is a "concierge," (office,) where the porter or porteress (for they are generally females) gives you the desired information respecting the locality of any tenant whom you may desire to visit. I made very extensive purchases, and have already shipped to America, through our consul, Mr. Draper, some of the most extraordinary, ingenious and beautiful pieces of mechanism I ever saw. I have also several artists at work in completing others, which will be shipped from time to time as they are finished. After completing our business, the doctor and myself devoted the remainder of our time in Paris to visiting its stupendous works of art. . . .

AUGUST 18, 1844

London. . . . I think I mentioned in a former letter that the "Grand Exposition, or quinquennial exhibition of the products of national industry," is held in the Elysian Fields, in an immense temporary building erected for the purpose. Several elegant cafes and restaurants are erected in various parts of the Champs Elysees; also, a building for the exhibition of panoramas, and a magnificent edifice for Franconi's summer circus.[63] I attended the circus one night, and was delighted with the interior of the building, and the grand display and effect of the large audience, from the peculiar manner in which the seats are arranged. The edifice is a spacious polygonal building of sixteen sides, built of stone, with a pedimented porch to the east, surmounted with a bronze figure of a horse. Panels with horses' heads (medallion) ornament the sides. The interior presents the appearance of an immense Moorish hall, the roof being supported by light iron columns, and painted, together with the panels, in rich colors, with gilding. The ceiling is tastefully arranged in compartments representing equestrian figures, and from its center, over the circle or ring, hangs a chandelier with 130 gas jets. Round the entire circus are ranged sixteen circles of seats, holding 6000 persons; and when these seats are all filled, as they were on the night that I attended, the scene is imposing in a great degree. The eight lower seats are fitted up with stalls, and the price to them is two francs; the upper seats are one franc. In America, the lower seats are called the pit and pay the least price; but here the positions and prices are reversed, and I think very correctly. Opposite the entrance is the orchestra, occupying the length of 20 feet and the depth of ten ranges of seats. The performances were very good, and one feat struck me as very extraordinary, viz.: the leaping of one horse over the backs of two horses, standing side by side. The circus, theater, and all places of amusement, are open in Paris on Sunday night, and are generally better attended than on any other night of the week. . . .

AUGUST 25, 1844

Norwich. Messrs. Editors–The last letter which I wrote you was dated London, and was really *commenced* there, but it was continued in Liverpool, received a few additional lines in Manchester, still more at Birmingham, a few at Ipswich, and was finished at Yarmouth. So you see what opportunities I have of "writing at my leisure," as I had expected to do, after Mr. Sherman arrived from America.[64]

I find that it will be necessary occasionally to write an *extra* letter, a kind of "supplement," treating on English matters, and thus forming a slight break in the descriptions of what I saw at Paris. Otherwise my letters would, for the next six or eight weeks, treat entirely of Paris, and the little incidents which might be occurring within my notice in England, would be left unrecorded. So you may as well mark this down as a "supplement."

General Tom Thumb has now been exhibited at the west end of London for *four* successive months, with a continued and unabated procession of crowded houses. In fact, no exhibition in London was ever before so absolutely popular and successful as the General's has proved. And what is still more gratifying is, that much the largest class of visitors have been persons of the highest rank and refinement. He has been petted by, and received presents from, ladies and gentlemen of the highest distinction, from the queen down. I have now a trunk full of letters from persons of influence in all parts of England, Ireland and Scotland, inviting us to visit them, and offering large pecuniary inducements for doing so. Still I am anxious to return home, and shall do so as soon as we can give a hop, skip and jump through the principal towns in England, Scotland, Ireland, and possibly France. At present it would be the height of folly and madness to run home when we can take $500 per day here, and that we can do with all ease, and have averaged more than that sum daily since the General's first visit to the queen, and the watering places are all now crowded with visitors. Being myself, as you know, a decidedly modest individual, I shall not attempt to *brag* of my exploits, nor say that I have got as much money as I want–(few men ever get *enough*)–but I cannot deny that I feel as if perseverance, industry, and perhaps "good luck," have placed me above the apprehension of want in this world; still, I assure you that, although I can make more money with General Tom Thumb in two months than I can in the American Museum in a year, yet my whole pride lies centered in the museum, and it will be ever a source of pride and pleasure to me to make it a place of universal resort, and one which, in point of respectability, shall not be surpassed in the world. I purchased that establishment under peculiar circumstances, when it was losing money; but by constant and unremitted industry, I made it a profitable concern, and, in my endeavor to gain an honest livelihood, I was nobly supported by a generous public. I *then* catered for the purpose of *making money;* and while I repeat that I neither now have, nor never expect to possess quite "enough," it is obvious that the pecuniary profits of the museum are small compared to what I can make in other ways, and therefore must be of little comparative importance to me; but I pledge my honor that I would give up all other hopes of emolument which I possess in the world, rather than part with the American Museum; for now, having secured an independence, I am determined to gratify my own pride and the pleasure of my patrons at the same time, by making that institution the most attractive and valuable establishment of the kind in the world. I have visited foreign institutions of the same description, and prepared to make every kind of improvement that could suggest itself to my mind, by viewing them attentively; and as I have opportunities for securing curiosities and performers which no other American has ever possessed, if my life is spared me, I will ere long, (if I have not already done it,) make that establishment a source of pride to our city and country, and render it an acknowledged and universal proverb, "that more beautiful and wonderful things can be seen and heard there for twenty-five cents than at any other place in America for a dollar," and the public shall go, not to benefit the manager, but to *benefit themselves*–blending rational amusement with valuable instruction for themselves and children; and thus will I show my gratitude to that public who, when I *needed* its assistance, came forward to and nobly sustained a man whom they saw was toiling night and day for his own support and their pleasure and gratification. In Europe, these institutions are owned, protected and fostered by *government*–but I will show the citizens of the Old World that, in good and glorious republican America, the aid of government for such a purpose is not required, but that, under our form of government, *individual enterprise* can effect what even the government itself cannot accomplish in other countries. . . .

NOVEMBER 24, 1844

Steamship Acadia, on the Atlantic. Messrs. Editors–You will hardly be more surprised than I am, to learn that I am so suddenly returning to America. Business, however, rules "men of business" with despotic sway; and men of the world who have as many irons in the fire as I have, learn that it is perfectly futile to calculate where they may be a few months future from any given time. . . .

On the second or third day out, before the passengers had become thoroughly acquainted with each other, I heard a couple of gentlemen talking of Gen. Tom Thumb and his successes in England. "Ah, no wonder he succeeded," said one, "for that Barnum has the impudence of the devil, and would have got before the queen if he had been obliged to do as the boy Jones did—crawl in at the back window." "Do you know him?" asked the other. "Not personally—but I keep a carpet store near the American Museum, and know him well by report." "Is he, then, as impudent as you say?" "Impudent! why, he was the exhibitor of old Joice Heth; and when traveling with that and various other exhibitions, he use to *preach* when the show business was bad, and thus raise money to carry him from town to town!"

This was getting quite rich, so I joined the gentlemen in conversation, and assured them that I knew Barnum very well, and that he was the greatest humbug who ever went unhung. The carpet man was delighted to find one of Barnum's acquaintances, who knew him so well, and I gave them rayther a dark picture of Mr. B's character.

"It is strange to me that so many patronize his museum," said the carpet man, "for we all know that it is Humbug Hall; in fact, one of the penny papers, that could not get Barnum's advertisements, christened it by that name." "Yes," I replied, "and well it might be called so. Don't you remember the mermaid?" "To be sure I do," replied the carpet man, "and I went with my two daughters to see it, expecting to find the animal alive, with the body of a beautiful woman and the tail of a fish, like the painting of it in front of the museum; but the thing was dead and stuffed, and I think it was the poorest show I ever *did* see." "Why don't you make him give your money back?" I inquired. "Oh, because we wanted to see the rest of the museum, and I must say that I never laughed in one night before, as I did at the performances in the lecture-room on this occasion. My daughters, too, were delighted."

"So, you partly got the worth of your money?" I asked. "Oh, yes—quite—quite; and my daughters have made me take them there a dozen times since; but that's no excuse for his humbugging the people. Now, I have been told that General Tom Thumb is a humbug." "To be sure he is," I replied. "Is it possible! In what respect is he a humbug?" asked the carpet man. "Because he is no more *alive* than the mermaid was," I replied. "Not alive! Why, you astonish me; for I have been told that he talks." "Certainly he does—or, rather, *it* does; for it is a wax figure filled with machinery, which is so constructed as to make it move about with the grace of a living being—and the voice is thrown into the body by Barnum himself, who is the best ventriloquist of the age, though it is not generally known; and thus he is constantly devoting his powers to imposing on the public."

"Wonderful!" exclaimed the carpet man and his credulous companion. "I thought," continued Mr. Carpet, "that it was impossible a human being could be as *small* as they say Tom Thumb is. Pray, where was this machine made?" "In

Bridgeport, Connecticut," I replied, and, turning on my heel, left the two gentlemen to continue their conversation regarding the great humbug. The next day the carpet man heard that Mr. Barnum was on board, and asked to have him pointed out. He was told that I was the individual. He would not believe, and gave his reasons, viz.: that I had told him about the impositions of this same man. "Just like him," was the reply; "he has been humbugging you–for it certainly *is* Barnum."

The carpet man approached me. "Is your name Barnum?" he asked. "It is," I replied. "And you keep the American Museum?" "I do." He was surprised, and attempted to make an apology. I begged him not to think of it–that he had nothing to apologize about, for it was all true except the preaching. "Well, really," he replied, "I heard in New York that you did sometimes preach." "I give you the credit for getting the news before I did," I replied; "it's no doubt true, but I never heard of it before." From that time we were all good friends; and on taking leave of the carpet man on our arrival in New York, he gave it as his decided opinion that I was *not a cloven foot,* as he had supposed before meeting me. Thine, as ever, P.T.B.

P.S.–You discover that this letter, commenced "at sea," was finished in New York.

JANUARY 5, 1845

Steamship Great Western, At sea. Messrs. Editors–After remaining a couple of days in New York, and passing unscathed through Miller's "last day,"[65] I began to arrange and carry out the various plans and improvements which have led me so suddenly to visit America; one of which I hope the public have learned before this time, was the permanent and extensive enlargement of the lecture room of the American Museum, by throwing two stories into one, in order that the various magnificent exhibitions which I had engaged in Europe could be brought out to better advantage. The particulars, however, of that and other important improvements you will learn by visiting the museum itself, and I trust that you will do your duties as public journalists too well to let the world remain long in the dark on that subject.

A source of great amusement to me on my return to New York, was the discovery of so many *new* friends. I could hardly credit my senses, when I discovered so many wealthy men, who compose the codfish aristocracy of New York, extending their hands to me, and expressing their great delight at seeing me again, although before I left New York those same nabobs would have looked down on me with disdain if I had presumed to have spoken to them.[66] I really forgot, till they forced the truth upon my mind, that since I left them I had accumulated a few more dirty dollars, and that now, therefore, we were upon *equal* ground! Bah! the very thought of money being the standard of merit makes me sick; and the fawning, canting obsequiousness which I witnessed from *many* during my flying visit to America, made me despise the sycophants, and almost wish I was not worth a shilling in the world! On the other hand, I met some good honest friends in humble circumstances, who almost appeared to approach me with awe–and then again I felt ashamed of human nature. What a miserable, pitiful and disgraceful state of society is it, which elevates a booby or a tyrant to its highest summit, provided he has more gold than others; while a heart or a wise head is trampled in the dust, if their owner happens to be poor.

No man can be happy who, because he happens to be rich, mounts upon stilts, and attempts to stride over his fellow man. For my own part, the only possible benefit which I can conceive wealth can confer on an individual is, that while it enables without ostentation to secure the comforts of life for himself and family, it also gives him the pleasure of contributing to the necessities and comforts of his fellow beings. My sincere prayer is, that I may be reduced to beggary rather than be made a pampered, purse proud and overbearing aristocrat, by the influence of wealth. This coat, I am sorry to say, is intended for and will fit many of my acquaintances in New York. I beg them, for their own sakes as well as mine, to *wear* it. I wish them and all the world to know that my father was a *tailor*, that I am a *showman* by profession, and all the *gilding* shall make nothing else of me. When a man gets above his business, he is a poor devil, who merits the detestation of all that know him. The idea that a shoemaker or a tinker cannot be a *gentleman*, is supremely ridiculous; but it is not so much so that which assumes every man *necessarily* to be a gentleman, if he happens to be wealthy. Both notions are false and wrong, and never should be encouraged in a country like ours. It leads to the most deplorable results; for frequently some clown, who happens to be fortunate, amasses great wealth, sets up for a gentleman, and being a great man, his friends will do whatever he pleases, and thus he is allowed to bore all who know him for the remainder of his life. Perhaps his ambition happens to take a political turn, and lo! we are cursed with a Dogberry of a judge, or an ass of a legislator, who would disgrace a legislative body composed of boys of ordinary intelligence ten years of age. . . .

I arrived in America a few days before the presidential election, and was sorry to see so much excitement on the subject. Those large and repeated "mass meetings" in all parts of the country are pernicious in their consequences, because they take so many thousands of persons away from their business, and the time thus lost would make an aggregate of great value. Should the excitements at our presidential elections continue to increase as they have done during the last eight years, the citizens of America will soon be spending nearly half their time in political meetings, instead of devoting their energies to legitimate and profitable business. These parades are very well for children, but should seldom be resorted to (for political purposes) by grown-up men. Again, they do no good; for if one party has a mass meeting, the other will do the same. If one party parades a coon on Monday, the other party will skin it on Tuesday; so that, on the whole, both parties will come back just where they started–nothing is gained, much valuable time is lost, and habits of idleness are engendered. The peaceable manner, however, in which the last election was conducted throughout the Union, reflects great credit on our country and its institutions, and will tend to no small degree to elevate us in the opinion of other nations. I most heartily rejoice at this. . . .

Edinburgh. Messrs. Editors–On the 26th of last month I took passage at Liverpool on board the splendid steamer Princess Royal, for Glasgow. The steamers on that line are unsurpassed in point of elegance by any that I have ever seen. On board the steamer were some forty passengers, consisting chiefly of Scotch and English. On learning that I was an American, a couple of the Scotchmen opened their batteries on me, regarding the existence of *slavery* in America. Were it not for slavery, they said, America would be the greatest, best, and justly the proudest nation in the universe; as it was, however, Americans should almost be ashamed to acknowledge their country. I replied that slavery was an evil fastened on us while under the English government; that many states, which formerly were slave-holding states, had abolished slavery, and that I believed very few slaveholders would own a slave a single day if they could give them their freedom with safety, but that it would be impolitic and unsafe to set free armies of ignorant negroes in such portions of the states that the whites were far inferior in point of numbers; besides, I thought these philanthropic gentlemen should remember that "charity begins at home," and they could talk with more consistency against the evil of American slavery when they had made the *poor working people* of England, Scotland and Ireland half so happy as were the southern blacks. I also told them that the masters of slaves were induced by interest alone, if they had no higher motive, to use their negroes well–to feed and clothe them well–and to administer to their wants when sick; and that the law compelled them to provide for their comfort in decrepitude and old age, and that, on the whole, they were much happier than the *starving workies* of this country, who could scarcely earn a subsistence while in health, and who in sickness and old age frequently died from starvation.[67]

"That is all very true," they replied; "and if your countrymen will come here and lecture on the situations of the laboring classes, they will be well received; and yet, in your boasted land of freedom of speech, you will not permit us to go into your southern states and expose the evils of slavery. Thus *ours* is the free country, and yours is *not* free."

I replied that if meetings were held in Birmingham and Manchester, to discuss the question whether the large manufacturers there really owned their establishments or not, and speeches were made informing the ignorant and starving workmen that *they* were entitled to take possession of the factories and kick their employers out–or, in the language of some abolitionists, that their masters "were man-stealers, robbers and murderers, who deserved to *change places* with them"–I thought the law would recognize all who joined in such meetings as *conspirators* who were trying to rob men of their property and to instigate ignorant individuals to riot and bloodshed. The Scotch gentlemen replied that no abolitionist would use such language–that they entertained no such feelings towards the owners of slaves, &c.; and after the controversy had been continued a couple of hours, I happened to remark that in a slave state or country where there were ten blacks to a white, I believed "if the blacks were unceremoniously set free, and there was no army to protect the whites, the blacks would murder them and take possession of their property," one of the gentlemen replied–"Well, it would serve them right, and I could not blame them for at last taking vengeance on their oppressors." "I firmly believe you," I replied, "and if you require 'the freedom of speech' which would permit you to preach that doctrine to the southern slaves, depend on it you will receive all the protection that you deserve!"–and thus the discussion ended.

I am no apologist for slavery, and I abhor its existence as much as any man; but the rabid fanaticism of some abolitionists is more reprehensible than slavery itself, and only serves to strengthen instead of weaken the fetters of the enslaved. . . .

JUNE 8, 1845

Paris. . . . We have now been in Paris nearly two months, and Gen. Tom Thumb's harvest is still *increasing!* The excitable Parisians talk of nothing but "General Tom Pouce, les tres jollie charmant enfant!" Not less than fifty different lithographs of the General, in his various costumes, have already been published by different artists in Paris, statuettes representing him in various characters are displayed in the shop windows, oil paintings of his splendid miniature equipage are starting from every corner, and the confectioners have served up "Petit Poucet" in all manner of forms for their gormandizing little customers, who seem as anxious to devour the General in sugar, as his thousands of female admirers are in reality.

A new and *taking* play has been written for the General; and besides his usual exhibitions, day and evening at the Salle Vivienne, he afterward appears in his new play every night at the Theater Vaudeville, where *every seat* is engaged from five to seven nights in advance! We only intended remaining here four or five weeks at farthest, but we shall now remain at least a month longer–making 12 or 14 weeks altogether. . . .

The Iowa Indians are here, under the management of Mr. Melody and Mr. Catlin.[68] The exhibition is not as successful as was anticipated, and, for the benefit of adventurers, I would advise that no more Indians be brought to England or France. It is a speculation that hereafter, for at least fifty years, will be a *losing* one in this country.

Brussels. Messrs. Editors—I have at last torn myself away from the glare and brilliancy, the beauties and gaieties, the enjoyments and enchantments of the gayest city in the world—Paris. Never did or could I spend four months more happily than the last four months have been spent in the French metropolis. All that is rich, beautiful, sublime, magnificent, and enchanting, are concentrated in Paris. In fact, the *world* is in Paris, and all its mysteries: and it would require volumes where Eugene Sue has only written lines, to open to view only a moiety of the "mysteries of Paris." But now I am fairly emerged from all the charms of French metropolis, my family having returned to America, Gen. Tom Thumb has commenced making the tour of France, Belgium, Germany, &c., and I am once more the simple showman, traveling through the country for the gratification of the public, who ought to feel under everlasting obligations to me for my *disinterested* motives in coming this great distance for the purpose of gratifying their curiosity.

We left Paris on the 23rd of June, for Rouen. We have since passed through Amiens and Lille, and from here we return through Paris to Orleans, from which town our route through France will be fairly commenced, and from which we proceed to Tours, Nantes, Bordeaux, Toulouse, Marseilles, Lyons, and, in fact, all the principal towns in France. During this tour I shall have time for scribbling occasionally, and shall therefore resume the liberty of sending said scribbling to you—it being, as usual, understood that they are to be printed or burnt—neither the public nor myself care which; so it all rests with you.

In Paris, I was introduced to Mr. Boucicault, author of "London Assurance," "Old Heads and Young Hearts," and other popular plays; and I subsequently had the pleasure of meeting him at several dinner parties.[69] He is one of the most sociable, open-hearted men I have met in this country. He is a young man of not more than twenty-six years, with a handsome countenance, a fine bearing, and a head which phrenologists would say "speaks for itself." He dresses in the height of fashion, and attends most of the fashionable parties; but there is a simplicity of manner, a freedom from all self-importance so unusual to young men of his standing, that an American is at once pleased with him: I mean, of course, such Americans as myself, who utterly despise the stiff forms and ceremonies—the mincing, simpering, namby-pamby nonsense too often prominent in those who *would* be aristocrats, *if they only knew how.*

I also had the pleasure of paying several visits to Madame George Sands, many of whose works have been reprinted in America.[70] She is not at all the person that the American public have been taught to believe. Her peculiar notions in regard to marriage and the domestic relations of life, have been wholly misrepresented. Indeed, after several hours of conversation on this very subject with her, and after having heard her publicly express her opinions at several different times on the same subject, I am satisfied that ninety-nine out of a hundred persons of sense would fully coincide with all that she professes.

She is, withal, one of nature's noblewomen. She is an ardent friend to the *mass*, and nearly all of her income, which is no small sum, is expended to protect the poor and unfortunate from the oppressions of the rich. If a laboring class feel that they are too much oppressed, and "strike" for higher wages, no matter if it is two hundred miles from Paris, Madame George Sands posts off directly to the spot, inquires into all the facts, and, if she finds the laborers in the right, she gives them every encouragement— gives them money to support their families, and fees counsel to protect them; for it is not at all unusual for the poor fellows, unless protected, to be punished for conspiracy. The consequence of this is, Madame Sands is beloved by the mass as she deserves to be, and is happy in being the possessor of the affections of an unfortunate and op- pressed, but industrious people. . . .

OCTOBER 5, 1845

Tours, France. Messrs. Editors—After getting the exhibition of Gen. Tom Thumb under fair headway, in Brussels, I concluded to assume the position of *avant courier* to the General, and, for this purpose, departed on my way to Bordeaux, repass- ing through Lille, Arras, &c. to Paris, Orleans, and Tours, and hence I purposed going to the various towns on my way to Bordeaux. The usual duties of the *avant courier* to an exhibition includes, among the most prominent, that of *raising an excitement*, by puffing the thing to be exhibited, and thus create, with the public an appetite for see- ing it. My duties are quite *the reverse!* My first business is to engage the largest theater or saloon to be found in the town, and then get out a simple placard, announcing that the General will appear on such a day; after which all my energies are devoted to *keeping the public quiet*, and begging them *not to get excited*, for we will endeavor to give them all a chance to see him—of course, provided "they down with the dust!" But there's no use in talking; they *will* get excited, and will keep talking about "the marvelous little General, who has delighted the principal monarchs of Europe, and more than a million of their subjects," and so they will continue to converse about the General and his magnificent presents, and his miniature equipage, &c., in *spite of all I can do to prevent it!* The consequence is that, when the General arrives we have a great deal of trouble in taking the money and finding places for all the people to get a look at him; but a man can stand almost anything when he gets used to it, so we bear our troubles with the calmness and the fortitude of philosophers and Christians. . . .

OCTOBER 19, 1845

Tours, France. . . . There was a great hurrah, a few years since, in Boston, when the Tremont theater was converted into a church.[71] The celebrated and revered Dr. Lyman Beecher was engaged to preach the first sermon in the theater; in the course of which he proved, beyond all question, that theaters had *fell*, and churches had "riz," in Boston, and in fact that, now that the church had got the theater building, theatricals in Boston were dead and "––" forever. To make the opening sermon doubly attractive, it was delivered in the interior of the building, in order to let the "sheep" see what a curious place the "goats" prepared for their wicked amusements. But the consequence of all this was just the same as that which followed the *burning* of a whole edition of a certain *book*, which proved obnoxious to a millionaire, and who, therefore, bought up the whole number extant and committed them to the flames. The author, realizing a good profit on his work, was enabled thereby to immediately republish a *much larger* edition! So by the Tremont theater. It was sold for a church at a great price. The scenery and wardrobe, which were valuable, were sold at auction by the church, and that shrewd Yankee, who always "has his top eye open," bought them for a song, and forthwith brought them into use, by making *theatricals* a leading feature in his Boston museum–a building situated about *five rods* from the theatrical church! Theatricals are as much the rage now in Boston as ever, notwithstanding the prophesying of the Rev. Dr. Lyman Beecher.

I have just seen, by the American papers, that Grace Church, in New York, is to be converted to the purpose of exhibiting an animate and inanimate "Chinese Collection"; so that it is not in France alone that churches are sometimes obliged to kick the beam to something more worldly in its nature. But this is all of little moment. It matters not whether a theater has been a church, or a church a theater; a good man can worship God as sincerely in one as the other, and a good actor will find little difficulty in brining his talent to the sticking point, because a preacher (perhaps as much an *"actor"* as himself,) has been there before him. For my part, I think that this strife between churches on the one hand, and theaters, "Chinese Collections," and diligence offices on the other, is like the strife between religious sects–a blessing to the country. It keeps the *balance of power* all right. The more sects there are, the less liable is a country to be ruined by that greatest of all curses, a union of church and state. . . .

Hotel Beford, Paris. . . . I was in London, a couple weeks since, and found much enjoyment in calling on old friends. My pleasure was not a little (though unexpectedly) enhanced by *falling* in with a jolly lot of Yankee brother "showmen."[72] Among them were Major Titus, the leviathan showman, one who has made and kept "more money than a horse can draw," and who, like that respectable darkey, "Mr. Brown," does not "mean to give it up so." Then, who else should I find but General Rufus Welch, the man who has scoured the world in search of, and to exhibit novelties–the *generous* Welch, who has got a heart like an ox, and is never happy unless he can see all happy around him. Then there was Yankee Carter, the "lion king"–in fact, he may be called king of all animals, for he confines himself no longer to lions alone, but is at home with animals of every description, wild or tame, savage or domestic. Indeed, he is at this moment the owner of the largest horse and largest dog in the world, besides any quantity of lions, tigers, &c. Carter's "big horse," which he has named General Washington, is indeed a magnificent animal, and one of the greatest curiosities that I have seen this many a day. . . .

Messrs. Titus and Welch both went by last steamer to America. The former had shipped animals enough to stock the Rocky Mountains if he would let them all loose. To get some of these animals, he and Van Amburgh have been to Africa; and, in their hunting expeditions in Algiers, it is said they have more than once sadly frightened Abd-el Kader, who took them for French foes, and at the same time (as usual) took to his heels, really thinking he was "come for." Titus also shipped eight of the mammoth Flemish horses, which are so celebrated as being used by the colliers and the brewers in London. They will cut a swell in America. They must necessarily fill a large space in the public eye, for they are the biggest horses ever seen on the American continent, but they are Tom Thumbs by the side of Carter's mammoth. . . .

On the whole, my brother showmen are doing themselves great honor in their shipments to America; and I am not so inclined to cruelty as to desire to put them all to shame, which I really should, were I to tell them what *I* have shipped from France and England to be brought out at the American Museum for the holidays. However, my friend Hitchcock will divulge the secret all in good time, and I will not indulge myself to say anything more about it, I drop the subject.[73]

London. . . . The universal Yankee nation is pretty well represented here at present, so far as amusements are concerned. Under this head may be named the Misses Cushman, Edwin Forrest, the Hutchinson Family, Dumbolton with the Ethiopian Serenaders, and, least as well as last, General Tom Thumb.[74] All of the above personages are successful, and will be able to pocket and carry back a few of the pounds which their brethren lavished upon foreign talent in America.

MAY 10, 1846

S teamship Great Western, at sea. Messrs. Editors–I little thought, when visiting you the last time from London, that within just a week from that day I should be on board an Atlantic steamer, with her bows turned towards the goodly city of Gotham. But so it is. A man of the world, and one who loves excitements and a diversity of occupations, seldom can *guess* on any given day what portion of the habitable globe he will be in within the next fortnight. To him the broad ocean is nothing; his ambition is not to be cramped, nor his way obstructed by the freezing, towering Alps–the burning Vesuvius–the scorching desert–nor the oceans roar. To him all climes and countries, if not exactly *attractive,* are at least bearable, if his interest is promoted therein; and while engaged in business pursuits he, like the bee which extracts honey from every flower, finds more or less pleasure in whatever quarter of the world he may be called. But let the man of the world take to himself all the philosophy he can become master of–let him lug himself into the belief that the cares of life sit easy on his brow–that he, being a cosmopolite, can enjoy himself anywhere, and that every portion of the world is the same to him, there are yet certain talismanic words which possess a charm for him unknown to one who has not learned them in the school of experience. These words are *"home"* and *"native land."* And more especially do these words come to the heart with the thrilling and all-powerful effect, when that home is the United States of America! the noblest, happiest land on the footstool of the Almighty! Other countries have their attractions–they may boast of their ancient institutions, their noble blood, their long list of family names, whose escutcheons have for hundreds of years been unsullied–they may boast of their powerful navies, their overwhelming armies, their power, their wealth and their might; but they must shut their eyes, and quail before the question, "Are not the people of the United States, as a body–are not the *masses*–the most free, independent, and happy upon earth?" The united voice of the world joins in the thundering, echoing and re-echoing answer, "YES!" In republican America, we cannot boast of mighty towers and gilded palaces–of trains of kinds, princes and all the gorgeous paraphernalia of royalty; but we can safely say, that we have a generally diffused education, and a generally diffused state of prosperity, that no other country can boast–that, while we cannot nor do not desire to boast of dukes and lords, whose annual income is some millions, we can safely say that, with us, (in contradiction to many other countries,) we have no cases of *starvation;* but, on the contrary, owing to the bountiful provisions of a merciful Providence, and the equality and justice of our institutions and laws, none need come to want and misery, unless brought to that state by their own idle or vicious habits. . . .

SELECTIONS FROM
Ancient and Modern Humbugs of the World
(1864–65)

During the spring of 1864, Barnum contracted with the *New York Mercury* to write his last major serial publication: *Ancient and Modern Humbugs of the World*.[75] Part of the attraction here, of course, was the pairing of author and subject. Much of Barnum's professional reputation had been built on producing humbugs for public consumption. But now he recast himself as a kind of expert, one who would serve the public interest by exposing and explaining the deceits of others.

Some of the most fascinating moments in the series come when these roles of trickster and expositor collide. Early on, for example, Barnum expends a great deal of energy challenging Webster's dictionary definition of humbug as "an imposition under fair pretences." In what contemporary business, the showman asks, is there not some form of humbug? Just as stockbrokers talk down the properties they most want to buy, savvy impresarios employ "novel expedients" and "glittering appearances" to attract the public eye. The argument ultimately boils down to a question of perceived value. If a salesman delivers a "full equivalent" for a customer's money, the public will condone even the most outrageous promotional tricks. But if the customer receives little beyond the pitch, the salesman is denounced as a "base, lying wretch."

It almost goes without saying that Bar-num's taxonomy of frauds was self-serving. One might argue, in fact, that the central agenda of the *Mercury* series was to redefine his early promotional deceits as adult common sense—as a way of doing business "generally accepted" in the sophisticated market economy of the mid-1860s. The *Mercury* essays thus provide a fascinating portrait of capitalist ideology in the making. First, the era's leading showman explicates some of the foundational techniques of promotion. Then he differentiates these techniques from more obviously criminal activities, using benchmarks generated by the market itself. Finally, he extends his defense of puffery by constructing elaborate analogies with other forms of mass persuasion (e.g., politics and religion). By the end of the series, cultural marketing and presidential electioneering look like much the same activity. Those who question the showman's epistemological distinctions are written off as naïve or self-deluding.

Yet, as Barnum himself admitted, this new way of thinking created its own kinds of managerial dilemmas. The series' third essay, "Humbugs–The Whale, the Angel Fish, and the Golden Pigeon," provides the most vivid examples. It begins with a brief anecdote about a "sharp Yankee lady" and her daughter, who arrive at the American Museum eager to see the showman's latest novelty, a Labrador whale. The whale,

Barnum explains, was kept in a large, top-lit tank in the museum's basement and rarely surfaced, which led some patrons to dispute its very existence. The Yankee lady, however, offered a different explanation: "'Mr. B., it's astonishing to what a number of purposes the ingenuity of us Yankees has applied india-rubber.' I asked her meaning, and was soon informed that she was perfectly convinced that it was an india-rubber whale, worked by steam and machinery." In the end, Barnum concludes that the Yankee lady "received double her money's worth in the happy reflection that she could not be humbugged, and that I was terribly humiliated in being detected by her marvelous powers of discrimination."

On one level, this amusing tale of consumer skepticism represented everything Barnum had worked for over the previous two decades. Here was a respectable "family audience" that understood humbug on almost precisely his own terms: not as criminal "swindling," but as a series of "novel expedients" devised by an honest impresario who delivers a quota of fun more than equal to the admission price. Yet this cash-value conception of truth came with one major (and unintended) consequence. Sometimes viewers saw rubber even when the whale was real. Sometimes the byproduct of modern humbug was reflexive cynicism.[76]

✳

The complete series *Ancient and Modern Humbugs of the World* includes dozens of essays on a wide range of frauds–from patent medicines and money manias to spiritualism and witchcraft. The selections here focus more specifically on Barnum's philosophy of promotion.

NEW YORK MERCURY,
MAY 21, 1864

Correspondence with P. T. Barnum

Mr. Barnum Consents to Write For The New York Mercury, At the Rate of Two Hundred Dollars a Week,

For One Year.

It will be seen from the subjoined letters that Mr. Barnum, at the earnest solicitation of the proprietors of The New York Mercury, has consented to write for the columns of this paper a series of articles entitled "The Ancient and Modern Humbugs of the World," for the sum of TEN THOUSAND FOUR HUNDRED DOLLARS.

New York Mercury Office,
113 Fulton Street, April 25, 1864.
P. T. Barnum, Esq:
Dear Sir: For what sum will you write for publication in the New York Mercury a series of fifty-two articles–one per week for one year–upon the "Ancient and Modern Humbugs of the World?" An early reply will oblige, respectfully, yours,
Cauldwell & Whitney,
Proprietors of the New York Mercury

American Museum, April 26, 1864

Gentleman: Yours of yesterday is received. I am quite too much occupied, not in humbugging, but in amusing and gratifying the public, to write for you on any terms. Truly, yours,

P. T. Barnum

New York Mercury Office, April 27, 1864

P. T. Barnum, Esq:

Dear Sir: Our object is the same as yours—to interest, instruct, and amuse the public. To this end, we devote our time, capital, and whatever talent and knowledge we possess. Yet we contrive occasionally to find leisure to visit your Museum. Can you reciprocate, and pay a weekly literary visit to our columns for the entertainment of hundreds of thousands of readers. With the hope that you will reconsider the matter, we make the following offer:

We will give you ten thousand four hundred dollars ($10,400), payable in weekly advance installments of two hundred dollars ($200) each for one article per week for one year, on the subject proposed in our former note—the articles to average respectively one column (or more). The topic, "Ancient and Modern Humbugs of the World," will give you an opportunity of explaining your views on a very curious and fruitful theme, and of illustrating them by incidents which have come under your observation during your extensive travels in both hemispheres, and while catering for the amusement of the public through a long series of years.

Your professional reminiscences, given in your peculiar, original, and humorous style, we have no doubt, form a rare chapter of Wit and Romance in the history of popular entertainments of every kind and class. In fact, we will not insist that all of your articles be confined to a History of Ancient and Modern Humbugs, but prefer rather that you shall not keep back a good anecdote or illustration, even if it is irrelevant to this particular subject.

Although the pecuniary consideration may be of small consequence to one who can make money so readily, perhaps the thought of ministering to the enjoyment of half a million of readers per week, for a twelvemonth, may induce you, on reflection, to comply with our request. Hoping for a favorable answer,

We remain sincerely yours,

Cauldwell & Whitney

American Museum, April 28, 1864

Gentlemen:

You are irrepressible. Were it not that I know you to be "live" men who publish a "live" paper, I should think your munificent offer a wild mistake; but as you generally know what you are about, I am bound to suppose that it is not made at random or on false grounds. This consideration is flattering, and affords me a more realizing sense of the value of notoriety than I have ever before experienced. Dismissing, therefore, my first idea, that you were blindly rushing into a hazardous speculation, and adopting *your* estimate of my commercial value, I frankly accede to your proposition. I have always held it as a maxim that a man should make a *profitable* use of his gifts, whatever they may be, always provided that he uses them legitimately; and I know of no way that they can be more legitimately employed than for the delectation of the people.

Holding myself in readiness to commence the series at any time, and accepting your suggestion to introduce prominently into the papers the fund of anecdote, incident, and information acquired during my long experience as a caterer for the world's amusement, I am, gentlemen,

Your considerably astonished friend and servant,

P. T. Barnum

New York Mercury Office, April 28, 1864

P. T. Barnum, Esq:

Dear Sir:

Perhaps it may relieve your mind to know that we expect to take the lion's share of the profits of your papers on the "Ancient and Modern Humbugs of the World."

Enclosed you will find our check for two hundred dollars ($200) for your first article, which be kind enough to send at your earliest convenience. Please supply us punctually with an article every week, and believe us,

Very truly, yours,

Cauldwell & Whitney

(Our readers will have already perceived that we are preparing for them an unprecedented literary feast. We shall have the pleasure of presenting No. 1 of "Ancient and Modern Humbugs of the World" in our next number, which we have arranged to make the best of all the interesting issues we have submitted to an appreciative public.)

ESSAY I, *NEW YORK MERCURY,*
MAY 28, 1864

Monsieur Mangin, The French Humbug.

One of the most original, unique, and successful humbugs of the present day was the late Monsieur Mangin, the black-lead pencil maker of Paris. Few persons who have visited the French capital within the last ten or twelve years will have failed to have seen him, and once seen he was not to be forgotten. While passing through the public streets, there was nothing in his personal appearance to distinguish him from an ordinary gentleman. He drove a pair of bay horses, attached to an open carriage with two seats, the back one always occupied by his valet. Sometimes he would take up his stand in the Champs Elysees; at other times, near the column in the Place Vendome; but usually he was seen in the afternoon in the Place de la Bastille, or the Place de Madeleine. On Sundays, his favorite locality was the Place de la Bourse. Mangin was a well-formed, stately looking individual, with a most self-satisfied countenance, which seemed to say: "I am master here; and all that my auditors have to do is, to listen and obey." Arriving at his destined stopping-place, his carriage halted. His servant handed him a case from which he took several large portraits of himself, which he hung prominently on the side of the carriage, and also placed in front of him a vase filled with medals bearing his likeness on one side and a description of his pencils on the other. He then leisurely commenced a change of costume. His round hat was replaced by a magnificent burnished helmet, mounted with rich plumes of various brilliant colors. His overcoat was laid aside, and he donned in its stead a costly velvet tunic with gold fringes. He then drew a pair of polished steel gauntlets upon his hands, covered his breast with a cuirass, and placed a richly mounted sword at his side. His servant watched him closely, and upon receiving a sign from his master, he too put on his official costume, which consisted of a velvet robe and a helmet. The servant then struck up a tune on the richly-toned organ which always formed a part of Mangin's outfit. The grotesque appearance of these individuals, and the music, soon drew together an admiring crowd. . . .

At last the prelude ended, and the comedy commenced. Stepping forward again to the front of the carriage where all the gaping crowd could catch his every word, he exclaimed:

"Gentlemen, you look astonished! You seem to wonder and ask yourselves who is this modern Quixote. What mean this costume of by-gone centuries–this golden chariot–these richly caparisoned steeds? What is the name and purpose of this curious knight-errant? Gentlemen, I will condescend to answer your queries. I am Monsieur Mangin, the great charlatan of France! Yes, gentlemen, I am a charlatan–a mountebank; it is my profession, not from choice, but from necessity. You, gentlemen, created that necessity! You would not patronize true, unpretending, honest merit, but you are attracted by my glittering casque, my sweeping crest, my waving plumes. You are captivated by din and glitter, and therein lies my strength. Years ago, I hired a modest shop in the Rue Rivoli, but I could not sell pencils enough to pay my rent, whereas, by assuming this disguise–it is nothing else–I have succeeded in attracting general attention, and in selling literally millions of my pencils; and I assure you that there is at this moment scarcely an artist in France or in Great Britain who doesn't know that I manufacture by far the best blackened pencils ever seen."

And this assertion was indeed true. His pencils were everywhere acknowledged to be superior to any other. While he was thus addressing his audience, he would take a blank card, and with one of his pencils would pretend to be drawing the portrait of some man standing near him; then showing the picture to the crowd, it proved to be the head of a donkey, which, of course, produced roars of laughter. "There, do you see what wonderful pencils these are? Did you ever behold a more striking likeness?"

A hearty laugh would be sure to follow, and then he would exclaim: "now who will have the first pencil–only five sous." One would buy, and then another; a third and a fourth would follow; and with the delivery of each pencil he would rattle off a string of witticisms which kept his patrons in capital good-humor; and frequently he would sell from two hundred to five hundred pencils in immediate succession. Then he would drop down in his carriage for a few minutes and wipe the perspiration from his face, while his servant played another overture on the organ. This gave his purchasers a chance to withdraw, and afforded a good opportunity for a fresh audience to congregate. Then would follow a repetition of his previous sales, and in this way he would continue for hours. To those disposed to have a *souvenir* of the great humbug he would sell six pencils, a medal and a photograph of himself for a franc (twenty cents.) After taking a rest he would commence a new speech.

"When I was modestly dressed, like any of my hearers, I was half starved. Punch and his bells would attract crowds, but my good pencils attracted nobody. I imitated Punch and his bells, and now I have two hundred depots in Paris. I dine at the best cafes, drink the best wine, live on the best of everything, while my defamers get poor and lank, as they deserve to be. Who are my defamers? Envious swindlers! Men who try to ape me, but are too dishonest to succeed. They endeavor to attract notice as mountebanks, and then foist upon the public worthless trash and hope thus to succeed. Ah! Defamers of mine, you are fools as well as knaves. Fools, to think that any man can succeed by systematically and persistently cheating the public. Knaves, for desiring the public's money without giving them an equivalent. I am an honest man. I have no bad habits; and now I declare, if any trader, inventor, manufacturer, or philanthropist will show me better pencils than mine, I will give them 1000 f.–no, not to him, for I abhor betting–but to the poor of the Thirty-first Arrondissement, where I live."

Mangin's harangues were always accompanied by a peculiar play of feature and of voice, and with unique and original gestures, which seemed to excite and captivate his audience. About seven years ago, I met him in one of the principal restaurants in the Palais Royale. A mutual friend introduced me. "Ah!" said he, "Monsieur Barnum, I am delighted to see you. I have read your book with infinite satisfaction. It has been published here in numerous editions. I see you have the right idea of things. Your motto is a good one–'we study to please.' I have much wanted to visit America; but I cannot speak English, so I must remain here in my dear belle France." I remarked that I had often seen him in public, and bought his pencils. "Aha! You never saw better pencils. You know I could never maintain my reputation if I sold poor pencils. But *sacre bleu*, my miserable would-be imitators do not know our grand secret. First, attract the public by din and tinsel, by brilliant sky-rockets and Bengola lights, then give them as much as possible for their money."

"You are very happy," I replied, "in your manner of attracting the public. Your costume is elegant, your chariot is superb, and your valet and music are sure to draw." "Thank you for your compliment, Mr. B., but I have not forgotten your Buffalo-hunt, your Mermaid, nor your Woolly Horse. They were a good offset to my rich helmet and sword, my burnished gauntlets and gaudy cuirass. Both are intended as advertisements of something genuine, and both serve the purpose."

After comparing notes in this way for an hour, we parted, and his last words were: "Mr. B., I have got a grand humbug in my head, which I shall put into practice within a year, and it shall double the sale of my pencils. Don't ask me what it is, but within one year you shall see it for yourself, and you shall acknowledge Monsieur Mangin knows something of human nature. My idea is magnifique, but it is one grand secret." I confess my curiosity was somewhat excited, and I hoped that Monsieur Mangin would "add another wrinkle to my horns." But, poor fellow! Within four months after I bade him adieu, the Paris newspapers announced his sudden death. They added that he had left two hundred thousand francs, which he had given in his will to charitable objects. The announcement was copied into nearly all the papers on the Continent and in Great Britain, for almost everybody had seen or heard of the eccentric pencil maker. His death caused many an honest sigh, and his absence seemed to cast a gloom over several of his favorite halting-places. The Parisians really loved him and were proud of his genius.

"Well," people in Paris would remark, "Mangin was a clever fellow. He was shrewd, and possessed a thorough knowledge of the world. He was a gentleman and a man of intelligence, extremely agreeable and witty. His habits were good; he was charitable. He never cheated anybody. He always sold a good article, and no person who purchased from him had cause to complain."

I confess I felt somewhat chagrined that the Monsieur had thus suddenly taken "French leave" without imparting to me the "grand secret" by which he was to double the sale of his pencils. But I had not long to mourn on that account; for after Monsieur Mangin had been for six months—as they say of John Brown—"mouldering in his grave" judge of the astonishment and delight of all Paris at his reappearance in his native city in precisely the same costume and carriage as formerly, and heralded by the same servant and organ that had always attended him. It now turned out that Monsieur Mangin had lived in the most rigid seclusion for half a year, and that the extensively-circulated announcements of his sudden death had been made by himself, merely as an "advertising dodge" to bring him still more into notice, and give the public something to talk about. I met Mangin in Paris soon after this event.

"Aha, Monsieur Barnum!" he exclaimed, "did I not tell you I had a new humbug that would double the sales of my pencils? I assure you my sales are more than quadrupled, and it is sometimes impossible to have them manufactured fast enough to supply the demand. You Yankees are very clever, but by gar, none of you have discovered you should live all the better if you would die for six months. It took Mangin to teach you that."

The patronizing air with which he made his speech, slapping me at the same time familiarly upon the back, showed in him the true character of egotist. Although good-natured and social to a degree, he was really one of the most self-conceited men I ever met. Monsieur Mangin died the present year, and it is said that his heirs received more than half a million of francs as the fruit of his eccentric labors.

ESSAY 3, *NEW YORK MERCURY*,
JUNE 11, 1864

Humbugs—The Whale, The Angel Fish, and the Golden Pigeon.

If the fact could be definitely determined, I think it would be discovered that in this "wide awake" country there are more persons humbugged by believing too little than too much. Many persons have such a horror of being taken in, or such an elevated sense of their own acuteness, that they believe everything to be a sham, and in this way are continually humbugging themselves.

Several years since, I purchased a living white whale, captured near Labrador, and succeeded in placing it, "in good condition," in a large tank, fifty feet long and supplied with salt water, in the basement of the American Museum. I was obliged to light the basement with gas, and that frightened the sea monster to such an extent that he kept at the bottom of the tank, except when he was compelled to stick his nose above the surface in order to breathe or "blow," and then would go down again as quick as possible. Visitors would sometimes stand for half an hour, watching in vain to get a look at the whale; for, although he could remain under water only about two minutes at a time, he would happen to appear in some un-looked for quarter of the huge tank, and before they could all get a chance to see him, he would be out of sight again. Some impatient and incredulous persons after waiting ten minutes, which seemed to them an hour, would sometimes exclaim "Oh, humbug! I don't believe there is a whale here at all!"

This incredulity often put me out of patience, and I would say: "Ladies and gentlemen, there is a living whale in the tank. He is frightened by the gaslight and by visitors; but he is obliged to come to the surface every two minutes, and if you will watch sharply, you will see him. I am sorry we can't make him dance a hornpipe and do all sorts of things at the word of command; but if you will exercise your patience a few minutes longer, I assure you the whale will be seen at considerably less trouble than it would be to go to Labrador expressly for that purpose."

This would usually put my patrons in good humor—but I was myself often vexed at the persistent stubbornness of the whale in not calmly floating on the surface for the gratification of my visitors.

One day, a sharp Yankee lady and her daughter, from Connecticut, called at the Museum. I knew them well; and in answer to their inquiry for the locality of the whale, I directed them to the basement. Half an hour afterwards, they called at my office, and the acute mother, in a half-confidential, serio-comic whisper, said: "Mr. B., it's astonishing to what a number of purposes the ingenuity of us Yankees has applied india-rubber." I asked her meaning, and was soon informed that she was perfectly convinced that it was an india-rubber whale, worked by steam and machinery, by means of which he was made to rise to the surface at short intervals, and puff with the regularity of a pair of bellows. From her earnest, confident manner, I saw it would be useless to attempt to disabuse her mind on the subject. I therefore very candidly acknowledged that she was quite too sharp for me, and I must plead guilty to the imposition; but I begged her not to expose me, for I assured her that she was the only person who had discovered the trick.

It was worth more than a dollar to see with what a smile of satisfaction she received the assurance that nobody else was as shrewd as herself; and the patronizing manner in which she bade me be perfectly tranquil, for the secret should be considered by her "strictly confidential," was decidedly rich. She evidently received double her money's worth in the happy reflection that she could not be humbugged, and that I was terribly humiliated in being detected by her marvelous powers of discrimination! I occasionally meet the good lady, and always try to look a little sheepish, but she invariably assures me that she has never divulged my secret and never will!

On another occasion, a lady equally shrewd, who lives neighbor to me in Connecticut, after regarding for a few minutes the "Golden Angel Fish" swimming in the Aquaria, abruptly addressed me with: "You can't humbug me, Mr. Barnum; that fish is painted!" "Nonsense!" said I, with a laugh; "the thing is impossible!" "I don't care, I know it is painted; it is as plain as can be." "But, my dear Mrs. H., paint would not adhere to a fish while in the water; and if it would, it would kill him. Besides," I added, with an extra serious air, "we never allow humbugging here!" "Oh, here is just the place to look for such things," she replied with a smile; "and I must say I more than half believe that Angel Fish is painted."

She was finally nearly convinced of her error, and left. In the afternoon of the same day, I met her in Old Grizzly Adams' California Menagerie.[77] She knew that I was part-proprietor of that establishment, and seeing me in conversation with "Grizzly Adams," she came up to me in some haste, and with her eyes glistening with excitement, she said: "O, Mr. B., I never saw anything so beautiful as those elegant

'Golden Pigeons' from Australia. I want you to secure some of their eggs for me, and let my pigeons hatch them at home. I should prize them beyond all measure." "Oh, you don't want 'Golden Australian Pigeons,'" I replied; "they are painted." "No, they are not painted," said she, with a laugh, "but I half think the Angel Fish is."

I could not control myself at this curious coincidence, and I roared with laughter while I replied: "Now, Mrs. H., I never let a good joke be spoiled, even if it serves to expose my own secrets. I assure you, upon honor, that the Golden Australian Pigeons, as they are labeled, are really painted and that in their natural state they are nothing more nor less than the common ruff-necked white American pigeons." And it was a fact. How they happened to be exhibited under that auriferous disguise was owing to an amusing circumstance, explained in another chapter. Suffice it at present to say, that Mrs. H. to this day "blushes to her eyebrows" whenever an allusion is made to "Angel Fish" or "Golden Pigeons."

ESSAY 6, *NEW YORK MERCURY*,
JULY 2, 1864

Definition of the Word Humbug— Warren, Of London—Genin, The Hatter— Gosling's Blacking.

When I come to sit down earnestly to fulfill my engagement with the publishers of the Mercury, to write for them a series of articles upon the "Humbugs of the World," I find myself somewhat puzzled in regard to the true definition of that word. To be sure, Webster says that humbug, as a noun, is an "imposition under fair pretences"; and as a verb, it is "To deceive: to impose on." With all due deference to Doctor Webster, I submit that, according to present usage, this is not the only, nor even the generally accepted, definition of that term.

We will suppose, for instance, that a man with "fair pretences" applies to a wholesale merchant for credit on a large bill of goods. His "fair pretences" comprehend an assertion that he is a moral and religious man, a member of the church, a man of wealth, etc., etc. It turns out that he is not worth a dollar, but is a base, lying wretch, an impostor and a cheat. He is arrested and imprisoned "for obtaining property under false pretences," or, as Webster says, "fair pretences." He is punished for his villainy. The public do not call him a "humbug"; they very properly term him a swindler.

A man, bearing the appearance of a gentleman in dress and manners, purchases property from you, and with "fair pretences" obtains your confidence. You find, when he has left, that he paid you with counterfeit bank-notes, or a forged draft. This man is justly called a "forger" or "counterfeiter"; and if arrested, he is punished as such; but nobody thinks of calling him a "humbug."

A respectable-looking man sits by your side in an omnibus or rail-car. He converses fluently, and is evidently a man of intelligence and reading. He attracts your attention by his "fair pretences." Arriving at your journey's end, you miss your watch and your pocket-book. Your fellow-passenger proves to be the thief. Everybody calls him a "pickpocket," and not withstanding his "fair pretences," not a person in the community calls him a "humbug." Two actors appear as stars at rival theaters. They are equally talented, equally pleasing. One advertises himself simply as a tragedian, under his proper name—the other boasts that he is a prince, and wears decorations presented by all the potentates of the world, including the "King of the Cannibal Islands." He is correctly set down as a "humbug," while the term is never applied to the other actor. But if the man who boasts of having received a foreign title is a miserable actor, and he gets up gift-enterprises and bogus entertainments, or pretends to devote the proceeds of his tragic efforts to some charitable object, without, in fact, doing so—he is then a "humbug" in Dr. Webster's sense of that word, for he is an "impostor under fair pretences."

Two physicians reside in one of our fashionable avenues. They were both educated in the best medical colleges; each has passed an examination, received his diploma, and been dubbed an M.D. They are equally skilled in the healing art. One rides quietly about the city in his gig or brougham, visiting his patients without noise or clamor—the other sallies out in his coach-and-four, preceded by a band of music, and his carriage and horses are covered with handbills and placards, announcing his "wonderful cures." The man is properly called a quack and a humbug. Why? Not because he cheats or imposes upon the public, for he does not, but because, as generally understood, "humbug" consists in putting on glittering appearances—outside show—novel expedients, by which to suddenly arrest public attention, and attract the public eye and ear.

Clergymen, lawyers, or physicians, who should resort to such methods of attracting the public, would not, for obvious reasons be apt to succeed. Bankers, insurance-agents, and others, who aspire to become the custodians of the money of their fellow men, would require a different species of advertising than this; but there are various trades and occupations which need only notoriety to insure success, always provided that when customers are once attracted, they never fail to get their money's worth. An honest man who thus arrests public attention will be called a "humbug," but he is not a swindler or an impostor. If, however, after attracting crowds of customers by his unique displays, a man foolishly fails to give them a full equivalent for their money, they never patronize him a second time, but they very properly denounce him as a swindler, a cheat, an impostor; they do not, however, call him a "humbug." He fails not because he advertises his wares in an *outré* manner, but because, after attracting crowds of patrons, he stupidly and wickedly cheats them.

When the great blacking-maker of London dispatched his agent to Egypt to write on the pyramids of Ghiza, in huge letters, "Buy Warren's Blacking, 30, Strand, London," he was not "cheating" travelers upon the Nile. His blacking was really a superior article, and well worth the price charged for it, but he was "humbugging" the public by this queer way of arresting public attention. It turned out just as he anticipated, that English travelers in that part of Egypt were indignant at this desecration, and they wrote back to the London *Times* (every Englishman writes or threatens to "write to the *Times*," if anything goes wrong), denouncing the "Goth" who had thus disfigured these ancient pyramids by writing on them, in monstrous letters, "Buy Warren's Blacking, 30, Strand, London." The *Times* published these letters, and backed them up by several of those awful, grand, and dictatorial editorials particular to the great "Thunderer," in which the blacking-maker, "Warren, 30, Strand," was stigmatized as a man who had no respect for the ancient patriarchs, and it was hinted that he would probably sell his blacking on the sarcophagus of Pharaoh, "or any other" mummy—if he could only make money by it. In fact, to cap the climax, Warren was denounced as a "humbug." These indignant articles were copied into all the provincial journals, and very soon, in this manner, the columns in every newspaper in Great Britain were teeming with this advice: "Try Warren's Blacking, 30, Strand, London." The curiosity of the public was thus aroused, and they did "try" it, and finding it a superior article, they continued to purchase it and recommend it to their friends, and Warren made a fortune by it. He always attributed his success to his having "humbugged" the public by this unique method of advertising his blacking in Egypt! But Warren did not cheat his customers, nor practice "an imposition under fair pretences." He was a humbug, but he was an honest, upright man, and no one called him an impostor or a cheat.

When the tickets for Jenny Lind's first concert in America were sold at auction, several business-men, aspiring to notoriety, "bid high" for the first ticket. It was finally knocked down to "Genin, the hatter," for $225. The journals in Portland (Maine) and Houston (Texas), and all other journals throughout the United States, between these two cities, which were connected through the telegraph, announced the fact in their columns the next morning. Probably two millions of readers read the announcement, and asked, "Who is Genin, the hatter?" Genin became famous in a day. Every man involuntarily examined his hat, to see if it was made by Genin; and an Iowa editor declared that one of his neighbors discovered the name of Genin in his old hat, and immediately announced the fact to his neighbors in front of the Post-office. It was suggested that the old hat should be sold at auction. It was done then and there, and the Genin hat sold for fourteen dollars! Gentlemen from city and country rushed to

Genin's store to buy their hats, many of them willing to pay an extra dollar, if necessary, provided they could get a glimpse of Genin himself. This singular freak put thousands of dollars into the pocket of "Genin, the hatter," and yet I never heard it charged that he made poor hats, or that he would be guilty of an "imposition under fair pretences." On the contrary, he is a gentleman of probity, and of the first respectability.

When the laying of the Atlantic Telegraph was nearly completed I was in Liverpool. I offered the company one thousand pounds sterling ($5000) for the privilege of sending the first twenty words over the cable to my Museum in New York—not that there was any intrinsic merit in the words, but that I fancied that there was more than $5000 worth of notoriety in the operation. But Queen Victoria and "Old Buck" were ahead of me. Their messages had the preference, and I was compelled to "take a back seat."

By thus illustrating what I believe the public will concede to be the sense in which the word "humbug" is generally used and understood at the present time, in this country, as well as in England, I do not propose that my letters on this subject shall be narrowed down to that definition of the word. On the contrary, I expect to treat of various fallacies, delusions, and deceptions in ancient and modern times, which, according to Webster's definition, may be called "humbugs," inasmuch as they were "impositions under fair pretences."

In writing of modern humbugs, however, I shall sometimes have occasion to give the names of honest and respectable parties now living, and I felt it but just that the public should fully comprehend my doctrine, that a man may, by common usage, be termed a "humbug," without by any means impeaching his integrity.

Speaking of "blacking-makers," reminds me that one of the first sensationists in advertising whom I remember to have seen, was Mr. Leonard Gosling, known as "Monsieur Gosling, the great French blacking-maker." He appeared in New York in 1830. He flashed like a meteor across the horizon; and before he had been in the city three months, nearly everybody had heard of "Gosling's Blacking." I well remember his magnificent "four-in-hand." A splendid team of blood bays, with long black tails, was managed with such dexterity by Gosling himself, who was a great "whip," that they almost seemed to fly. The carriage was emblazoned with the words, "Gosling's Blacking," in large gold letters, and the whole turnout was so elaborately ornamented and bedezined, that everybody stopped and gazed with wondering admiration. A bugle-player or a band of music always accompanied the great Gosling, and, of course, helped to attract the public attraction to his establishment. At the turning of every street corner your eyes rested upon "Gosling's Blacking." From every show-window gilded placards discoursed eloquently on the merits of "Gosling's Blacking." The newspapers teemed with poems written in its praise, and showers of pictorial handbills, illustrated almanacs, and tinseled souvenirs, all lauding the virtues of "Gosling's Blacking," smothered you at every point.

The celebrated originator of delineations, "Jim Crow Rice," made his first appearance at Hamblin's Bowery Theater at about this time. The crowds which thronged there were so great that hundreds from the audience were frequently admitted upon the stage. In one of his scenes, Rice introduced a negro boot-blacking establishment. Gosling was too "wide awake" to let such an opportunity pass unimproved, and Rice was paid for singing an original black Gosling ditty, while a score of placards, bearing the inscription, "Use Gosling's Blacking," were suspended at different points in this negro boot-polishing hall. Everybody tried "Gosling's Blacking"; and it was a really good article, his sales in city and country soon became immense; Gosling made a fortune in seven years, and retired; but, as with thousands before him, it was "easy come easy go." He engaged in a lead-mining speculation, and it was generally understood that his fortune was, in great measure, lost as rapidly as it was made.

Here let me digress, in order to observe, that one of the most difficult things in life is for men to bear discreetly sudden prosperity. Unless considerable time and labor are devoted to earning money, it is not appreciated by its possessor; and, having no practical knowledge of the value of money, he generally gets rid of it with the same ease that marked its accumulation. Mr. Astor gave the experience of thousands when he said that he found more difficulty in earning and saving his first thousand dollars than in accumulating all the subsequent millions which finally made up his fortune. The very economy, perseverance, and discipline which he was obliged to practice, as he gained money dollar by dollar, gave him a just appreciation of its value, and thus led him into those habits of industry, prudence, temperance, and untiring diligence so conducive and necessary to his future success.

Mr. Gosling, however, was not a man to be put down by a single financial reverse. He opened a store in Canajoharie, N.Y., which was burned, and on which there was no insurance. He came again to New York in 1839, and established a restaurant, where, by devoting the services of himself and several members of his family assiduously to the business, he soon reveled in his former prosperity, and snapped his fingers in glee at what unreflecting persons term "the freaks of Dame Fortune." He is still living in New York, hale and hearty, at the age of seventy. Although called a "French" blacking-maker, Mr. Gosling is in reality a Dutchman, having been born in the city of Amsterdam, Holland. He is the father of twenty-four children, twelve of whom are still living, to cheer him in his declining years, and to repay him in grateful attentions for the valuable lessons of prudence, integrity, and industry, through the adoption of which they are honored as respectable and worthy members of society.[78]

BARNUM'S FINAL WORD ON THE SUBJECT,
LATER PUBLISHED AS CHAPTER I OF *HUMBUGS OF*
THE WORLD (NEW YORK: CARLETON, 1865)

A little reflection will show that humbug is astonishingly widespread—in fact, almost universal. . . .

I apprehend that there is no sort of object which men seek to attain, whether secular, moral, or religious, in which humbug is not very often an instrumentality. Religion is and ever has been a chief chapter of human life. False religions are the only ones known to two-thirds of the human race, even now, after nineteen centuries of Christianity; and false religions are perhaps the most monstrous, complicated, and thorough-going specimens of humbug that can be found. And even within the pale of Christianity, how unbroken has been the succession of impostors, hypocrites and pretenders, male and female, of every possible variety of age, sex, doctrine, and discipline!

Politics and government are certainly among the most important of practical human interests. Now it was a diplomatist—that is, a practical manager of one kind of government matters—who invented that wonderful phrase—a whole world of humbug in half-a-dozen words—that "Language was given to us to conceal our thoughts." It was another diplomatist who said, "An ambassador is a gentleman sent to *lie* abroad for the good of his country." But need I explain to my own beloved countrymen that there is humbug in politics? Does anybody go into a political campaign without it? Are no exaggerations of *our* candidate's merits to be allowed? No depreciations of the *other* candidate? Shall we no longer prove that the success of the party opposed to us will overwhelm the land in ruin? Let me see. Leaving out the two elections of General Washington, eighteen times that very fact has been proved by the party that was beaten, and immediately we have *not* been ruined, notwithstanding the dreadful fatal fellows got their hands on the offices and their fingers into the treasury.

Business is the ordinary means of living for nearly all of us. And in what business is there not humbug? "There's cheating in all trades but ours," is the prompt reply from the boot-maker with the brown paper soles, the grocer with his floury sugar and chicoried coffee, the butcher with his mysterious sausages and queer veal, the dry-goods man with his "damaged goods wet at the great fire," and his "selling at a ruinous loss," the stock-broker with his brazen assurance that your company is bankrupt and your stock company not worth a cent (if he wants to buy it), the horse jockey with his black arts and spavined brutes, the milk man with his tin aquaria, the land agent with his nice new maps and beautiful descriptions of distant scenery, the newspaper man with his "immense circulation," the publisher with his "Great American Novel," the city auctioneer with his "Pictures by the Old Masters"—all and every one protest each his own innocence, and warn you against the deceits of the rest. My inexperienced friend, take it for granted that they tell the truth—about each other! And then transact your business to the best of your ability on your own judgment. Never fear but that you will get experience enough, and that you will pay well for it too; and towards the time when you shall no longer need earthly goods, you will begin to know how to buy.

Literature is one of the most interesting and significant expressions of humanity. Yet books are thickly peppered with humbug. "Travelers' stories" have been the scoff of ages, from the "True Story" of old Lucian the Syrian down to the gorillarities—if I may coin a word—of the Frenchman, Du Chaillu. Ireland's counterfeited Shakespeare plays, Chatterton's forged manuscripts, George Psalmanazar's forged Formosan language, Joe Smith's Mormon Bible (it should be noted that this and the Koran sounded two strings of humbug together—the literary and the religious), the more recent counterfeits of the notorious Greek Simonides—such literary humbugs as these are equal in presumption and in ingenuity too, to any of a merely business kind, though usually destitute of that sort of impiety which makes the great religious humbugs horrible as well as impudent.

Science is another important field of human effort. Science is the pursuit of pure truth, and the systemizing of it. In such an employment as that, one might reasonably hope to find all things done in honesty and sincerity. Not at all, my ardent and inquiring friends, there is a scientific humbug just as large as any other. We have all heard of the Moon Hoax.[79] Do none of you remember the Hydrarchos Sillimannii, that awful Alabama snake? It was only a little while ago that a grave account appeared in a newspaper of a whole business of compressing ice. Perpetual motion has been the dream of scientific visionaries, and a pretended but cheating realization of it has been exhibited by scamp after scamp. I understand that one is at this moment being invented over in Jersey City. I have purchased more than one "perpetual motion" myself. Many persons will remember Mr. Paine—"The Great Shot-at" as he was called from his story that people were constantly trying to kill him—and his water-gas. There have been other water-gases too, which were each going to show us how to set the North River on fire, but something or other has always broken down just at the wrong moment. Nobody seems to reflect, when these water-gases come up, that if water really could be made to burn, the right conditions would surely have happened at one of the thousands of city fires, and that the very stuff with which our stout firemen were extinguishing the flames, would have itself caught and exterminated the whole brave wet crowd!

Medicine is the means by which we poor feeble creatures try to keep from dying or aching. In a world so full of pain it would seem as if people could not be so foolish, or practitioners so knavish, as to sport with men's and women's and children's lives by their professional humbugs. Yet there are many grave M.D.'s who, if there is nobody to hear, and if they speak their minds, will tell you plainly that the whole practice of medicine is in one sense a humbug. One of its features is certainly a humbug, though so innocent and even useful that it seems difficult to think of any objection to it. This is the practice of giving a *placebo*–that is, a bread pill or a dose of colored water, to keep the patient's mind easy while imagination helps nature to perfect a cure. As for the quacks, patent medicines and universal remedies, I need only mention their names. Prince Hohenlohe, Valentine Greatrakes, John St. John Long, Doctor Graham and his wonderful bed, Mesmer and his tub, Perkins' metallic tractors–these are half a dozen. Modern history knows of hundreds such.

It would almost seem as if human delusions became more unreasoning and abject in proportion as their subject is of greater importance. A machine, a story, an animal skeleton, are not so very important. But the humbugs which have prevailed about that wondrous machine, the human body, its ailments and its cures, about the unspeakable mystery of human life, and still more about the far greater and more awful mysteries of the life beyond the grave, and the endless happiness and misery believed to exist there, the humbugs about these have been infinitely more absurd, more shocking, more unreasonable, more inhuman, more destructive.

I can only allude to whole sciences (falsely so called), which are unmingled humbugs from beginning to end. Such was Alchemy, such was Magic, such was and still is Astrology, and above all, Fortune-telling.[80]

But there is a more thorough humbug than any of these enterprises or systems. The greatest humbug of all is the man who believes–or pretends to believe–that everything and everybody are humbugs. We sometimes meet a person who professes that there is no virtue; that every man has his price, and every woman hers; that any statement from anybody is just as likely to be false as true, and that the only way to decide which, is to consider whether truth or a lie was likely to have paid best in that particular case. Religion he thinks one of the smartest business dodges extant, a first-rate investment, and by all odds the most respectable disguise that a lying or swindling businessman can wear. Honor he thinks is a sham. Honesty he considers a plausible word to flourish in the eyes of the greener portion of our race, as you would hold out a cabbage-leaf to coax a donkey. What people want, he thinks, or says he thinks, is something good to eat, something good to drink, fine clothes, luxury, laziness, wealth.

If you can imagine a hog's mind in a man's body–sensual, greedy, selfish, cruel, cunning, sly, coarse, yet stupid, short-sighted, unreasoning, unable to comprehend anything except what concerns the flesh, you have your man. He thinks himself philosophical and practical, a man of the world; he thinks to show knowledge and wisdom, penetration, deep acquaintance with men and things. Poor fellow! He has exposed his own nakedness. Instead of showing that others are rotten inside, he has proved that he is. He claims that it is not safe to believe others–it is perfectly safe to disbelieve him. He claims that every man will get the better of you if possible—let him alone! Selfishness, he says, is the universal rule—leave nothing to depend on his generosity or honor; trust him just as far you can sling an elephant by the tail. A bad world, he sneers, full of nastiness—it is his own foul breath that he smells; only a thoroughly corrupt heart could suggest such vile thoughts. He sees only what suits him, as a turkey-buzzard spies only carrion, though amid the loveliest landscape. I pronounce him who thus virtually slanders his father and dishonors his mother, and defiles the sanctities of home, and the glories of patriotism, and the merchant's honor, and the martyr's grave and the saint's crown—who does not even know that every sham shows that there is a reality, and that hypocrisy is the homage that vice pays to virtue—I pronounce him—no, I do not pronounce him a humbug, the word does not apply to him. He is a fool.

Looked at on one side, the history of humbug is truly humiliating to intellectual pride, yet the long silly story is less absurd during the later ages of history, and grows less and less so in proportion to the spread of real Christianity. This religion promotes good sense, actual knowledge, contentment with what we cannot help, and the exclusive use of intelligent means for increasing human happiness and decreasing human sorrow. And whenever the time shall come when men are kind and just and honest; when they only want what is fair and right, judge only on real and true evidence, and take nothing for granted, then there will be no place left for humbugs, either harmless or hurtful.

Barnum's Promotions

Barnum's vast promotional paper trail offers an exceptionally rich and diverse body of primary source material. Many of the texts in this gallery can be read on four different levels: as an effort to represent a particular product; as an attempt to build a particular audience; as a prescription for a particular set of consumer behaviors; and as an indirect record of the tastes, values, fantasies, and prejudices that Barnum's consumers brought with them into the exhibition hall.

There are, however, considerable analytical challenges involved in working with these materials. One is the sheer volume of Barnum's promotional output. This gallery provides a broad sampling of the showman's puffery across different eras, institutions, and themes. But it represents just a small portion of Barnum's overall production. Often, Barnum produced multiple promotional pamphlets for the same exhibition; and this is to say nothing of the

thousands of newspaper advertisements, playbills, lithographs, posters, and souvenir photographs produced in conjunction with the pamphlets. There is also the question of who actually authored the promotions. In some cases, the language is so close to that of the showman's private letters and published memoirs that it is unlikely anyone could have served as ghostwriter. In other cases (especially in his later circus newsletters), there is clear evidence that he commissioned and/or edited promotional copy written by someone else.[1]

Such ambiguities of authorship are part of the story here. Over the course of his career, Barnum employed a growing army of press agents, assistant managers, and advertising writers. Still, he continued to exert control over the corporate script. An 1885 account by one of his circus agents provides a sense of the collaborative process:

Every line of the stock letter press that is prepared in the winter he sees and criticizes and he is not loath to drop a word of judicious praise. It is related that once late-in-the-winter-time the manuscript for the couriers and quarter-sheets was sent up to Bridgeport for his perusal and, as the scribes did not enthuse over the "Greatest Show on Earth" with any degree of uniformity of statement, the whole mass was packed up in a soap box and shipped to Madison Square Garden with the request, "Please lie with some uniformity."[2]

This leads to perhaps the most complex question of all: whose values were expressed in the promotions? The showman's own values are in there somewhere, of course. Yet we know that many of his deepest personal convictions were inextricably bound up with his promotional goals.

During the late 1840s, for example, Barnum did not simply embrace temperance principles and sign the teetotaler pledge. He also framed his pledge and hung it in the entrance to his museum, hoping to recruit a more "respectable" class of consumer. Barnum's efforts to regulate public taste, moreover, necessarily coexisted with his market-driven need to appease, flatter, and indulge. It is far too simple, then, to describe these texts as the ideological expressions of any particular individual or interest. Long before the advent of focus groups, Barnum recognized one of the core principles of mass marketing. The most successful puffs crystallize a public's collective, inchoate desires. In some cases, they even bring a public into being.[3]

JOICE HETH

The Life of Joice Heth, The Nurse of Gen. George Washington, (The Father of Our Country,) Now Living at the Astonishing Age of 161 Years, and Weighs only 46 Pounds.
Price 6 cents (N.Y.: printed for the publisher, 1835).

THE LIFE OF JOICE HETH.
The Nurse of George Washington.

Joice Heth, the subject of this short memoir, was born on the Island of Madagascar, on the Coast of Africa, in the year One Thousand Six Hundred and Seventy-four. Of her parents little or nothing is known, save what she herself relates of them, in which her recollections are so indistinct, that but very little can be satisfactorily learnt. At the age of fifteen, she was cruelly torn from the bosom of her parents and her native land by one of those inhuman beings, who, in those days, to enrich themselves, made merchandise of human flesh.

She was imported to America, and sold as a slave to Thomas Buckner, an extensive planter of Virginia. She remained with him several years, when she came into the Washington family, who were then living on an extensive domain, called the Chotank Plantations. About this time, or soon after, she was married to a slave named Peter, belonging to Mrs. Atwood, a relative of the family of Washington, and living with the next door neighbor.

In this condition she lived until she became the mother of fifteen children, being the property of Augustine Washington, the father of George Washington, (or little Georgy, as she now calls him,) and was the first person who put clothes on the unconscious infant, who was destined in after days to lead our heroic fathers on to glory, to victory, and to freedom.

In the mean time she made a public profession of religion, and about the year Seventeen Hundred and Twenty, was baptized in the Potomac River, and became a member of the Baptist Church.

By her trusty and faithful discharge of such duties as were assigned her, she gained the full confidence of all the family, and was treated by them more as an hired servant than a slave. To her was trusted the full care and management of both the nursery and kitchen. At the age of fifty-four years she was formally sold and transferred, by a regular bill of sale, for the price of thirty-three pounds, to Mrs. Atwood, who was the then owner of Peter, her husband. This was not done on the account of the value of the services she might render, as to accommodate her in the enjoyment of the constant company of her helpmate, (Peter,) who was also at this time something in years, and a favorite domestic servant. By this arrangement, they were permitted to be constantly together, both employed in the lighter services in and about the house.

At the decease of Mrs. Atwood, she fell into the hands of Mr. Boling, he being one of the heirs to the estate. Some years after, Mr. Boling emigrated to Kentucky, and settled in the town of Paris, Bourbon county. He took with him Joice and her husband, who then, from the infirmities of old age, were unable to do much labor; they, however, being old domestic servants, were kindly provided for during the life of Mr. Boling. Soon after his death, died Peter, her husband, at a very advanced age, leaving Joice a single and only witness of the events of the preceding century.

From that time she has followed by legal succession, the branches of the family down to the present time.

Some of the time since, according to her own story, she has been very much neglected, laying for years in an outer building, upon the naked floor. In speaking of her past condition, she expresses great thankfulness, that Providence should so kindly provide the comforts of life, and make infinitely better her condition as she approaches towards the close of it.

She would not return to her former residence on any account, and is highly pleased with the idea of her remaining as she is, until death may finally close this mortal scene with her. She has a nurse, whose sole and only business is to dress, feed, and take care of her, who is very kind and attentive, and leaves nothing undone which could make her more comfortable and happy. Her diet consists of a little weak tea and corn bread, with rare cooked eggs, which is served her three or four times a day. Coffee made very sweet as often as she asks for it. She seems extremely fond of animal food, frequently asking for it; and when denied it, telling her the doctors say that it is not good for her, she will make a quick and spirited reply; "I guess I have lived long enough to know what is good for me, as well as the doctors; if I had minded them I should have been dead long ago." She says that she has never in her life taken any medicine, nor ever will.

Her greatest temporal enjoyment seems to be contained in her pipe and tobacco, the use of which for the last one hundred and twenty years has been constant. Her general health has been perfectly good, her pulse ranging from sixty-five to seventy; full, strong, and perfectly regular. She is, in her intellect, uncommonly bright; hears and understands perfectly all conversation, when not wearied by company. She takes great interest in conversing with pious persons, upon the subject of religion. She will repeat and sing hymns and psalms for hours together, while alone, that were commonly learnt and sung a century and a half ago; converses freely about death, and is willing to meet it, often saying, "Oh! That the Lord would in his mercy and goodness receive me home quickly."

She has certificates in her possession from some of the oldest and most respectable planters in the section of the country where she has lived for the last sixty or seventy years, who without any hesitation, give her a most excellent character for truth, honesty, and exemplary piety. The following are some of the certificates she has with her, which she values very highly, and nothing gives her greater trouble than to be informed they will be taken from her:

This may certify, that I was born and have always lived in Bourbon county, Kentucky; that I am now sixty-seven years of age, and ever since my remembrance have known Joice Heth, the colored woman, now visiting Cincinnati, as being one hundred and sixty-one years old. I have no doubt but this is her correct age, for as early as I can remember, she was totally blind from age, and so infirm as to be unable to do any labor. She was always called in our neighborhood, Aunt Joice Heth. She has ever been celebrated for her piety, and I believe no reward or threat could be offered which would induce her to tell a falsehood. She always since my remembrance was fond of relating anecdotes concerning George Washington, whose nurse she always claimed to be, and I never doubted it myself, or heard it doubted by others.
Signed in the presence of, &c.

This shall certify that I, the subscriber, was born in the town of Paris, in the state of Kentucky. My age is seventy-one years on the 17th of February, 1835. I have ever known Joice Heth, the old colored woman. When I first remember Aunt Joice, as we called her, she was totally blind and unable to work, which must have been fifty-five years ago. It was always understood that Joice was the nurse of George Washington, and slave of his father. She is very religious and honest, and I believe the most implicit confidence may be put in her word, for nothing in my opinion would tempt her to utter a falsehood.

Signed, &c.

Within the last two or three years, she has traveled through many of the States, visited most of the principal cities, and been seen by multitudes, with perfect wonder and astonishment, no one doubting on seeing her, but that she is what she herself claims to be, the nurse of Washington and 161 years of age. The most learned and scientific men in this country have visited her, and after conversing with and examining her, all without exception, declare her to be the greatest curiosity in the world.

In giving the foregoing brief sketch of the life and character of Joice Heth, the writer of this has but one single motive, and that is of charity towards the descendants of this living monument of antiquity.

She has outlived all her descendants save five, and they are her great grand-children, who are now held in bondage by a highly respectable gentleman of Kentucky, who has generously offered to set them free on being paid two-thirds what they cost him. This work, together with what may be collected from her exhibition, after deducting expenses, is expressly for that purpose, and will be immediately done whenever there can be realized the sum sufficient to do it. Two of them are said to be uncommonly intelligent and active, quick to learn, and great favorites of their master. In consequence of his partiality towards them, they have been instructed to read, and have acquired by their assiduous application upon the Sabbath, a knowledge of the scriptures, of which they are very fond to learn. It is designed that they shall be instructed in the glorious truths of the gospel, so as to become fully qualified to teach their poor unfortunate race the true way to future happiness.

If such should be the case, the writer of this little work would feel himself amply compensated for all his labor, by the happy reflection of having been instrumental, through the favor of the Lord, in opening a new channel through which might flow freely and effectually to those unfortunate beings, the glorious blessing derived from the knowledge of the gospel.

Persons are now engaged in collecting facts relative to the history of this old woman, which will be published as soon as they can be authentically gathered.

The following are notices, which some of the public journals have taken of her:

From the New-York Sun.
Joice Heth.–The arrival at Niblo's Gardens, of this renowned relic of the olden time, has created quite a sensation among the lovers of the curious and the marvelous; and *a greater object of marvel and curiosity has never presented itself for their gratification.* From the length of her limbs and the size of the bones, it is probable that she was a large, stout woman, in her day; but now, she comes up exactly to one's idea of an animated mummy. Her weight is said to be less than

fifty pounds. Her feet have shrunk to mere skin and bone, and her long attenuated fingers more resemble the claws of a bird of prey than human appendages. The presumed date of her birth is 1674–which would make her age, at present time, upward of 161!!–Notwithstanding her burden of years and infirmities, she is lively, and seems to retain all her senses wonderfully. Her hearing is almost as acute as that of any person of middle age.

From the New-York Evening Star.
The "old one" has arrived, and crowds of ladies and gentlemen have visited her at Niblo's. She is lively, and answers of questions cheerfully. From the bill of sale of the old lady from Gen. Washington's father, *we can have no doubt that she is 160 years of age.* Her appearance is very much like an Egyptian mummy just escaped from the Sarcophagus.

From the New-York Sunday News.
Joice Heth.–This living *mummy,* on whose head 161 winters have sprinkled their snows, is now exhibiting at Niblo's Garden. She was born in the year 1674, during the reign of Charles the 2d of England, and Louis the 14th of France, and independently of her great age, she is an object of curiosity and interest to the American public, as having been the nurse of great Washington.

From the New-York Commercial Advertiser.
Antediluvians.–We venture to state, that since the flood, a like circumstance has not been witnessed equal to one which is about to happen this week. Old Joice Heth, whom we mentioned on Friday, holds a drawing room at Niblo's this day, which is to be continued till Saturday. Ancient or modern times furnish no parallel to the great age of this *woman.* Methuselah was 969 years old when he died, but nothing is said of the age of his *wife.* Adam attained nearly the age of his antiquated descendant. It is not unlikely that the sex in the olden time were like their daughters at the present day–unwilling to tell their age. Joice Heth is an exception; she comes out boldly, and says she is rising at 160.

From the Providence Daily Journal.
Joice Heth, the nurse of Washington, will pass a few days in this city next week. She has been several weeks in New-York, and been visited by thousands of ladies and gentlemen. Joice Heth was born in the island of Madagascar, on the east coast of Africa, in the year 1674, and has consequently now arrived at the astonishing age of *one hundred and sixty-one years.* She weighs but forty-six pounds, and yet is very cheerful and interesting, converses freely, sings numerous hymns, relates many interesting anecdotes of the *boy* Washington, *the red coats,* &c., and when speaking of her young master, George Washington, says, *she raised him.*

⟞⟝

THE FEEJEE MERMAID

From *A Short History of Mermaids, Containing Many Interesting Particulars Concerning Them. Also, A Description of the One Now Exhibiting at the Boston Museum* (Boston: Marden and Co., Printers, 1842).[4]

> However naturalists may doubt of the existence of mermen or mermaids, if we may believe particular writers, there seems testimony enough to establish it.
>
> *−Chambers. History of Mermaids.*

> Thou remberest
> Since once I sat upon a promontory,
> And heard a Mermaid on a Dolphin's back,
> Uttering such dulcet and harmonious breath,
> That the rude sea grew civil at her song.
>
> *−Shakespeare.*

Naturalists for the most part not only discredit the existence of mer-people, but assume that the existence of beings so organized is an anatomical impossibility. The same is their argument against the Centaur, which is, no doubt, a fabulous Creation; not that we consider its existence anatomically impossible but that we cannot find any link in the chain of organic life to connect such a being with the animal kingdom. But that beings of human conformations, formed from the regions of the pelvis, inhabit certain parts of the oceans, we are as firmly convinced as there are black swans in Australia or giants in Patagonia.

At all events our faith is sustained by the testimony of travelers and others in all ages of the world, and that is as good authority as we have for the existence of many of the wonders that we constantly hear of, and which are fully accredited. Besides they are actually required to make the chain of mechanic life perfect, for there are sea lions, sea wolves, sea horses, sea dogs—in fact sea animals of all the varieties that we have on land; and hence, though we should argue by inference alone, it is natural to suppose that there are sea men and sea women. The argument of anatomical impossibility is sufficiently answered by the fact, that the polypii constructed apparently without any design, is a living animal; as is also the *sponge;* and when the mechanism of such beings are formed conformable to the purposes of life, who can believe that a creature formed as the mermaid, could not enjoy a breathing existence.

Further, it is no argument against mer-people that they are not more frequently seen; but perhaps the wonder is that they are seen so often as they are—or at all. The sea is their atmosphere, and no doubt a subtler fluid is unnatural to them. Hence it were as much to expect them to rise to our breathing world, as for us to go down into theirs. "But," may add the reader, "according to the testimony of hundreds they have been seen on the surface of the ocean, which destroys this hypothesis." Our answer is—not at all; for though men cannot breathe salt water, individuals of the human race existed from time to time who could, and who have remained under the waves hour after hour—nay, in two or more instances—day after day in the unrestricted enjoyment of their faculties; and arguing from analogy it is to be presumed that rare instances may occur in which individuals of the sea people have the gift of existing in an atmosphere differing from that of their own. As well in fact might mermen and women argue against the existence of the human race, because they have been visited by so few of its representatives, as we to argue against theirs for the same reasons.

Moreover, notwithstanding the progress of navigation, and the great intercourse of nations, men know but little indeed of what is going forward on or in the various oceans. Our ships do not traverse them in all directions, but keep in lines, as in beaten tracks through immense forests—so that—granting that they were equal to the respiration of our upper air, which we doubt in the aggregate—the mer-people may float about in myriads on the surface of the, by man, unfrequented parts of the seas, for aught we know to the contrary; and indeed, there are not wanted many grave, and fairly authenticated traditions to bear us out in the assumption that such might be the case. . . .[5]

The following letter concerning the one now in this country is from an eminent Professor of Natural History in the city of New-York.

Notwithstanding the majority of naturalists have doubted the existence of the mermaid, I never have found any good reason or ground for these doubts, and certainly I have always been far from believing their existence to be a physical impossibility. Linnaeus, one of the first naturalists in the world, believed in their existence, as did also the poet and historian Southey, Sir John Sinclair, and many others whose opinions are worthy of consideration.

I have this morning seen, and very critically examined the animal belonging to J. Griffin, Esq., an English naturalist, who has spent the last five years in traveling on the western part of the American continent, for the purpose of collecting curiosities for the Lyceum of Natural History in London. The animal, though possessing by no means a repulsive appearance, is far from being the beautiful and captivating creature represented by the many pictures found in old books which profess to treat of mermaids.

The head, breast, arms, hands, fingers, and indeed all the upper part of the body, bear a close resemblance to those of a human being, certainly considerably nearer than the monkey or ourang-outang, as the palm and fingers of those animals are invariably much longer than those of the human species, while the hand of this creature is as perfectly and beautifully proportioned as that of an infant. The lower portion of the body is supplied with scales, fins, and tail, precisely like that of a fish, with the exception that the fins are placed in different positions from those of any species of fish ever yet discovered.

That the animal has lived, moved, and had its being, *as it is,* ADMITS NOT THE

SHADOW OF A DOUBT, as all must acknowledge who see it; and that it is the animal heretofore described as the MERMAID, and hitherto considered as a fabulous creature, is equally certain. It is decidedly a wonderful production of nature, and as it fully establishes a long disputed point, it is a subject of deep interest to all persons, and of great importance to naturalists throughout the world.

Since closely examining this creature, I have wondered that its existence should so long have been doubted. I see nothing more extraordinary in the existence of a connecting link between the fish and the human species than in the continued chain found binding together the whole animal kingdom. We have the flying fish and the flying squirrel; these animals connect the bird with the fish and the quadruped; also the bat, the bat fish, the penguin, the porcupine fish, the seal, the sea lion, sea horse, sea wolf, the ourang outang, and an endless number of other animals, all evidently forming connecting links in the various species of animated creation. The Platypus, or *Ornithorincus Paradoxus,* from New Holland, is an animal with a body resembling the seal or otter, and the webbed feet and bill of the goose.

Indeed the works of creation are without end, and could they all be displayed to human vision, I am convinced that we should discover that no animal or form has ever been conceived by man which has not actually been endowed with life by the infinitely Wise and Omnipotent Creator of this and myriads of other worlds.

THE HOBOKEN BUFFALO HUNT

From the *New York Herald,*
August 30, 1843.

GRAND BUFFALO HUNT,
(FREE OF CHARGE,)
At Hoboken, near the Ferry, on Thursday, August 31st, at 3, 4, and 5 o'clock PM.
Mr. C. D. French, one of the most daring and experienced hunters of the west, has arrived thus far on his way to Europe, with a
HERD OF BUFFALOES,
Captured by himself near Santa Fe. He will exhibit the method by hunting the Wild Buffaloes, and throwing the Lasso, at Hoboken, on Thursday; and in order to place this novel exhibition within the means of every man, woman, and child, it will be FREE TO ALL, and will come off on a fine piece of ground within a few rods of Hoboken Ferry, capable of accommodating 100,000 persons.
THREE DISTINCT RACES
Will take place at 3, 4, and 5 o'clock P.M. On each occasion a herd of 15 to 20 Buffaloes

will let loose. The City Brass Band is engaged. Extra Ferry Boats will be provided. For particulars see bills. If the weather should be stormy, the sport will come off at the same hour the first fair day.

BARNUM'S FIRST SELF-PROMOTION

From the *New York Atlas*, April 20, 1845.[6]

Our Foreign Correspondent.

We have received from an intimate friend of Barnum's, a very loving one, apparently–the following particulars:

Mr. Barnum was born in Danbury, Bethel parish, and he is at this moment *one hundred and seventy-nine years of age.* This averment may possibly excite a smile of incredulity; but we beg our readers to indulge us for a moment, and they will agree that we are right regarding Barnum's longevity. Not that he has literally lived that number of years upon the earth, (for he was born in 1810,) but in this age of go-aheaditiveness, when machinery is propelled by thunder and lightning–when locomotives go sixty miles an hour, and when it is no longer asked "how far" it is from one place to another, but the question is, "how many hours is it," &c.–when distance is reckoned by *time* instead of miles, it is but just and proper that a man's age should be computed by the incidents of his life, his experience in the world, &c., rather than by the number of years which he may have breathed the breath of life. Now we say that men have lived to the age of 80 or 90 years, and sank down into the grave without seeing or dreaming of a *tithe* of what Barnum has experienced as a *propria personae* although he is now in his thirty-fifth year. Our readers, therefore, upon perusing the following brief sketch of only a few prominent incidents in his history, will agree that we have marked his present age in about the right notch, 179 years.

His father (as Barnum himself boasts) was a *tailor.* He gave his son an ordinary district school education, and at the age of eleven years he was placed as clerk in a country store, and there he continued dealing in tacks and tapes, cloths and curry-combs, gin, gridirons, grindstones and gingerbread, till the death of his father in 1824. Our hero was thus left without a protector or a penny at the age of fourteen; but he earned a good livelihood by his clerkship. At sixteen he importuned his mother to let him hire out as secretary to a traveling caravan of wild animals; but the good old lady put her veto on this early desire to become a showman, by telling him that these straggling people were a wicked and desolute race of beings, and would ruin him if he joined them. At the age of 18, therefore, our hero opened a small store in his native town on his own account. In the course of that year he began paying his addresses to a young lady, to which his mother objected because the girl had not got enough money to suit her ideas; but our hero, thinking a want of riches no crime, became indignant at the parental opposition, and in the spirit of *go-ahead* which is one of his most striking characteristics, he ran away with the girl, and coming to this city was married, and returned home a husband at nineteen!

At the age of twenty-one he had built two fine houses in his native town, in one of which he resided, rented the other, and was "well to do in the world." At about this time some person in the town had been guilty of one of that kind of mean and dirty actions which no law can touch, and which public opinion alone can punish, upon which Barnum wrote an article setting forth all the facts, and took it to the village paper for insertion. The editor refused to publish it, pretending to fear a prosecution for libel; the writer then offered bonds, indemnifying him against the effects of such a prosecution for libel; but the editor persisted in his refusal, upon which Barnum became indignant, and declared that the editor did not conduct a free press, and if he did not publish the article he would publish it *in his own paper* within two weeks. The editor laughed at what he supposed was an idle threat; but Barnum hastened to this city, purchased a press and type, engaged workmen, and, in two weeks from that day, he published the first number of a paper called the Herald of Freedom," which afterwards proved a fatal rival to the old paper. We have an old copy of the "Herald of Freedom" before us. The motto at the head of the editorial columns is, "Truth, Liberty, Justice," while under the title of the paper, on the first page, is a motto adopted from Jefferson: "I have sworn upon the altar of God eternal hostility to every form of tyranny over the mind of man."

As might have been expected, the Herald sometimes blew some strange blasts, startling the sedate citizens of Connecticut from their propriety. In one year, however, Barnum (at the age of 22) was prosecuted in the name of the state for a libel on the deacon of the church. He proved the truth of his publication; but the judge contended for the doctrine "that the greater the truth the greater the libel," and Barnum was convicted, fined, and imprisoned sixty days in the county jail!

This event was one of the most fortunate that could have occurred for our hero, for the people, who always arose to put down injustice and persecution, came in thousands to his support. On the first day of imprisonment his apartment was elegantly carpeted, papered and decorated, his library removed into it, and, for two months, he held a constant succession of *levees*, his apartment being continually thronged with friends, and new friends forming every day. While in prison he continued to edit his paper, the circulation of which became immediately augmented by several thousand new subscribers. At the expiration of sixty days, a great public celebration of his emancipation from prison took place, at which thousands attended, some coming the distance of fifty miles. An oration of the "Freedom of the Press" was delivered in the same court house, where, two months previously, he had been sentenced, a public dinner was partaken of, toasts given amid the roar of cannon and playing of a large band of music, and, at the conclusion, Barnum was escorted to his house, a distance of three miles, in a splendid carriage drawn by six horses, preceded by a band of music, and followed by a large concourse of friends in carriages and on horseback. In reply to a toast given that day, Barnum made a speech, in which he asserted that the preceding sixty days had been the happiest and proudest of his life, and that his press should continue a *terror* to evil doers–a supporter to those who did well, etc.

In 1832 or 33, he removed to this city, and opened a wholesale grocery store at 156 South Street. From 1835 to 38 or 39, he was concerned in circuses, caravans, the Zoological Institute, etc., etc., traveling through every portion of the Union. In fact, we have heard him assert that there was no town in the United States or Canada, containing 3000 inhabitants, which he had not visited personally, and in which he had not a friend with whom he could hold a correspondence should business require it. During one of these peregrinations, he came across the famous Joyce Heth, in Kentucky, and his profitable adventurers with her he has more than once given to the public.

In 1838, Barnum was traveling with a circus company in Mississippi, coining money with great rapidity. In February the roads throughout the country became almost impassable, on account of the great depth of mud peculiar to some portions of that state in winter. Barnum had arrived at Vicksburg and found that he must lie still a couple of months, on account of the heavy traveling. He could not tolerate that idea, so he stepped down to the wharf and purchased the steamboat Ceres, with all its equipments, then plying Vicksburg and New Orleans. On board this steamer he took his circus company and stud of horses. He also purchased a negro in Vicksburg to attend him as servant. They then went up and down the river in the steamer, and, landing at the principal towns, put up the large tent on shore, sent the music car and band around the town, opened the show, at the conclusion of which all would again be placed on the steamer, and perhaps the next day this aquatic company would be performing two hundred miles from the place where they played the evening previous! At Natchez Barnum missed several hundred dollars from his pocket. His negro had stolen it while brushing his master's clothes before he was up in the morning. Barnum suspected the "nigger," searched him, found the money, gave him fifty lashes, and took him to New Orleans, where he was sold at auction.

When the Ceres arrived at New Orleans, the papers announced her arrivals as follows: "Arrived from Natchez, steamboat Ceres, *Captain Barnum*–cargo, an equestrian company." In the spring Barnum visited what is called the "Attakapas" country, passing down "Bayoutash" to St. Martinsville, Opelousas. At the latter town he sold his steamer and all his horses, receiving in payment cash, sugar, molasses, and *a negro woman and child*. He shipped his sweets to New York, sold his negroes in St. Louis, and arrived in this city in June, after a very successful tour.

In 1840, he engaged in business at 101 Bowery, but was sadly swindled by his partner, Proler, who escaped to Germany with all the property he could lay his hands on. The same year Barnum was manager of the Vauxhall Gardens, and here first brought out the famous dancer, Master John Diamond. The year following he was principal agent for the sale of *Sears' Pictorial Bible!* In 1841 or '42, he purchased the American Museum from the heirs of its founder, John Scudder; and although the museum had been a losing concern for some years, Barnum at once gave new life to it, and by managing it with tact, liberality and energy, he has rendered it far the most profitable establishment of the kind in America—perhaps in the world. During the last year he has been in Great Britain, where he has cleared about $100,000 by the exhibition of General Tom Thumb, with whom Barnum has been three or four times before Queen Victoria and the court, and has visited most of the mansions of royalty and nobility in England.

Barnum is possessed of an enterprise that is *indomitable.* He has a spirit of perseverance seldom equaled; but the grand secret of his success is, that he has a *genius* corresponding with his high aspirations. He sees a subject in all its details at a single glance—his first impression always governs him—his motto, like that of Crockett, is "go ahead," and he lays it down as an established fact, that a man of sound sense of efficient enterprise can accomplish anything which that "sense" will lead him to undertake. He therefore never commences a project without persevering to the end, for the idea of defeat never enters his mind.

Barnum is a man of liberal principles, and a friend of equal rights. He is a jovial companion, always in high spirits; and possessing a large fund of anecdotes, with a good knack of relating them, he is sure to keep a company in good humor. Although he delights in making money, he could never be happy if he could not spend it freely. He is free, open-hearted, generous and charitable almost to a fault.

In the heyday of his prosperity he joined the Odd Fellows. A friend said to him one day—"What inducement had you for becoming an Odd Fellow! Certainly you never expect to need their assistance?" "No," was the reply, "*but they need mine,* and I want no greater pleasure than that which a man feels when he is bestowing his charity where he knows it is needed and deserved; and in these days of humbug it is quite a blessing to be able to expend money for charity, and to know that the recipients of your bounty are not a set of swindlers, who live by begging in the name of some charitable institution with a fine title."

Barnum has also appropriated some money to the Fourierites. When a friend told him that he feared it was a visionary scheme, he said that if there was one chance in one hundred of it succeeding, he should not regret having contributed his funds—for, if it succeeded penury and want would be unknown, and no chance to bring about so great a desideratum ought to pass unimproved.

In business, Barnum prides himself in allowing no man to overreach or deceive him, and woe to him who succeeds in doing so. Barnum, who does his business openly, frankly and above-board, will neither sleep nor slumber till he has revenged himself on any man who deceives him.

One of Barnum's greatest foibles is his love for a *practical joke*. In the attainment of this desired object, he will spare neither friend nor foe, but this mania often leads him to injure the feelings and sometimes the regard of his best friends. Unlike most practical jokers, however, he is fond of what he calls "a good joke," even if it is practiced on himself. The consequence is, many of his friends never hesitate to "sell" him if they get a chance; and when he has been "sold," he knows no greater enjoyment than to relate the trick which has been played at his expense.

GENERAL TOM THUMB

From *Sketch of the Life, Personal Appearance, Character, and Manners. of Charles S. Stratton, The Man in Miniature, Known as* GENERAL TOM THUMB, *Twenty-Eight Inches High, and Weighing Only Fifteen Pounds. With Some Account of Remarkable Dwarfs, Giants, and Other Human Phenomena, of Ancient and Modern Times. Also, General Tom Thumb's Songs* (New York: Van Norden and Amerman, Printers, 1847).[7]

Some Account of General Tom Thumb, The Man in Miniature

Ever since the commencement of the world, there has existed, amongst all races of men, a common average as to height, size and proportion; and so little has it been found to vary, that we might refer the dimensions of our race to an almost universal standard, regarding striking and casual deviations from the usual order of things, as only exceptions to the general rule. The mummies which have been removed from the places of their long repose in the tombs of the Pharaohs; the skeletons which have been found in dim old charnel houses, which were constructed years before our history takes note of their existence; the bones dug out of Indian mounds, which rise abruptly in the forest or on the prairie: the relics of antiquated religious houses, and the remains found on battle fields of only a few years' notoriety—all show the average length of six feet. Climate and other circumstances may have modified the size of men, but a consistent uniformity of height has characterized man in all ages of the world.

In the volumes of Sacred History we have presented to our view nations and individuals who have attained notoriety in consequence of their remarkable deviations from the usual order of things. For instance, we are told of a race of giants who existed before the universal deluge, and who afflicted the earth with war and bloodshed. "There were giants in those days" has passed into a familiar proverb. By means of ancient, and even in modern history, and through the revelations of tradition, we have been informed that at certain periods giants and monsters existed; for which stories, it is unreasonable to suppose no foundation whatever existed. Bunyon, the prince of fable writers, has taken advantage of popular belief, to weave one of his most powerful allegories; and the old Greek poets frequently introduce giants into their narratives. On the vast continent of the New World, skeletons have been found in such numbers, as to justify the assumption that, at some former and very remote age, there must have existed an entire race, who average stature was nearly eight feet. . . .

On the other hand, those who have failed to attain the usual stature, and have fallen much under it, have also proved exceptions to the general law; and these instances, though, perhaps, not so numerous as the added size, have been far from few. As there were nations of Giants, so there have been, and are, communities of Dwarfs and Pigmies. In the regions of the extreme North, the frigid climate and the peculiar modes of living have reduced the stature of whole nations. Recent and former navigators in the Arctic Seas have assured us that the Esquimaux are generally beneath five feet in height. The Laplanders are still smaller, for they scarcely average four; and in the wilds of Sought Africa, a pigmy nation, even inferior to their Northern brethren, exists. . . .

In our own day, Count Borulaski was the greatest little man. He was very little, very amiable, and very accomplished; but he was a head and shoulders higher than General Tom Thumb. Count Borulaski, like the General, was a special favorite of royalty, for he frequently visited George the Fourth. The late inimitable Charles Mathews was also extremely attached to him. He died only a few years ago.

Major Stevens, the American Dwarf, is about forty inches in height and a fine accomplished little gentleman; has been exhibited in nearly every city of the United States. Other dwarfs, of about the same dimensions, male and female, have been exhibited within a few years, and regarded with no little wonder and curiosity. Many of these tiny gentlemen have been much or partially deformed, and so pain has been felt whilst looking at them. But in the case of the hero of our narrative no such drawback exists, even to the approach of a defect. All former dwarfs were, in shape as in size, far his inferiors. We now proceed to give some account of this most extraordinary human being.

GENERAL TOM THUMB,

As he is best known, but whose real name is Charles S. Stratton, first saw the light in the town of Bridgeport, Connecticut, U.S.A. His parents are persons about whom there exists no peculiarity, either in their mental or physical organization. At his birth, the General (for so he has been styled by the united voices of his thousands of friends and admirers) weighed nine pounds and a half—which is rather above the usual weight of children at birth, so that he bid fair to become—indeed *was* a bouncing boy. He grew, as other children do, day after day, until he attained to the age of seven months, when nature put a *veto* on his further upward progress, and ordered him forever afterwards to remain in *status quo.* People, when he was twelve months' old, fancied that he had never grown an inch for some time; measures (tape ones) were resorted to for the purpose of ascertaining his stationary condition; but although in *every other* respect he grew day by day, with great rapidity, never a hair's breadth more was added to his length. No longer—no shorter—no heavier—but much handsomer—a great deal sharper, and considerable stronger; this was how matters stood. His appetite increased, although his stomach refused to grow larger; he never complained of sickness, partook freely of the dishes found upon the tables of the laboring classes, enjoyed refreshing sleep, *and has always exhibited the most perfect health,* with the exception of those slight colds to which the most robust are liable. His parents have had two other children, who are well grown, interesting girls of nine and eleven years of age. In fact, there is nothing in his history or appearance, or in that of his family, which furnishes the slightest clue to the astonishing phenomena which are presented by his miniature features and frame.

That trite but expressive saying, "He must be seen to be believed in," holds good in General Tom Thumb's case, for it is extremely difficult to form a proper idea of the personal appearance of this extraordinary being from descriptions, or even from drawings; all representations of him have an exaggerated appearance. The imagination cannot conceive the possibility of such extreme littleness; and we find it difficult, with the best artistic aids, to picture on the mental retina a perfect MINIATURE MAN, only TWENTY-EIGHT INCHES HIGH, perfect and elegant in his proportions, and weighing only FIFTEEN POUNDS!

When standing on the floor, or parading the room, which he does, dressed in a style of Bond-street elegance, and with all the grace, dignity and ease of a finished gentleman, his head scarcely reaches to the knees of a person of ordinary stature, and is about on a level with the seats of the chairs, sofas and ottomans of the drawing-room. Unlike many other dwarfs, the General is exquisitely proportioned, his head being not large, but of the proper symmetry, and beautifully developed, and his hands and feet the prettiest ever seen. His boots are perfect Wellingtons, made of the softest kid, by the most fashionable artists; his clothes are the product of the most distinguished tailors, and his gloves are of necessity furnished to order, for nothing so small and fairy-like were ever before manufactured. His canes, of which he has several, are from ten to twelve inches long, and his hats, for the various costumes, are of themselves curiosities.

The General has a fair complexion, light hair, fresh, rosy cheeks, large beautiful dark eyes, a fine forehead, a handsome mouth, and great vivacity of expression and hilarity of manner.

The Editor of the "Courier and Enquirer," Colonel Webb, whom the General visited soon after his arrival in New-York in 1841, thus describes him in that paper:

SOMETHING NEW UNDER THE SUN—While quietly discussing our dinner, we were honored with a very unceremonious visit from no less a personage than the distinguished *General Thomas Thumb*. We were somewhat annoyed at the interruption at first, but discovering its cause, and the honor conferred upon us, very quietly proceeded in the operation of carving a turkey, which the companion of the General assured us weighed more than his Grace. We were somewhat disposed to question this; but, when informed that GENERAL THUMB *weighs precisely Fifteen Pounds Two Ounces!* we admitted the truth of the assertion, and placed the General alongside of our plate to superintend the operation of carving. He took his station with great *sang froid,* and, amid the roar of our little ones, quietly kicked aside a tumbler of water, which he considered dangerous in the event of his falling into it! As soon as we carved the turkey to his satisfaction, he very gracefully walked around the table, at the risk of being drowned in a wine glass, paid his respects to all who were sitting around it, and selected a seat for himself, in which he ate a very hearty dinner, and drank the health of all present in a glass of *Malmsey.* All this may appear *fiction* to the reader, but it is sober truth. GENERAL THUMB weighs fifteen pounds two ounces, and is exactly *twenty-eight inches high!* Beyond all question, he is the *greatest* PIGMY of whom we have any account, being smaller than Sir GEOFFREY HUDSON, who was actually served up in a *pie* for the amusement of guests, and alongside of whom Major STEVENS declares himself to be a *giant!* Of a verity, he is the greatest curiosity we have ever seen; and we are quite sure that all who omit to pay their respects to him, at the *American Museum,* will for ever regret it. . . .

He is magnitude in miniature, *multum in parvo;* not exactly an abridgement of human nature, for the fellow's *amplitude* is undeniable, but one of Nature's *indices,* in which the principal features of the race may be looked at with one glance, without turning over interminable folios to see "what man is made of." He is a sort of mental and physical concentration, a chemical synthesis, in which manhood has been *boiled down;* a son of Anak reduced to his lowest term; the cube root of all creation! In sober seriousness, this dwarf is an amazement, and no one who has the opportunity, should fail of seeing him; for, besides being, as we verily believe, the smallest specimen of humanity that ever before visited the earth, he is an exceedingly *pretty* boy, *symmetrical in all his proportions,* and altogether free from the deformities which generally disfigure such manikins. In short, he is a sight worth going a great way to see. . . .

In strength, activity and vivacity, the General is remarkable. He often amuses himself by taking hold of a cane with one or both hands and being carried about the room, which a man can easily do with one hand. He is constantly engaged in walking about, talking, and in various pastimes and employments, from early in the morning till late at night, without showing any signs of fatigue, and seems the happiest little fellow in the world.

His personations of what are generally termed the "Grecian Statues," are among the most beautiful and wonderful portion of his performances. His "tableau" of Cupid, with his wings and quiver, is inimitable—his size and form being so perfect for that representation, that he looks as if he had just been removed from an Italian image-board. His "Samson carrying off the gates of Gaza" is a most extraordinary representation. His attitude is perfect, and the spectator for the moment loses the idea of the diminutive size of the representation of the *strong* man, so perfect is the representation. His personations of the "Fighting Gladiator," "The Slave whetting his knife," "Ajax," "Discobulus," "Cincinnatus," "Hercules with the Nemaean Lion," &c., exhibit a correctness of attitude, and develop in his motions a firmness and strength, combined with a spirit and intelligence, which prove his age beyond all question to be as represented. At times the General dresses as a sailor, and dances a hornpipe to perfection. Again, we find him dressed as an English Fox Hunter, with his red coat, drab breeches, and top boots, the feet of which are three inches long, and one and a quarter inches wide!!!

His personations of NAPOLEON BUONAPARTE, and of FREDERICK THE GREAT, are perfection itself. His court costumes are elegant, but dressed as a HIGHLAND CHIEFTAIN, he carries his visitors by storm. Nothing can be conceived more perfect or more lovely.

Never was a human being, of any size, blessed with a kinder heart, or more excellent disposition. He never forgets an acquaintance, and cherishes his friends with the greatest affection. There is something extremely winning in his manners, and this, with his strange beauty, has made many persons, and especially ladies, so strongly attached to him as to become his almost daily visitors. Children are always delighted with him, and little girls are his especial favorites. He receives all his visitors with a cordial and courtly grace; shaking hands and kissing the ladies, which it is difficult to prevent his doing, and which he appears to enjoy, especially when done roguishly, or by stealth, with extreme gusto. During his Southern Tour, early in the Spring of 1843, when he was visited by immense crowds in every Atlantic city, he boasts, among his other adventures, of having kissed six thousand ladies. The number now, (1847,) exceeds a million and a half!

It is natural to suppose that the smallness of the brain should limit the development of his intellectual faculties; such, however, is not the case; but, from obvious circumstances, the General's education has, until recently, been neglected. There is no lack of intelligence or aptitude to learn, and the General is now advancing in reading, writing, music, &c., with every prospect of rapid proficiency.

It is gratifying to add, that the utmost care is devoted to his moral and religious education, and that his ideas regarding the Deity, and the essential requisites of the Gospel, are as lucid and correct as those of many a mature age. The General was never known to utter a falsehood, and his language is always unexceptionable.

Of course General Tom Thumb has been the greatest attraction, made a strong sensation, and drawn admiring crowds in every place which he has visited. At the

American Museum, in New-York, he was seen, during a few weeks, by more than eighty thousand persons. In Philadelphia, Boston, Baltimore, Charleston, &c., his success was not less remarkable. It is true that the other attractions of the American Museum are of the highest order, and that under the management of Mr. Barnum, it ranks with the first establishments of the kind in the world; but unquestionably General Thumb has proved, in all his engagements, its greatest card. . . .[8]

"General Tom Thumb's Visit to the Queen of England, at Buckingham Palace, 1844." Written by Mr. James Morgan, of the Imperial Hotel, Liverpool, at the General's particular request.[9]

> Tune: Yankee Doodle.
>
> I'm General Thumb, just come to town,
> Yankee Doodle Dandy,
> I've paid a visit to the Crown,
> Dressed like any grandee:
> *The Queen* has made me presents rare;
> *Court Ladies* did salute me;
> *First rate* I am, they all declare,
> And all my dresses suit me.
> Yankee Doodle loves you all,
> Yankee Doodle Dandy,
> Both young and old, and short and tall,
> Declare that I'm the Dandy.
>
> *The Prince of Wales*–dear *little* boy–
> Yankee Doodle Dandy,
> When we first met, was rather shy,
> And could not understand me;
> But since, we've been the best of friends,
> And play'd at romps together;
> I wonder when he next intends
> To mount another feather.
>
> (chorus)
>
> *Prince Albert* speaks so kind and free,
> Yankee Doodle Dandy;
> He's taller *very much,* than me,
> Although I'm neat and handy;
> He loves the Queen, and so do I–
> They both say I'm a beauty:
> I'm much obliged to all–good bye–
> To-day I've done my duty.
>
> (chorus)

THE AMERICAN MUSEUM

From *Sights and Wonders in New York; including a description of the mysteries, miracles, marvels, phenomena, curiosities, and nondescripts, contained in that great congress of wonders, Barnum's Museum. . . .* (New York: J. S. Redfield, 1849).[10]

UNCLE FIND-OUT had two nephews, who, losing their parents in infancy, became the inmates of his abode, subject to his guardianship and protection. He was a man most exceedingly kind in point of disposition, beloved by all who had the pleasure of his acquaintance, and admired and beloved by none more sincerely and deservedly than by the members of his own family, which consisted of himself, an old bachelor, the two nephews already alluded to, his faithful Tom, and Maggy the housekeeper. Uncle Find-out loved his nephews and they in return loved him; who could help it?–for he was a good-hearted, kind old gentleman, and made everybody about him happy. He was in the habit of visiting the city of New York occasionally, and, as the time for doing so had arrived, he concluded his nephews would be pleased to accompany him to the empire city, to behold the sights to be seen there, as well as to witness the tricks upon travelers, so expertly performed in a thousand different ways.

He accordingly accosted his nephews, who had just entered his snug, old-fashioned parlor: "Well, boys, what say you for a journey to New York with your uncle to-morrow?"–"To-morrow never comes, uncle, so they say," replied the elder, whose name was Charles. The other one, Alfred, reproved his brother for supposing his uncle would propose anything he did not intend to carry into effect, and, turning to his uncle, replied, "My brother and I will be most happy to accompany you, dear uncle, and I trust we shall convince you how highly we value your kindness by our good conduct, not only during our stay in New York, but also upon our return to our rural hermitage on the banks of the Passaic." Charley asked his uncle if he would go with them to the various places of amusement. Uncle Find-out replied that he intended they should see all the places of amusement where boys ought to go, but that they must bear in mind that there were some places he should decline taking them to. The boys nodded a cheerful assent to the remarks of Uncle Find-out, and Alfred then said, "You will perhaps take us to the 'Museum' under the control of Mr. BARNUM."–"To be sure I will, and there you will see 'all the world in Bingham' in that ark of the city that has something of everything in it worth looking at. But, boys, first of all, let me know what is the meaning of the word 'museum.'" Charley replied that it was used to describe a building set apart as a repository for such things as related to the arts and sciences, or, in other words, a cabinet of curiosities.

"You are right, my boy. Originally it was the name given to an institution founded by Ptolemy Philadelphus, about two hundred and eighty years before the birth of Jesus Christ, for the promotion of learning and the support of learned men. We learn from Strabo that the museum formed a part of the palace, and that it contained cloisters or porticoes, a public theatre or lecture-room, and a large hall where the learned men used to dine together. The museum was supported by a common fund supplied from the public treasury, and the whole was under the superintendence of a priest, who was appointed by the king, and, after Egypt became a province of the Roman empire, by the Caesars. Botanical and zoological gardens appear to have been attached to the museum; other additions were also made by Claudius."

The time to go to rest having arrived, the boys took leave of their uncle with a hearty "Good-night," and a kiss printed warmly upon the good man's cheek; and up the stairs they ran to their slumbers—impatient enough, you may be sure, for the morning light, and ardently praying for a bright, clear day for their journey.

The boys had their wish: the morning broke in upon their slumbers with a bright sun and a cloudless sky. Breakfast was soon disposed of. Down to the steamboat they went with their uncle; the bell for starting rang; the passengers hurried on board; the captain called out "All aboard!" and in a minute old Dame Steam assured them they were onward for New York. A couple of hours passed merrily on, when the mighty city with her steeples in the distance, her shipping in the foreground, flags flying, guns firing, Trinity bells ringing' and a host of people with happy faces, met their astonished gaze. Landing at Pier No. 1, the party made the best of their way through the motley groups of coach and cab men, boarding-house runners, &c., "Coach, sir?"–"Cab, sir?"–"Take your luggage, gemmen?"–"Our card, sir?"–"The Globe, sir?"–"Astor House the best, sir"–"It's no such thing, sir! the Irving's the best!"–"The Times, Herald, Tribune, Ned Buntline's Own, sir, four for six cents!" and a thousand other cries, led the boys to suppose that the city was a Tower of Babel. A few minutes more, and the party arrived at the Museum. The musicians were playing the national air, "Hail Columbia, happy Land!" Large transparencies adorned the exterior of the buildings, representing the largest man in the world, Mr. Hale, being eight feet high, and weighing five hundred and eight pounds; Miss Eliza Simpson, the giantess, also eight feet high, and weighing three hundred and thirty-seven pounds; the fairy queen "Titania," twenty-four inches in height, The "Great Western," in his varied characters: and all these, with hundreds of thousands of curiosities, to be seen within the walls of this magnificent museum.

Having received their tickets of admission the party proceeded to room No. 1–and didn't the boys stare with all the eyes they had? They saw so much to look at, that if their heads had been full of eyes they would not have had eyes enough to see all that was there staring them in the face. At the top of the room was a case of beautiful birds, among which was the green stork of the East Indies, the scarlet flamingo of

South America, the pouched stork, or adjutant, of the Indies. Uncle Find-out informed them that the flamingo was from three to four feet high, purple-red on the back, and rose-colored wings; that they formed lines for the purpose of fishing, and, when they reposed on the shore, the same disposition to be in files or troops remained; that they appointed a sentinel for their common security, who, upon alarm, makes a braying cry similar to the noise of a trumpet, which is the signal for departure from danger. The tongue was considered a delicacy among the Romans. They build their nests in the form of a sugar-loaf, about twenty inches high. In consequence of their long legs, they straddle over their nests, their legs hanging down on each side and resting on the ground. "Is there anything particular in the pouched stork?"–"The feathers from beneath the wing form the beautiful light plumes which the French call *marabeaus.* The flamingo is found in Senegal and India. When standing in long rows upon the shore, they have the appearance of soldiers in full feather."

He then called their attention to the albatross, the great petrel, cormorant, booby, gamut, and frigate pelican. This last, he informed his nephews, was called the man-of-war bird, from the rapidity of its flight, being met with frequently four hundred

FIGURE 5

A rare illustration of the American Museum interior (From *Gleason's Pictorial Drawing Room Companion,* January 29, 1853, © collection of the New-York Historical Society, neg. #40655). This engraving depicts the museum's central room, the Second Saloon.

leagues at sea, and was the active warrior against the flying-fish. These birds attack the boobies, and, striking them upon their bodies, force them to disgorge the product of their fishing, which they dexterously seize before it falls in the water. The latter bird takes the name of booby from its stupidity submitting to the attacks of both men and animals.

The case opposite the latter next attracted the attention of our wondering admirers. It contained a beautiful variety of ducks, from various parts of North America, Europe, and the cape of Good Hope. Their uncle then drew their attention to a fine specimen of the joints from the Giants' Causeway in Ireland. From this they turned to a native rock crystal, weighing two hundred and twelve pounds, found in a silver-mine about five hundred miles from the city of Mexico; and also to a case of imitation diamonds, after those in the possession of various crowned heads in Germany, Russia, Portugal, &c., with their relative sizes and values—and oh! Didn't they wonder that such an immense value should be put upon such diamonds?

The next attraction presenting itself to their notice was the cameleopard, or giraffe. Uncle Find-out told them that it was a native of Africa: when full grown, its height is about twenty-two feet—its skin is a beautifully-spotted brown upon a white ground. Its favorite food is the leaf of the acacia and ash trees.

He then called them to look at the case of plovers, widgeons, geese, goosanders, &c.; but Alfred called to his uncle and his brother to look at the beautiful infant sleeping with hummingbirds hovering around her. "Oh, what lovely birds!" exclaimed one. "What beautiful plumage!" cried the other. From this their attention was drawn to a variety of beautiful engravings of Queens Adelaide and Victoria, Prince Albert, the duchess of Kent, &c., all of England; but our heroes thought much more of the likeness of General Tom Thumb and of P. T. BARNUM, ESQ., the indefatigable manager, who so unceasingly caters for the amusement, gratification, and instruction, of his young visitors, and who, in his journeyings with Tom Thumb, visited and conversed with all the principal crowned heads of Europe—and they concluded that his Museum was worth all the kings, queens, and nabobs, of the world. . . .

At length they came to the last case of the birds, larks, fly-catchers, field-fairs, &c., when, highly delighted with what they had seen, Uncle Find-out, taking the lead, introduced them to room No. 2. There they beheld the portraits of all our great men, from Washington downward—generals, orators, statesmen—who have left names deeply engraved in the hearts of a brave and great nation; patterns and examples worthy of imitation by those who will have to play their parts in the great drama of life. Also the wax profiles of some thirty Mexican generals, enclosed in a handsome frame. Mrs. Pelby's celebrated groups of wax figures then came in for a share of deep and thoughtful consideration by the whole party.

And first, the Intemperate Family. The group composes one family: the old man at the table, with the bottle in his pocket, is the father of the dying man; both are drunkards. The fruits of the poisonous bottle are too clearly depictured in the misery, poverty, and wretchedness, around the unfortunate group. "Look well, my boys, on that picture of woe–remember an uncle warns you–see that you touch not, taste not, handle not, the contents of the intoxicating bottle, lest your condition be as unfortunate as the one you are now gazing upon." They shuddered, and passed to the other side, to the groups representing the Last Supper of our Lord with the disciples.

Uncle Find-out informed his nephews that the moment selected by the artist was where Jesus says–"One of you shall betray me." He then drew their attention to the countenances of the disciples, and requested them to point out the one that appeared the most faithful delineation of the betrayer of Jesus. In a few minutes the boys recognized Judas, and each exclaimed, "That, uncle, is the man!"–and he quietly nodding his assent, they passed on to the groups representing the trial of Jesus before Pontius Pilate. "There, my children," exclaimed Uncle Find-out, "is a solemn representation of the Son of God, standing as a prisoner, bound as a criminal, the object of Jewish hatred and revenge. I need not pass any further remarks upon it; you are sabbath-school scholars, and well know the history of this trial, of one of the best of beings, the friend of sinners."

"Oh, yes," cried Charley, "our teacher has often talked with us upon the Redeemer and his sufferings,"

"Yes, brother; and he always used to beg of us never to forget what Jesus had done for us, poor children of the dust." Here Uncle Find-out purchased, for six cents, a pamphlet describing all the wax statuary, and also containing a copy of the "DEATH WARRANT OF OUR SAVIOR." "Let us turn, children, now, to a more pleasing subject. Behold the newborn babe of Bethlehem, whose birth made heaven echo, and angels shout, 'Glory to God in the highest–peace on earth–good-will to men!'" "This is a beautiful scene, uncle," exclaimed the boys. "Yes it is, my boys. Can you recite any passage of Scripture that will suit the representation before you?"

"And she brought forth her first-born son, and wrapped him in swaddling-clothes, and laid him in a manger." "Very good, Alfred. I am glad you have fixed upon a passage so appropriate. Do you remember the cause that compelled the mother to shelter the babe in a manger?" "Oh, yes sir. Because there was no room in the inn."

In passing from these interesting subjects, their attention was drawn to a magic dial, which, to all appearance, presented no evidence of any connection between the hand of the dial and the machinery in the base. This excited their surprise; and after some reflection, they concluded they would both have to find that out when they had more time and ability than at present. At any rate, it was passing strange to them, and as hard to find out as double rule of three, tare and tret, or vulgar fractions. Having taken a view of the last objects in the room, their uncle led them to room No. 3, when their attention was called to the great polar bear, of Greenland, the black bear and cub, of North America, and the badger, of Europe. Alfred was tickled almost to death at the sight of such strange-looking creatures. . . .

Uncle Find-out further stated, that in consequence of the great facilities enjoyed by Mr. Barnum for furnishing instruction and amusement for the public, (he having agents traveling in Europe and all parts of the world, selecting and forwarding the richest specimens of all that is novel and curious), he has taken the NEW MUSEUM IN PHILADELPHIA,–a most magnificent building, *five* stories high, recently erected by Dr. Swaim, on the corner of *Seventh and Chestnut streets,*–and fitted it up in a style superior to that of any establishment of the kind in the world.

The citizens of the Quaker city now pride themselves on having the greatest and best assortment of natural curiosities ever exhibited in one museum, and as interesting entertainments as are furnished in any city.

Mr. Barnum deserves their everlasting gratitude for opening this splendid establishment; and Philadelphians and their visitors will reward him for his eminent exertions; while the ladies and children, in particular, will enjoy the most pleasing performances, which are chaste and entirely free from any immoral influences.

Mr. Barnum (continued Uncle F.) is an advocate of the principles of teetotalism, and is a blessing to the country round about by his persevering efforts in the cause of temperance. His heart and purse are always open to the worthy unfortunate; and the gratitude and prayers of the widow and orphan, assist him in living up to the singular but appropriate motto–"LOVE GOD AND BE MERRY."

Thus you see, my boys, what persevering industry will do. Prosecute faithfully, as Mr. Barnum has done, the duties that fall to your lot; be vigilant, active, and industrious, as he has been; and, with the smiles of Fortune, you will find your highest hopes crowned with success. That this may be the case, will ever be the ardent wish and prayer of your affectionate uncle,

TIMOTHY FIND-OUT.

Open every day in the year, except the Sabbath, from 7 o'clock, A.M. till 10 P.M. Such regulations are established and enforced, as render it perfectly safe for LADIES and CHILDREN to visit the Museum in the daytime, though unaccompanied by gentlemen. Exhibitions and performances in the Lecture Room TWICE *every Day,* and oftener on Holydays. *The Price of Admission to the whole Museum, including the Entertainments, in the Lecture Room and all, is* TWENTY-FIVE CENTS. *Children under 10 years of age Half Price.*

THE "LECTURE ROOM" THEATER

From *Barnum's American Museum Illustrated*
(New York: William Van Norden and Frank Leslie, 1850).

BARNUM'S AMERICAN MUSEUM, ILLUSTRATED. A PICTORIAL GUIDE TO THAT FAR-FAMED ESTABLISHMENT; CONTAINING MUCH INTERESTING MATTER, AND HIGHLY USEFUL TO VISITORS.

Open from 8 A.M. until 10 P.M.

The alterations and improvements of this magnificent establishment are at length completed, and the Museum as it now stands, outrivals anything of the kind in the United States. . . .

Of the interior we shall frequently have to speak in detail; we may, however, allude in this place to the good taste displayed in the arrangements. As the attractions of the Museum are intended for the moral and the intelligent, in contradistinction to those who seek unwholesome excitement, no bar for the vending of intoxicating liquors is to be found upon the premises; but ample accommodation is offered to those persons who may desire the refreshing and healthful drinks of the season. As a further guarantee of the propriety which pervades the entire establishment, the amusements presented in the elegant Lecture Room (which we shall have to describe in full) are of that pure and domestic character, which cannot fail to improve the heart, while they enlarge the understanding. The most fastidious may take their families there, without the least apprehension of being offended by word or deed; in short, so careful is the supervision exercised over the amusements, that hundreds of person who are prevented visiting theaters, on account of the vulgarisms and immorality which are sometimes permitted therein, may visit Mr. Barnum's establishment without fear of offence on that point.

Instead of ascending a flight of stairs, as we were obliged to do before the late alterations were made, our way is direct before us, through a kind of vestibule. On the left are the Manager's private office, and place of the money taken; on the right, at the extremity of the entrance, the check-taker's. A row of gas burners, enclosed in ground gas globes, ornaments each side, and shed a beautiful illumination, more in harmony with this portion of the Museum, though less brilliant, than the two new gas lamps of green and gold which have been put up before the front, in the street. . . .

Having briefly enumerated the principal objects to be seen in the collection, we must now request the visitor to descend into either the Cosmoramic, the Third, or the Second, from either of which he will find two entrances into the beautiful new

Lecture Room, which, for amusement, now claims our attention and admiration. In every detail, it is most gorgeous, and reminds of the like erections in the palaces of European sovereigns and nobles. Our first sentiment on entering is approval of the great pains that have evidently been taken, so far as ventilation and the facilities of ingress and egress are regarded. The windows and doors are numerous, and to add to the coolness and pleasantness of the atmosphere, the parquette and balconies are not partitioned. The proscenium consists of stage doors and private boxes, between pilasters of the Corinthian order of architecture, the whole being white and gold. Rich draperies grace the arch above the stage, displaying numerous American and (out of compliment to the aid rendered the country by the French on the occasion of the Revolution) tri-colored flags, surrounding a bust portrait of Washington. The back drop gives us a view of the Capitol, a graphic delineation, and at the bottom is inscribed in large gilt letters, the appropriate words, "We study to please." The orchestra, like the balconies, is open trellis work, and white, the latter being gilt and burnished. Rich crimson damask paper covers the walls, while velvet of the same hue adorns the seats. The center of the ceiling is elaborately gilt and radiated, while all without is a blending of beautiful and varied colors, intervening with sixteen medallion compartments, each containing a portrait of some American worthy. We immediately distinguish the Presidents Jackson, Van Buren, Tyler, the two Adams, and "though last but not least," General Lafayette, Washington Irving, and Cooper. In the orchestra is a magnificent Piano-forte made by Chickering of Boston, expressly for this Lecture Room, at a cost of $1000; Master B. Wolf is engaged to preside at this instrument; while Mr. C. W. Clark, the well known comedian, late of Burton's Theater, has the superintendence of the dramatic department. . . .

A magnificent gilt chandelier is suspended on each side of the proscenium. It is lighted with gas of a peculiarly pure and steady flame, as also are the lamps with ground glass globes, which are ranged round from the balcony. On the opening night we had an opportunity of proving the free ventilation of the Lecture room. The weather was warm, and every seat was occupied, but, notwithstanding, there was none of that oppression or sensation of faintness which are concomitant to most crowded assemblies, especially at this season of the year. In the audience part of the building every thing was brilliant, and gay; before the stage lamps, every body was emulous to do his or her best. A spirit stirring overture was played, after which the curtain was raised, to enable Mrs. Rodgers to deliver a well written and appropriate address. Subsequently we were treated to a sweet melody, and then the drama of the *Drunkard* was commenced. This is not the place in which to criticize the performance of an ordinary night; the occasion, however, of which we are writing, is beyond the application of the rule, and we may, therefore, be pardoned if we indulge in a few words. The acting throughout was capital, while the *dramatis personae* were varied and nicely blended. A respectable matron, keenly alive to the moral interests of her daughter; a loving bride; a manly, honest lover; a chicaning lawyer; a vain old maid; a maniac girl whose affianced husband has been lured to his destruction by means of drink; and her brother, a real Yankee, with exuberant animal spirits, and a heart almost too big for the place that holds it–these are the persons with which the dramatist has had to do; and much beholden is he to the representatives of them on the evening of Mr. Barnum's reopening of his Museum. . . .

As for Mr. Barnum, he has more than realized expectation–a rare thing for any man to do. In speaking of his establishment in future, we must no longer use the indefinite article, for it is, without doubt, *the* Museum of America. On the part of the public, too, we may congratulate Mr. Barnum, and convey to him the assurance that endeavors like his are sure to meet their reward. In his announcements of the opening of his Museum, he has laid considerable stress upon the moral tone of the entertainments given in his Lecture Room; for that and the obvious intention he has to carry out the plan in its fullest extent, he is doing much to enhance the estimation in which he is held by the really respectable portion of the community.

JENNY LIND

From *Programme of Mademoiselle Jenny Lind's Concert*
(New York, 1850).

The Hall of the Castle Garden, has been selected by Mademoiselle Lind herself, as the best Concert-room at present existing in New York. Considerable difficulty was caused Mr. Barnum, in arranging it for the Concert, owing to its occupation until Monday by the Italian Company, who have been recently performing there. This, however, has been obviated by the greatest industry in the preparations. The stage has been thrown across the orchestra, for the purpose of improving its capabilities for the voice, and every arrangement has been made to secure the accommodation of the public. . . .

The proceeds of the Tickets sold at auction on the Saturday, were $9,119. The number of Tickets which produced the amount, was 1,429. On the Monday, 3,055 were sold. The proceeds of the sale amounted to $15,359; so that it may fairly be concluded, that the proceeds of the first Concert will considerably exceed $35,000.

A plan of Seats is given at the end of the Book, with directions, by which the Ticket holders may take their seats. To prevent confusion, the holders of Yellow Tickets will be admitted at 5 o'clock. The holders of Red and Blue Tickets, will be admitted at [blank] o'clock. The holders of Promenade Tickets, will be admitted at

7 ½ o'clock. It is respectfully requested of them, that they will take their position as directed by the usher, and not occupy the aisles between the seats, arranged in the center of the Hall. . . .

SKETCH OF THE LIFE OF JENNY LIND.

This greatest of modern singers, was born in Stockholm. Her parents filled a comparatively humble position in life, and when Jenny first came into the world nothing augured her future reputation. She was a lovely and modest child, and from her earliest days was passionately fond of melody. Her first accents were almost made in music. One day, when she was merely five or six years of age, a Swedish actress heard her singing, and was so surprised by the almost marvelous purity of her voice and the talent and native skill even then displayed by the child in its management, that she spoke of it to Herr Croelius, a music master, then resident in Stockholm. He came and heard the child sing, and instantly determined on presenting her to the Count Puke, as a candidate for admission to the musical school attached to the Royal Theater, of which he was the manager. The Count Puke at first made some difficulties, but after hearing her sing, was even more astonished than Herr Croelius had been, and consented to her admission. She accordingly entered the conservatory at this early age, and was placed under the tuition of Erasmus Berg, a profound and skillful musician. After studying under this master for several years, the public was surprised at seeing a child appear in a *vaudeville* in which she had to sing. This child was Jenny Lind. Such was her success, that she became a public favorite, and after a short time, began to appear in opera. At this period in her life, everything seemed to bid fair for the future, and the child looked forward to the day in which she might hold a high position in her art. This, however, was a dream that was destined to be dispelled by a misfortune to which she had not looked forward. It was the loss of her voice, when she was about fourteen years of age. She was compelled to retire from the theater, and again practice her art alone, and in the privacy of her own apartments.

At length her voice returned to her, but it was no longer the voice which she once had, nor had it acquired the wonderful beauty and purity which now marks it. She now managed to go to Paris, and place herself under the tuition of Signor Garcia, who, however, at first little foreboded the future eminence which his pupil was to obtain. And very frequently has he said: "If Lind had more voice at her disposal, nothing could prevent her from becoming the greatest of modern singers; but as it is, she must be content with singing second to many who will not have one half her genius."

Her voice, nevertheless, gradually strengthened, and she was at length summoned back to Stockholm. Here she again entered the Theater, and speedily became again a public favorite in Sweden. But during her residence in Paris, she had made the acquaintance of Giacomo Meyerbeer, the celebrated composer. This great man

FIGURE 6

A portrait of Jenny Lind, the Swedish
opera star, from her 1850 U.S. tour,
published by Napoleon Sarony (Library
of Congress, Prints and Photographs Division,
reproduction number LC-USZ62-1129).

had formed a friendship for Jenny, and e'er two years had elapsed, she received an
invitation from him to join the opera in Berlin. To this she consented, and soon after
repaired to Berlin, in 1842 or 1843. We are unable to name the precise year, but it
was in one of these that she first appeared there. At the commencement, she made
little impression upon the public, for her voice had not completely returned to her.
One evening, however, when she was singing in *Robert le Diable*, she felt that it had
returned, and inspired by the consciousness, sang the music of *Alice* with such a force
and power, combined with the sweetness to which the public has become accustomed,
that she electrified them and astonished Meyerbeer, who from that moment regarded
her as the first of modern singers. Everything was now changed for her. She rapidly
progressed in public estimation, and her reputation soon spread through the whole
of Germany, which at present is perhaps the most musical nation on Continental

Europe. Soon after this, a musical festival was held at Bonn, upon the Rhine, and the Queen of England, who was then on a visit to His Prussian Majesty, attended it. Jenny Lind was engaged at the festival, and the English critics who attended it, wrote back such warm accounts of her genius, that it was not difficult to foretell that she would soon come to England. Accordingly, towards the end of the year, M. Belinaye came to Berlin, and through the medium of Lord Westmoreland, was presented to Jenny Lind, whom had the satisfaction of engaging to appear, under Mr. Lumley's management, the following season.

England

Her success in England was such as at once to rank her in the estimation of London as the very first of modern singers, and this too at a season when Alboni made her first appearance there, and Viardot Garcia had returned to the English stage in all the triumph of a continental reputation. From this period her reputation has been unchanged. Incredible sums have been paid for the purpose of hearing her–sums, in comparison with which the $225 paid for the first seat which was on Saturday exposed to auction in the Castle Garden, can indeed scarcely compare. She has sung in Vienna and in every capital of Germany with the same extraordinary success. In Edinburgh at the two concerts in which she sang, near £ 2000 were cleared above every expense by Mr. Howard Glover, who was the *entre preneur;* and at her Majesty's Theater crowds have been in attendance round the pit and gallery doors as early as three in the afternoon on the nights on which she was to appear. She has sung before the Queen of England repeatedly in private, and has indeed appeared in all the Courts in Germany and northern Europe, excepting that of Russia; nor has she been merely received as a singer, but as a woman the spotless virtue of whose life and whose extraordinary and splendid charities equally entitle her to the admiration and love of the public. While she lives her talents and genius will constitute the highest of her claims to public admiration, and after her death she will be remembered by those to whom her voice has been productive of so much and such abundant advantage.

THE GRAND NATIONAL BABY SHOW

From the *New York Daily Times,* May 10, 1855.

GRAND NATIONAL BABY SHOW AT BARNUM'S AMERICAN MUSEUM, in New-York, June 5, 6, 7, and 8, 1855–Twenty one premiums, amounting in all to over $1,000 in cash! The portion of the premiums to be given, if preferred, in gold or silver plate, at its exact cost. This Baby Show, the first exhibition of the kind ever held in New York, will be open to Children (under five years of age) from all parts of the world! Retiring rooms, cradles, &c., will be provided for one hundred Babies and their attendants. Ladies of the first respectability have consented to serve as Judges on the occasion. All persons competing for the above premiums must obtain at the Museum a numbered Certificate, depositing for the same One Dollar, which dollar will be returned on the second day of the exhibition. The number of Babies exhibited at this Baby Show is limited to one hundred. The names of the competing children, may or may not be given for publication, at the option of the parents.

WHAT IS IT?

From *Illustrated Memoir of an Eventful Expedition into Central America Resulting in the Discovery of the Idolatrous City of Iximaya . . .*
(New York: Wynkoop, Hallenbeck, and Thomas, Printers, 1860).[11]

THE WHAT IS IT? OR, MAN-MONKEY!, a most singular animal, which, though it has many of the features and characteristics of both the human and brute, is not, apparently, either, but, in appearance, a mixture of both—the connecting link between humanity and the brute creation.

In regard to this wonderful freak of Nature, the keeper thus addresses, on all explanatory occasions, his crowded audience:

"This nondescript was captured by a party of adventurers who were in search of the Gorilla. While exploring the River Gambia, near the mouth, they fell in with a race of beings never before discovered. They were six in number. They were in a PERFECTLY NUDE STATE, roving about among the trees and branches, in the manner common to the Monkey and Orang Outang. After considerable exertion, the hunters succeeded in capturing three of these oddities—two males and a female. All of them were forwarded to this country, but, unfortunately, two of them sickened and died on the voyage across. The present one is the only survivor. When first received here, his natural position was ON ALL FOURS; and it has required the exercise of the greatest care and patience to teach him to stand perfectly erect, as you behold him at the present moment. But a few weeks have elapsed, in fact, since he first assumed this attitude, and walked about upon his feet. If you notice, you will perceive that the WALK OF THE WHAT IS IT is very awkward, like that of a child beginning to acquire that accomplishment. When he first came, his only food was raw meat, sweet apples, oranges, nuts, &c., of all of which he was very fond; but he will now eat bread, cake, and similar things, though he is fonder of raw meat or that which, slow-cooked, is rare. If you notice the formation of this non-descript, you will observe that it is something very peculiar, indeed. The formation of the head and face combines both that of the native African and of the Orang Outang. The upper part of the head, and the forehead in particular, instead of being four or five inches broad, as it should be, to resemble a human being, is LESS THAN TWO INCHES! The HEAD OF THE WHAT IS IT is very small. The ears are set back about an inch too far for humanity, and about three-fourths of an inch too high up. They should form a line with the ridge of the nose, to be like that of a human being. As they are now placed, they constitute the perfect head and skull of the Orang Outang, while the lower part of the face is that of the native African. In the next place, the teeth, instead of standing erect, occupy a slanting position, like those of the horse or the sheep, slanting to a great distance under the tongue, and into the roof of the mouth. The teeth are double nearly all around, and the creature is not able to close its mouth entirely, owing to the formation of the jaws, which are crooked instead of straight, thus leaving the front of the mouth open about half an inch. THE ARMS OF THE WHAT IS IT are much too long in proportion to its height—at least some three inches. They are also crooked like those of the Orang Outang, and it is not able to straighten them. He has great strength in his hands and arms. Anything he can get hold of he will cling to quite a length of time. There is apparently more strength in his hands and arms than in all the rest of his body combined. In the next place, his legs are crooked, like those of the Orang Outang. He cannot make them straighter than you see them now. He has no calf to his leg, but exhibits a gradual taper from the knee to the ankle joint. THE WHAT IS ITS FOOT is narrow, slim, and flat, and has a long heel, like that of the native African. The large toe is more like a man's thumb. The others are bent under, and the distortion appears to be natural. He is supposed to be twenty or twenty-three years old, but there is nothing positive known in regard to his age. He may be older, or possibly younger than that. He stands about four feet high, and weighs fifty pounds. He has been examined by some of the most scientific men we have, and pronounced by them to be a CONNECTING LINK BETWEEN THE WILD NATIVE AFRICAN AND THE BRUTE CREATION; and the formation of the head and limbs is such as to leave beyond any doubt whatever the characteristic claims of the WHAT IS IT?"

ZOBEIDE LUTI

From *Biographical outline of the beautiful Circassian girl, Zobeide Luti, or, "Lady of Beauty," together with "A Brief Sketch of the Manners, Customs, and Inhabitants of Circassia"*
(New York: Barnum and Van Amburgh Museum and Menagerie Co., 1868).

The subject of this little sketch, Zobeide Luti, was born in the town of Kizlaar, Circassia, near the river Terek, which rises in the Caucasian Mountains, and is by far the most important water-course of the country.

While Zobeide was of a very tender age, Circassia was convulsed by one of those terrible Russian invasions, which, during the period of which we write, had been as frequent as they were devastating, and which drove many of her country in almost hopeless despair to seek a doubtful refuge in the dominion of the Sultan of Turkey. The parents of Zobeide beheld their fields desolated and their flocks more than decimated by the Czar's subjects, and their own lives and those of their kindred imperiled. To them there was no alternative but to gather their little remnants of property and with their children seek a refuge, amid the mosques and minarets of Constantinople, from their ruthless and remorseless foe.

It was here that Mr. John Greenwood, who was making an Oriental tour of profit and pleasure, first saw Zobeide, a lovely infant, in its mother's arms.[12] Nature had never been more dainty, more lavish in her handiwork; had created nothing so transcendentally beautiful as this little Circassian child. Proverbial as is the splendor of the Circassian women and female children, Mr. Greenwood saw none, amid the hundreds of her country people that thronged the thoroughfares of the Turkish metropolis, possessing anything like so wonderful and lovely a *tout ensemble.*

The dreamy and lustrous beauty of her eyes was extraordinary, while her luxuriant tresses, which were of the same singular but very becoming conformation that characterized Zalumma Agra, adorned her classic and exquisitely modeled head like the aureole of a saint. No Praxiteles or Titian had conceived or executed, nay, even dreamed of such perfection in form and feature: no poet ever sang the praises of so enchanting an ideal.

Mr. Greenwood, by dint of energy and persuasion, had already succeeded in the benevolent object of rescuing Zalumma Agra from the probable fate that was pending over her, and of inducing her parents and the Turkish authorities to allow him to bring her to the United States: and the wish was father to the thought that he might be as equally successful in saving Zobeide from the ignorance of Paganism and the atrocities of a harem. Through the aid of an interpreter he made known his wishes to Zobeide's parents; but Nature was enthroned too firmly in their hearts for them to hearken to the proposition. No art of persuasion, no argument, however deftly presented or patiently urged, could induce them to acquiesce in his charitable design, and his proposal was routinely rejected, if not indignantly spurned. "Zobeide," in their language of beautiful metaphor, "was the light of their eyes and the sunshine of their hearts," and nothing should deprive them of her. She was their darling, their pet, their comfort, and their pride. Her infant prattle was to them the most delicious music, and her beauty was a marvel in the eyes of the world, and a pride in their own. Oh, no! Never, for a single moment, would they entertain the thought of allowing a stranger to guide the future footsteps of their darling, to alienate and estrange her affections. Courteous but unyielding, they ended their interview with a peremptory denial. Convinced that any further endeavor was futile, Mr. Greenwood very reluctantly abandoned the idea of inducing Zobeide's parents to permit her to accompany him to America; but his interest in the beautiful child was in no wise diminished by his rebuffs.

It happened that Herr Presnitz, at that time Austrian Consul to Constantinople, had had his attention drawn by Mr. Greenwood to Zobeide, and had made strenuous endeavors to aid him. Finding that his interest was awakened in the child's welfare. Mr. Greenwood besought the Consul to care for her, and, if possible, to give her the advantages of a Christian education. Mr. Presnitz was only too happy in seconding Mr. Greenwood's intentions, and, with commendable zeal and enthusiasm, entered heart and soul into the undertaking. Leaving him to assume what guardianship was practicable over the child, Mr. Greenwood reluctantly pursued his journey.

It is not our purpose to dwell on events, nor will the limits of this sketch permit it. We have only space to state that after an interval of years an opportunity presented itself for Mr. Greenwood to revisit the Turkish Empire, and inclination induced him to accept it. The steamer "Quaker City" announced a trip to Palestine, including the various cities of the Orient. The excursion would be a delightful one in many points of view, and besides, he had an unabated desire to learn what had been the fortune of Zobeide. He accordingly became one of the party of excursionists, and on arrival at Constantinople he at once made inquiry for Mr. Presnitz, and learned that he had retired from the Austrian Consulate, removed from Constantinople, and was then a successful merchant at Ispahan. Disappointed but not discouraged on learning that Mr. Presnitz had departed, and with him all traces of the Circassian girl, as soon as opportunity and convenience would permit, he proceeded to Ispahan, and found not only Mr. Presnitz, but Zobeide; not the beautiful and charming little Zobeide, however, of his remembrance, but a full-grown, voluptuous, and ravishingly beautiful woman.

Mr. Presnitz had proved himself in every way worthy of the charge imposed on him, and had devoted nearly every leisure hour in improving and cultivating her mind and rendering her capable, mentally as well as physically, of being an ornament to any society. It may be as well to state that, within a very short period after Mr. Greenwood returned home from his first visit to Constantinople, but the parents of Zobeide had been stricken down by a prevailing epidemic and had died. Mr. Presnitz, true to his trust, took the orphaned Zobeide to his own home and educated her in the manner stated; not only perfecting her thoroughly in the German language, but giving her a very fair knowledge of the English. She had several times been to Circassia, and her reminiscences of her native land, as she relates them, will serve to impart much knowledge of the history and geography of her distant country, and the manners and customs of its inhabitants.

The people of Circassia, as she relates, are exceedingly nomadic, and, except the residents of the towns, seldom dwell long in one place, but live in tents or huts according to the season of the year, and remove from one place to another like their neighbors of the adjoining country of Astrakan. They are possessed of immense herds of cattle, which they drive before them, remaining no longer in one place than they can find pasture. Nothing can be more agreeable than the prospect of Circassia from its variety of mountains, valleys, woods, lakes, and rivers, with which it is everywhere diversified. It is fertile almost beyond imagination, and most of the cereals are successfully grown by merely once turning the soil.

The hair and eyes of the inhabitants are generally black, and not a cripple or deformed person ever appears amongst them. The women are always closely veiled when they go abroad. The people, she says, are extremely hospitable, and will not suffer a traveler to pay anything for the entertainment of himself, his servants, or his horses, but will contend, frequently, who shall have the honor of serving him. They carry no provisions with them on their journeys, but are as welcome at any house they arrive at as they would be at their own.

Though the Circassian Princes are exceedingly honored and respected by their subjects, yet such is the independence of the people that they are not obliged to do anything at their command, but are guided by their own inclination; and whatever presents the Czar of Russia sends to the Princess of Circassia, their respective subjects expect a part. If the presents cannot be conveniently distributed, they will have an equivalent in specie or such commodity as may be easily parted among them. The spoils taken in war are divided among the troops, the sovereigns being excluded from any share.

The people have a great veneration for ancient houses, and are extremely tenacious of their family honor. The contract for marriage is entered into by the parents or guardians, after which the young couple are presented to each other, and after a few visits the affair is concluded, and the bride is sent home, attended by her women. The bridegroom is obliged to make valuable presents to the bride's relatives of horses, dromedaries, camels, etc. The general food of the Circassians is mutton, beef, poultry, wild fowl, and venison; but a piece of young colt is preferred to any of these. Their bread is made into thin cakes either of barley-meal or millet, which they bake on the hearth. Their usual drink is water or mare's milk. They sit cross-legged, and have a carpet or piece of Russian leather spread before them, and little wooden tables at their meals, but neither linen nor plates. They observe no regular hours for eating, drinking, or sleeping, but just as they have inclination or opportunity. Polygamy is permitted to such of the Circassians as profess the Mohammedan religion.

But we have only space to relate in a few terse sentences that Zobeide shared in the desire of Mr. Greenwood that she should visit the United States; and Mr. Presnitz, though loath to part with her, was unwilling that any proposition for her further advancement should be trammeled by any objections that he might urge. She accordingly accompanied Mr. Greenwood on his return voyage, and at the period of indicting this sketch has been two or three weeks in America.

In company with her protector she paid a visit to Barnum's Museum, where she saw, for the first time within her remembrance, the Circassian girl Zalumma Agra. Their meeting was friendly and cordial and exceedingly gratifying to both, and although Zalumma's recollections were very clouded and obscure, yet, they were speedily attracted to each other by the ties of nativity. To gratify her own inclinations and those of Zalumma, she concluded, with the consent of Mr. Greenwood, to become the companion of her new-found friend: and now once more appareled in the costume of her native land, she can be seen at Barnum's Museum at any time during exhibition hours.

THE TOM THUMB TOUR COMPANY

From *Gen. Tom Thumb's Three Years' Tour Around the World, Accompanied By His Wife–Lavinia Warren Stratton, Commodore Nutt, Miss Minnie Warren, And Party*
(New York: S. Booth, 1872), 64–70.[13]

The excitement amongst the natives at the sight of the ponies and carriage, as it circulated through the streets, and such glimpses as they caught of the "little people," as they rode to and from the theater, daily grew apace. A great stir was made amongst the patrons of the several Chinese theaters, soliciting the managers to engage the little people. Consequently I was eagerly sought after. The first who made application was the manager of the "Kwin-Kwae-Hien," "Foo-Kein Road," the largest and finest theater in Shanghae. He was introduced to me by a European merchant, who assured me that his theater was the "Drury Lane" of the city, being under the immediate patronage of mandarins and other high officials. He had learned to speak English quite correctly. Before I had arranged terms three other managers were in waiting. Anxiety was at fever heat. I finally concluded with him upon the following terms: the prices to be doubled, he to advertise to his people and to furnish me an interpreter, and I to receive seventy per cent of the gross receipts.

A description of this theater will apply to all the theaters in China, the difference being in size only, the construction the same. The "Kwin-Kwae-Hien" is in the heart of the city. It is built of teakwood frame, the interstices filled with brick, the front stuccoed, and it has a tile roof. The interior is about eighty feet long, sixty feet wide, and forty feet high. The stage is a raised platform, thirty feet wide, twenty feet deep, and five feet high, with a total absence of scenery. A gallery extends around the sides, the portion directly opposite the stage divided by railings into boxes, the center one being the manager's box, and used only by him or by any dignitary visiting the theater. The body of the hall was enclosed by a railing, extending from each corner of the stage towards the door to the distance of forty feet. Outside of the railing, upon each side, were raised seats, and also at the back near the door. Within the railing were a number of tables, around each of which were placed four bamboo chairs; the boxes in the gallery contained the same. These tables are graced by the presence of the small-footed, almond-eyed beauties with their attendant amahs. Upon the tables are placed tea and fruits, and as the ladies also indulge in smoking, between the tea and the pipe they have much to soothe their minds. . . .

To return to our appearance at the Kwin-Kwae-Hien Theater. The manager had two large banners painted in Chinese characters, announcing the appearance, which was carried upon poles by Chinamen, behind the little carriage as it peregrinated the city. Calling at the theater early in the morning, I was informed that it was impossible to obtain an interpreter. "You speak English—you must do it," said I. He seemed almost paralyzed by the bare idea; he informed me that he associated with mandarins; they would scorn him were he to appear upon the stage. I did not wish to refuse to perform—he was a manager in difficulty—he felt distressed; but, I, too, was in a quandary. A sudden thought struck me. "We will do without an interpreter," said I. His countenance brightened. "Get me six pieces of thick paper," said I. He disappeared and shortly returned with them. In the meantime, I wrote out the names, ages, birth-place, and description of the little people, also a description of the ponies and carriage. "Have that," said I, "painted separately, in Chinese characters, upon those cards." He looked his gratitude.

When I arrived at the theater, one hour before the proper time of opening, I found it literally crammed and no money taken. "I could not keep them out," said the manager. There was no alternative but to go through and collect the money. I obtained from the manager a quantity of his regular tickets—long strips of paper with painted characters upon them; as each person paid I stuck a ticket in his hand and motioned to him to hold it up conspicuously. I then formed our men in a line across the building, at the door, and ordered an advance to collect the tickets. I could not help laughing at the sight of so many outstretched arms, holding the different colored tickets. If any were found without a ticket they were compelled to pay. I took this precaution, as it was probable I would miss a great number in such a dense crowd. Some protested, "My payee, all same like dat," pointing to the silver in my hand. When the ticket was demanded, the reply "no got" settled it—as I seized them by the shoulder, as if to eject them, they would speedily produce the price.

The ponies and carriage, with Rodnia Nutt as the coachman in full-dress livery, stood upon the stage, at the back. The music of the melodeon excited their curiosity. When the four little people entered in full costume, and advanced to the front, a buzz of admiration emanated from the immense throng. I had taken the precaution, not being a Chinese scholar, of writing the name of each person on the back of their descriptive card, or otherwise I might have made a grievous mistake—perhaps holding the one describing ponies over Mrs. Stratton, and Minnie's description over the General. Mrs. S. advanced a couple of paces; I held the card over her head so that it could be read, then walked to each side for the benefit of the galleries. All eagerly read; if any at the back of the theater were too distant to discern, they were quickly informed by the others—thus I exhibited each separately. When Mrs. Stratton sang, the sound of her voice seemed to entrance them; they sat in breathless attention; they did not even take a single puff at their pipes. At the conclusion of her song they chatted, they nodded, they laughed, and expressed in various ways their extreme delight. The Commodore, in his dancing, drumming, crow, and comicalities, excited their risibilities; they gazed open-mouthed in wonder at the General in his characters. A little pantomime play amused them exceedingly, and their enthusiasm was unbounded when, after taking a number of little children upon the stage and comparing statures with Minnie, I retained one boy five years old, and placing her hand in his, she paraded to and fro with him. The little fellow, with his pigtail touching the floor, strutted about with her to the intense delight of all. America and China clasping hands! When I returned him to his parents, he was fondly caressed by them and passed hither and thither, and showered with kisses, as one who had been highly honored. At the conclusion of the performance I told the manager, who was seated in his box with several mandarins, enjoying their tea and bubble-pipes, that I would allow the audience the privilege of shaking hands with the little people; he leaned forward and in a mild tone informed them; there was a general rush for the stage, and all was confusion; but I speedily brought them under control, granting the ladies the first privilege. They could not sufficiently admire Mrs. Stratton's and Minnie's hands and feet; they patted them, laughed and chatted, some of them exclaiming, "Ah! Good! Little piecee 'oman! Good!"

I took precautionary measures in the evening against the afternoon difficulties. As we approached the theater, for the distance of an eighth of a mile we threaded our way through lines of sedan chairs and palanquins with their numerous attendants and bearers, who, having deposited their burdens at the theater door[,] had retired to give place to others; each attendant being provided with a lighted lantern, made a brilliant illumination. The building was apparently crammed to its utmost capacity, and still they came. After pushing our way to the stage, I managed by dint of packing and filling the stage to accommodate the late arrivals. Such a mass of shaven heads with lengthy pigtails, interspersed with the high and elaborate coiffures of the ladies, it is probable I will never again witness. The performance was received with even greater favor than in the afternoon. The manager was so delighted with his success that he presented the General with his beautiful and valuable silver bubble-pipe as a remembrance. . . .

AN ADVANCE COURIER FOR ONE OF
BARNUM'S RAILROAD CIRCUSES

From *Barnum's Illustrated News*
(Buffalo: Courier Company Show Printing House, 1879).[14]

P. T. Barnum's Address to his Patrons and the Public
On the inauguration of his one and only

GREATEST SHOW ON EARTH

FOR

HIS CLIMACTERIC SEASON OF 1879.

For a period of nearly fifty years I have been prominently before the public as a caterer for the instruction and amusement of my fellow men, and while I have been recognized more emphatically as a showman, I have combined with my vocation much else which has given me prominence in other directions. Journalism, Banking, Politics, Literature and Business Enterprises of various kinds have successively and successfully received my attention. From 1865 up to the present time, I have been chosen at various periods by my fellow citizens to represent the County of Fairfield in the Legislature of the State of Connecticut, and have also served as the Mayor of the City of Bridgeport, CT., while as a zealous advocate of Temperance, I have delivered thousands of lectures in various parts of the country upon that as well as upon other subjects.

But though I have won honors, the applause of my constituents, and "golden opinions from all sorts of people," my heart has always been in my vocation, and I have ever been, and shall always be prouder of the title of "Showman" than all the dignities and honors I have otherwise won and received.

Probably if I had been a Clergyman, a Physician, or a Lawyer, I should have exercised my natural energy and diligence in my profession, but I do not believe that my heart would have been so thoroughly in my work, or that I could have labored more earnestly and conscientiously to make the world better, than I have done as a caterer for the Public Recreation.

It has ever been my aim to exalt the character of Public Amusements. I have conscientiously refused to cater to low or depraved tastes, but have striven to cultivate a love and admiration for that which is pure and refined, and while I ever made instruction my chief aim, have not forgotten that "man is the only animal that laughs," and have, accordingly sought to combine with that which is didactic, a sufficiency of humor and piquant but refined fun, to inspire hilarity and cheerfulness. A hearty laugh is good for mind and body.

No exhibition, in which vulgarity, profanity, broadness or equivocation formed a part, or which was tainted in any degree with immorality, has ever received my sanction. Had I been less religious in the observance of this principle, I might have made more money, but I have not labored entirely for pecuniary profit, and when it is evident to me that the public, old and young, are not made wiser, happier and better, by the recreation I provide for them, my efforts in that direction will cease.

I have neither inclination nor space here, to go into the various details of my public career of half a century. My business has been, for many years, everybody's business. And as my autobiography entitled the "Struggles and Triumphs of Fifty Years," has had a sale in this country of over half a million copies, and several editions have been published in London, Paris, Leipzig (Germany) and Amsterdam, a popular journal may not be far from wrong in saying that "P. T. Barnum is the best and most pleasantly known man in America, if not the world."

My name in fact has been adopted as a part of our vernacular and "Barnum" is the recognized synonym of an enterprising and conscientious provider of wholesome public amusements. As journalist, businessman, politician, legislator, municipal officer, financier, and showman, I have endeavored to do my duty, remembering the lines of the Pope: "Honor and fame from no condition rise, Act well your part, there all the honor lies." And now a few words concerning my Greatest Show on Earth for the season of 1879.

My fifty years' experience has taught me that the only sure means of achieving success is to deserve it. Accordingly I have never remained satisfied with what I have previously accomplished, but have always striven to outdo myself—to make each exhibition larger, grander, more interesting, more novel and attractive, than that which preceded it. I never go backward. "Upward and Onward!" is the motto which I have followed. To accomplish this, several qualifications are required. Among these may be named:

FIRST. A knowledge of that which will please, where to get it, how to get it, and what to do with it when obtained.

SECOND. Capital, sufficiently large, disposition sufficiently liberal, and courage sufficiently great to invest it.

THIRD. A thorough acquaintance with all the great objects of interest in the various parts of the world, the haunts of strange animals, birds and reptiles, and a corps of agents, contractors, hunters, and trappers, to purchase or capture and transport them across continents and vast oceans.

All these requirements I claim to possess and do possess, for a continued success of half a century has enabled me to invest hundreds of thousands of dollars in attractive features, all of which I have concentrated in my One Single Greatest Show on Earth, in which will be found the most expensive, novel, and marvelous attractions in the world. No other showman in this or any country possesses my facilities or advantages, therefore it follows that my show is without parallel, and beyond and defiant of any and all rivalry. It has not equal, and I assert it never will be surpassed except by myself in the future. Whenever I discover something new, or hear through my agents of any novelty which I think will please my millions of patrons, I GET IT, whether it costs a thousand dollars or fifty thousand dollars, for I am determined the public shall see everything that is worth seeing, regardless of cost.

Among the principle features of My Greatest Show on Earth for the season of 1879, will be found the largest, most interesting, most costly, and beyond comparison the rarest aggregation of wild animals in any traveling menagerie in the world. To the perfecting of this grand ZOOLOGICAL COLLECTION, I have made Earth, Sea, and Air, pay tribute, and my brave rangers, hunters, and agents, have traveled to the uttermost parts of the earth to complete it; braving the dangers of the jungle, the miasma of the morass, the arid, burning plains, the snows of the Polar Circle, the simooms of the desert, the ferocious cannibals of the African forests, and "the pestilence that walketh by noonday" in the dread lagoons and poisonous swamps of India. This superb and only exhaustive Zoological Collection in the United States, contains more costly and rare specimens of natural history, more monsters of the deep, rare birds, strange fishes, reptiles, amphibia, and wild denizens of every clime and country, than have ever been before presented to the public, and form a VAST LIVING SCHOOL OF INSTRUCTION, where the student may spend hours in wondrous contemplation, looking "from Nature up to Nature's God."

In addition to magnificent specimens of the feline species, such as lions, tigers, etc.; graminivorous animals, such as the Eland and various beautiful species of Antelopes, the visitor will find the only TWO-HORNED Rhinoceros ever exhibited in America, which cost me $16,000.00; a BLACK, Double-Humped Camel, a most beautiful animal, covered with fine, glossy, silken hair, as dark as Erebus. And by his side, in strong contrast, another Double-Humped Camel perfectly WHITE. These are the only real genuine black or white camels which have been exhibited in America, and were imported this spring at a larger expense, than has ever before been paid by any one, and no one person could for $20,000 obtain a pair equal to them in all respects.

Another marvelous curiosity will be found in the remarkable anomalous pachyderm, from the interior of Africa, which even the *savants* of Europe have not been able to classify. It has the head of the hippopotamus, the tusk of the elephant, the hide of the rhinoceros, the body of the lion, and the feet of a camel. It weighs nearly two tons and has been named from its peculiar form and strange combination, the ELEPHANTUS-HIPPO-PARADOXUS; as it paradoxically combines several animals in one. In this collection will be found a herd of eleven elephants, from the ponderous full grown giant of Ceylon, to the diminutive African, standing but three feet in height, among them being the most perfectly trained, intelligent performing elephants in the world. A colony of two hundred monkeys, from the enormous orang-outang and chimpanzee to the baby monkey weighing less than a pound, together with many attractions which will be more fully described elsewhere.

While most exhibitions advertise more animals than they possess, and many which the advertisers never saw, I hereby solemnly agree to forfeit and pay $50,000.00 if the proprietors of any Menagerie now in the country can show that they have incurred the same expense, and if an equal number of rare animals was ever before seen in any traveling exhibition in this country or in Europe, or anywhere on the face of the whole earth. I am thoroughly in earnest in making this proposition, and pledge my honor and my money for its due fulfillment.

I desire also to call particular attention to what last season proved to be one of the most popular and interesting exhibitions I have ever brought before the public. I refer to my magnificent stud of twenty royal stallions, for which I paid $100,000. They are from the stables of the Emperor of Russia, late King of Italy, the imperial Ecuries of Poland, and those of the Grand Khan of Tartary. They have continued during the vacation under the charge of their accomplished trainer and exhibitor Mr. Carl Antony, and in addition to the wonderful and beautiful feats which elicited such universal admiration last season, will appear in a number of new and most interesting feats and evolutions.

The Colossal Pavilion containing the great ORIENTAL AND EUROPEAN MUSEUM, will afford more interest, amusement and instruction, than all the combined attractions of any other show that travels, comprising as it does a vast collection of natural curiosities, from all parts of the civilized and uncivilized world, from every zone and every country, together with life-like automatic, mechanical marvels; Col. Goshen, the great living giant; the tattooed Greek nobleman, and other human phenomena never before seen, and which no other exhibition can present. A feature of peculiar attractiveness is the wonderful anomaly called the "Mysterious Lady," who, while pleasing everyone by her exquisite and classical beauty, the bewitching expression of her face, the grace of her movements and the ineffable sweetness of her speaking eyes, leaves all in doubt whether it is a vision or reality—whether she is endowed with life or only a lovely myth—whether of exquisitely molded flesh and blood, or but a marvelous piece of most subtle and ingenious mechanism.

Determined that each of the departments of My Greatest Show on Earth shall excel in attractiveness anything I had ever before attempted, I have secured more novelties for 1879, in addition to those of last year, than comprise the entire stock of any other traveling show, and besides those already enumerated, I have added the Circus department, the greatest array of talent which was ever combined in one exhibition, simply because I have been able to outbid all competitors by paying more munificent salaries than were ever before paid to equestrian performers. In proof of this, I have only to mention my galaxy of Star Lady Riders, comprising the beautiful and all surpassing Mme. Dockrill, Miss Katie Stokes, Signora Linda Jeal and Miss Emma Lake–the four most beautiful, accomplished, and popular Equestriennes in the world. In the company will be found the most expert and dashing of Athletes, Wrestlers, Tumblers, Trapezists, Leapers, and Equilibrists, as well as the most witty and comical of Clowns, and most accomplished and facile general performers, forming an exhibition at once amusing, thrilling, beautiful and interesting, and free from every gross and questionable feature.

The expense of this vast conglomerate of novelties is not less than $3,500.00 per day. I state this for a fact! And will forfeit and pay $10,000 to any person that can show that the bare expenses of running my establishments during the past six years has not averaged more than *the entire gross receipts* of any show during the same time, which has ever traveled either in this country or Europe, and in making this offer, I promise every facility for learning the facts. *I never advertise anything I do not possess, and do not exhibit,* but I do not advertise more than one-half of the many things which are contained in my Own Greatest Show on Earth, for I have not the space to mention them. It will be readily seen by my patrons that I offer more for less money than anyone else in the business–and were my show diminished by two-thirds, it would still be larger than any other on the continent, and far better worth seeing.

Should any new and fresh attractions be found during the season, they will immediately be added, no matter at what cost of trouble or expense, for I am determined that the exhibition shall always be worthy of being called The Greatest Show on Earth. Elsewhere will be found more full descriptions of the various features and attractions. The show will travel under my immediate management and supervision, and I shall myself travel with it as much as possible, so that I hope to pay my respects in person to my kind patrons and friends, and if I cannot take them all by the hand, shall have the pleasure of assuring them of the best wishes and gratitude of their

Devoted and Faithful Servant,

Waldemere, 1879   P. T. BARNUM

* * * * * * *

MY AUTOBIOGRAPHY

"Struggles and Triumphs of Forty Years," is a book of 800 printed pages, profusely illustrated with wood engravings, by the best artists, and written up to the close of the year 1878. This book, 500,000 of which have been sold in America alone, is published at $1.50, but it is sold by my agents with the show for $1.00; giving to each purchaser a 50 cent ticket which admits to my entire show. It may also be had, wholesale or retail, from the Courier Company, Buffalo, N.Y.

* * * * * * *

THE MORALITY AND EXCELLENCE OF MY GREAT SHOW!

Among the hundreds of letters which I am constantly receiving from clergymen, endorsing the morality and excellence of my Greatest Show on Earth, I select the following, from which the public can judge of the estimate in which my efforts to amuse, elevate and instruct the public are held by such distinguished preachers of the Gospel as Rev. THEODORE L. CUYLER, D.D., and Rev. E. H. CHAPIN, D.D.

Brooklyn, January 13, 1878.

My Dear Old Friend: "The King never dies." This old maxim of royalty seems to apply to you as the King of the Exhibitors and Caterers, not merely to the public amusement, but to popular instruction. Millions of "little folks" may consider you their benefactor in affording them innocent gratification. I have several times taken my children to your Museums, Menageries and Exhibitions, and have not observed there anything profane or impure. I especially thank you for your allegiance (both in your practice and in your business) to the principle of *total abstinence from all intoxicants.*

With a thousand good wishes, and with kindest regards to your family, I remain,

Yours sincerely,

THEO. L. CUYLER

New York, January 15, 1878.

My Dear Barnum:

It gives me great pleasure to express my *sincere* opinion, that in the entertainment which you have furnished for the public, your patrons have always received a full and profitable money's-worth, and that they are fitted not only to amuse, but to *instruct,* and are certainly free from anything that can be in the least objectionable to any refined or religious person. I remain,

Truly yours,

E. H. CHAPIN.

* * * * * * * *

A Rule Never Broken.

No gambling—no "Prize Packages," no deceptions—by my own people or by camp followers, or immoral practices of any kind, are allowed in or about my show. We go in for a good time. Plenty of innocent recreation—wholesome amusement, lots of jolly but harmless fun, much instruction given in a pleasant, but enduring manner. In fact, a day to be remembered with great satisfaction, and not to be equaled, till Barnum comes round again with the new attractions he provides for every season.

* * * * * * * *

My Lady Riders.

"Pad-riding," or the use of a pad saddle is seldom seen in my exhibitions. I have not only by far the best lady riders in the world, but I have positively more real first-class lady riders on bareback horses than exist in traveling shows in America combined. I state this for a literal and positive fact. There are not more than two or three—I am not sure there is even one—first-class lady rider on a barebacked horse outside of my Great Show.

* * * * * * * *

Boldness in business is the first, second, and third thing.

* * * * * * * *

What it Costs.

"Barnum has ruined the show business!" This is the howl that has gone up from among the small-fry showmen, who are in the habit of gulling the public by advertising to exhibit what they never had or saw, who travel about the country with a few cages of mangy animals of the commoner sorts, broken-winded and dilapidated horses, a few ordinary performers and vulgar clowns, and go upon the principle that "a show is a show" whether it contains anything worth showing or not. I am glad to know that these fellows are right. Barnum has ruined that kind of show business, and I am proud of having done so. Since I came into the field with my gigantic consolidations, these one-horse concerns are forced to hide their diminished heads in the cross-roads and back woods, while my Greatest Show on Earth continues it triumphal career season after season.

* * * * * * * *

My Consolidated Shows.

The public expect more of Barnum than they do of anyone else. I have educated my patrons to believe that they are entitled to the best there is to be had, and they know that when they come to see my show, everything novel, interesting, attractive, instructive and amusing will be represented for their instruction and approval, no matter what it costs. Therefore the consolidation of the best features of all the principle shows of Europe and America, in my great show for 1879, is but in obedience to the demand of my patrons for the best, and for a larger, grander and more attractive exhibition than they have ever seen before, and such as no one else can possibly give. Of course I must fulfill the public expectation because my patrons wait for me, and by withholding their patronage from the smaller and less attractive shows while they turn out *en masse* to see my Greatest Show on Earth, foster and secure the "survival of the fittest."

* * * * * * * *

A Fact.

I gave Jenny Lind $1,000 per day by contract, and voluntarily added to that a share in the profits of the enterprise. My other expenses, including salaries to other artists, an orchestra of 100 musicians, the cost of transportation, printing, advertising, the rent of theaters, halls, &c. were perfectly enormous. The tickets to the Jenny Lind concerts were sold at auction, and brought from $4 to $30 each, and yet my entire expenses at that time were not one-half of the daily cost of my present "Greatest Show on Earth," to the whole of which the admission costs but 50 CENTS. But my great exhibition tent seats 10,000 persons, and is filled twice, and often three times each day, and thus the immense number of my patrons enables me to maintain the reputation I have enjoyed for so many years, of giving them ten times the worth of their money.

* * * * * * * *

My Patrons.

The reverend clergy, and school teachers of both sexes throughout our land, are among my firmest and strongest supporters of my great moral exhibition. I am both a husband and a father, and I will *never* place any entertainment before the public, that a Christian mother cannot patronize in every department, with her innocent daughters, with pleasure and profit.

* * * * * * * *

My Clowns.

My clowns are the most talented and funny ever seen, and the best of it is, they never make a joke or a gesture that could be objected to by the most moral and refined ladies.

* * * * * * * *

Special Notice.

No intoxicating liquors permitted to be sold on the grounds where my great show is encamped, nor games of chance of any name or nature allowed. We carry a special detective force, and the light fingered gentry will do well to give the Barnum show a wide berth.

* * * * * * * *

Reserved Seats.

I employ a corps of agents whose business it is to accommodate the public with tickets and reserved seats at one or more places in the various towns where my show is exhibited. I pay them liberal salaries, furnish them with transportation and board them, besides paying liberally for the privilege of selling tickets in the different stores, where they are advertised for sale. I do this simply for the accommodation of ladies and parties with children, who desire to avoid the rush of crowds at the ticket wagon on the grounds; and a small advance is charged which is scarcely sufficient to pay the expense of providing the public with these facilities. Those who desire to avail themselves of them, will always find tickets and reserved seats at the places designated in my regular advertisements.

* * * * * * * *

My Side Shows.

Through my agents in all parts of the world, I am continually in receipt of rare and attractive objects and performers, which it would be impossible to exhibit in my principal pavilion under several hours. Therefore, in order to keep away the catch-penny, vulgar, immoral gambling and swindling side shows, I have combined many of these extra attractions in a Grand Side-Show of my own, and have engaged the celebrated

Geo. B. Bunnell, proprietor of the American Museum in New York, to manage and superintend it. This exhibition will be open the entire day and evening at a small price of admission, and is well worthy of the patronage of all classes of people, as it presents a host of new and pleasing features.

* * * * * * * *

Nuisances Abolished.

There is no nuisance of which the patrons of circuses complain as much as that of peddling candies, lemonade, &c., &c., on the seats. I have abolished it altogether, and will not allow it at all, as I will not allow my patrons to be disturbed or their attention distracted from the wonderful and delightful performances in the great arena. Those who wish a glass of water or a glass of really *good* wholesome lemonade, will find it in stands in each pavilion. But no peddlers will be permitted to go among the audience, under any pretense whatever.

JUMBO THE ELEPHANT

From *The Book of Jumbo: History of the Largest Elephant That Ever Lived*
(n.p., probably 1882).

No period of the past has ever furnished a sensation like Jumbo. If anybody has anything stupendous, no matter what nature the enterprise, undertaking or object, it is at once styled Jumbo. Jumbo means a big thing now-a-days. It is a new and popular word for everybody's every-day lexicon, and it is not specially confined to Jumbo himself. Jumbo also means success of a Herculean order, and delight, instruction and recreation to the millions everywhere, besides certain destruction to all pretenders and would-be competitors, who foolishly get under his feet or within sound of his trumpet-trunk. Six million Americans saw and admired him in the Eastern States last year, and almost as many more attempted, but failed to get an eye on him. The rush was greater than could be accommodated.

Jumbo is said by the people and the press to be a Feature that more than fills the bill. His mastadonic size and really mastadonic shape overwhelm the beholder. And he has grown several inches, his tusks have pushed out nearly a foot, and he weighs a full ton more than last year. He is gradually increasing his already monstrous and phenomenal development. There never was but one Barnum—there is but one Jumbo. They are inseparable, and irrevocably the property of history, and *the* products of the century—and each so familiar to the reader of the current events of the age that further description here is unnecessary. Say "Jumbo"—and there is a volume of comment in silence, because it is the one accepted synonym in all the world for magnitude.

Eighteen years ago, the Royal Zoological Garden, Regent's Park, London, England, purchased from the Jardin des Plants, Paris, the Elephant "Jumbo," of the African species, and an account, of apparent authenticity, says: "When he arrived from Paris he was a wee little pachyderm, not more than five feet high; but he has since attained a height over twelve feet, and weighs nearly ten tons. He is already more huge in his proportions than the monster that Ptolemaeus states was brought by Caesar to Britain in 54 B.C., and terrified the inhabitants greatly; and he is more colossal than the 'elephant of enormous size' which was presented by the King of France to our own Henry III, in 1252."

Sir Samuel Baker says he was acquainted with the history of Jumbo's earlier existence. He asserts that he was captured when very young by the Hamran Arabs, who brought him down from the Settite River in Abyssinia, and disposed of him to a Bavarian collector named Johann Schmidt. Jumbo was then less than four feet high, and traveled with another elephant about his own tender age, which has since died. Even if this is true, and there is no reason to dispute it, there is still no accurate data upon which to make a calculation as to his age. He was obtained at the Jardin des Plants, Paris, in 1861, and after years of rapid growth was transferred to the Royal "Zoo," London. As zoologists have learned from close observation that the African species of elephant grows almost imperceptibly for many years of its youth, requiring a much longer time to attain maturity than its Indian kindred, it will be seen how impossible to guess rationally at Jumbo's age. He is probably much older than generally believed.

Jumbo's prodigious size has been the wonder of all Europe for years. It is probable that half a million Americans saw and admired him during his sojourn at the Royal London "Zoo." It is estimated by the managers of the "Zoo" that in seventeen years a million and a quarter of children have ridden gleefully on his broad back, including the most noted among the royalty of England and other European powers. He was a gigantic favorite with everybody, and was fed by his friends with barrels of buns, precious bits and sweet morsels every day.

P. T. Barnum, and his associates, J. A. Bailey and J. L. Hutchinson, have for two years had argus eyes on the elephantine monster, and a trusted agent was sent to England to purchase him, if possible. The Council, in whose hands the business of the Zoological Society is placed, was called together by the Superintendent, Mr. Bartlett, and Barnum, Bailey and Hutchinson's agent told them if they would set a price on Jumbo, that he would convey their determination to his employers. After consultation and much delay, they named the enormous sum of TWO THOUSAND POUNDS AS THEIR PRICE FOR THE GIANT BEAST. When the information was conveyed to the managers by the agent, they concluded to accept the terms, and at once communicated their resolve to the Council of the Zoological Society of England. Preparations were inaugurated for the removal of Jumbo to America. It was found that the hatchways of the largest ship would have to be cut away, and the upper deck raised in order to admit the great brute, which many well-informed persons believe to be the mastodon of by-gone ages. This difficulty surmounted, the agents, with a corps of experienced elephant keepers, at once set sail for England. In the meantime, the press had taken up the theme on the other side of the Atlantic, and there went up such a remonstrance and resistance against the sale and removal of the favorite Jumbo, as the world has seldom heard of before. Hundreds of cables were received by the great showman and his partners, offering almost any consideration if they would cancel the sale. Tearful requests from thousands of children and anxious ladies appeared in the columns of the British public prints. Her Majesty, the Queen, and the Prince of Wales joined the entreaties and regrets with the anguish of the whole of England. The illustrated newspapers published serious pictures and ludicrous cartoons of poor Jumbo, and the craze swept with the rapidity of lightning. Hundreds of columns and editorials appeared in the leading press daily, and the weeping nation poured in wagon loads of protesting letters by every mail. Letter heads, cards, ladies' charms, umbrellas, fans, hats, bonnets, boots, gloves, overcoats, etc., were got up in London with the portrait of Jumbo on them. His picture was sold by the hundreds of thousands on the street. The Royal Zoological Gardens added nearly $50,000 to its receipts from those who wanted to make a final farewell visit to Jumbo. The excitement spread even to the House of Commons, was discussed in Parliament and every section of Great Britain. The people, through the London *Daily Telegraph,* offered Mr. Barnum any sum in reason to cancel the contract and permit Jumbo to remain. The children wrote him thousands of letters, offering to pay him any amount if he would leave them in possession of their dear old favorite, Jumbo.

Every obstruction possible to invent was put in the way of the agents and keepers by the people, who censured no party to the transaction save the directors of the Zoological Society. Queen Victoria and the Prince of Wales requested the Garden to refuse to deliver Jumbo, and let Barnum collect his damages, which the British nation would pay. Mr. Ruskin did the same thing. Our Ambassador, Mr. Lowell, said in public speech: "The only burning question between the nations is Jumbo." Mr. Laird, builder of the rebel war steamer *Alabama,* wrote Mr. Barnum a letter in like tone and manner. To all these appeals Mr. Barnum gave courteous attention but turned a deaf ear. He was firm as Gibraltar, and stood boldly and courageously for his rights, answering the London *Daily Telegraph* by cable: "Fifty millions of American citizens awaiting Jumbo's arrival. My forty years' invariable practice of exhibiting the best that money could procure, makes Jumbo's presence here imperative. Hundred thousand pounds would be no inducement to cancel purchase."

Among the elephants in the Garden is a female called Alice, which, from the affection which has many years existed between the two, has been known as Jumbo's wife. When the Americans appeared and chained the huge monarch, preparatory to taking him through the streets to Millwall Docks, nine miles away, he utterly refused to leave his companion, making the saddest demonstrations of grief. At the gate he laid down, and no power of the keepers could compel him to move further. After days of ineffectual attempts, it was at last decided to build a huge trolley, or truck, with low wheels, the weight of which was eight or more tons, and gradually educate and accustom him to the great, strong and heavily-ironed box, prepared and placed on the vehicle. Weeks of valuable time was consumed in preparation, and for a season it seemed as though all effort to get Jumbo to America must fail. At last, however, after sinking the wheels in the ground as described elsewhere, he entered the box, and was drawn by forty draught horses to the vessel, *Assyrian Monarch,* of the Monarch Line, and taken to New York. Of course, the cost of freight, duties and other expenses have been very great, but are nothing as compared with the value of this stupendous animal, which is without question the largest elephant in or out of captivity. These pages faithfully detail the sad regrets with which his English friends parted with him, and there can be no shadow of doubt but that the American public will esteem so distinguished and treasured a visitor with a regard fully as great. Tremendous and unparalleled is Jumbo in stature, and broad as the world is his fame. He is today the largest known animal that walks the earth.

Barnum's
Gallery
of Wonders

It seems almost inevitable that Barnum would have chosen to work with Nathaniel Currier (1813–88) and James Merrit Ives (1824–95). For most of their careers, these early masters of middlebrow amusement occupied Lower Manhattan business quarters within a few short blocks of one another and traveled in similar social circles.[1] Barnum and Currier launched their cultural careers the same year (1835), owed their early success to the same promotional engine (the penny press), catered to the same basic demographic (the white middle class), and traded in the same kind of product (cheap visual entertainments designed for "family audiences").[2]

Fires destroyed most of the internal records from the companies of both men, so we know relatively little about the day-to-day logistics of the collaboration. It seems to have begun in 1848, four years before Ives joined Currier's firm, and continued for over two decades. Modern catalogs show that Currier and Ives created at least thirty-five different prints for the showman, most of which were part of a series known as Barnum's Gallery of Wonders.[3] Variations between the prints are often subtle. The two Stratton portraits reproduced in this book as figures 7 and 16, for example, follow much the same format: similar pose, similar props, similar border. But one is not a copy of the other. The print entitled *Barnum's Gallery of Wonders No. 1* (fig. 7) has a copyright date of 1848 and advertises a specific touring company, Barnum's Traveling Museum and Menagerie. The second portrait (fig. 16), by contrast, makes no mention of the touring company, features a portrait of a more mature Stratton, and offers a new biographical detail (that Stratton is twenty-two years old), all of which would suggest a publication date during the late 1850s.

These small variations can make cataloging a major challenge. Still, they help us to recognize something fundamental about the larger production process. Simply put, all of the lithographs that Currier and Ives produced for Barnum involved some sort of recycling. *Gallery of Wonders No. 1* was actually a lithographic reproduction of an earlier daguerreotype by John Plumb.[4] Other lithographs recycled particular exhibits. The Wonderful Albino Family, for instance, appeared in at least three different Currier and Ives portraits, each time with a slightly different compositional format and promotional spin. Still other lithographs recycled particular motifs. Thus we find much the same generic white patrons ogling the Aztec Children and What Is It? The great irony here is that both firms liked to market themselves as restless innovators and champions of consumer choice. Their vast product inventories, however, lead to a more ambiguous conclusion. As popular entertainment entered the age of mass production, novelty and formula became twin pillars of the same promotional philosophy.

A similar point can be made about the subject matter of the Gallery of Wonders. At first glance, the only constant seems to be novelty itself. Barnum's conception of wonder includes anything and everything: animals as well as human beings; cultural as well as physical anomalies; bell ringers as well as military heroes. Upon closer inspection, though, more subtle continuities begin to emerge. One involves the particular mode of spectatorship encouraged by the artists. Barnum's human anomalies appear not as social beings but as objects of scrutiny. Curious-looking people have the same ontological status as curious-looking animals. Driving the curiosity, moreover, is a deep and abiding fascination with difference. A wonder can be large or small; fat or tall; male or female; white or black; European, African, Chinese, or Aztec. But the basic ideological exercise remains much the same. Again and again, the lithographs work to establish a normative sense of self by picturing what the viewer is not.[5]

This process of cultural differentiation

was not without a few interesting wrinkles. None of the performers pictured here, for instance, can be described as "other" in the strict sense of absolute opposite or antipode. More typically, Barnum's characters straddled the conventional boundaries between young and old (Tom Thumb), male and female (the Swiss Bearded Lady), black and white (William Cammell), man and animal (What Is It?), one self or two (Chang and Eng). Part of the attraction, in other words, was the opportunity to contemplate figures that resisted final categorization. It was precisely their ambiguous status vis-à-vis the normal that Barnum liked to emphasize. In some cases, too, Barnum developed contradictory promotions for the very same figure. This pattern is particularly striking in the two lithographs of What Is It? (see figures 19 and 24). Whereas the former depicts the character as a menacing "African savage," the latter promises "he is playful as a kitten and in every way pleasing and amusing."

The most surprising irregularity may concern the remarkably ordinary portrait of William Tillman (see figure 26), an African American Civil War hero who appeared at Barnum's Museum during the early 1860s. What qualified Tillman for public exhibition was not his race per se. More specifically, promotions emphasized Tillman's central role in recapturing a hijacked New York schooner from a "rebel privateer." This must have been a thoroughly reassuring image for Barnum's wartime audiences. Here was a faithful "colored steward" who risked his life to save his white crewmates, not to mention one of the Union's most important commercial shipping lines. The fact that Tillman was also saving himself from slavery is never explicitly acknowledged.[6]

It is worth noting, finally, that gaps remain in our understanding of this intriguing collaboration between printers and showman. How were the prints sold and distributed? Where did consumers display the images? How many copies of each print were produced? And why is the text for one of the lithographs, *Old Neptune, the Great Black Sea Lion,* given in both English and Spanish?[7] After a century of research on Barnum's career, many unanswered questions await the detective work of future scholars.

✳

As far as possible, I have arranged the lithographs in this gallery chronologically to demonstrate how the series changed over time. Some of the surviving prints, however, lack a printed copyright date. In such cases, the dates in parentheses within the captions represent educated guesses based on Barnum's exhibition schedules.

ward

FIGURE 7

Barnum's Gallery of Wonders No. 1, Charles Stratton as General Tom Thumb,
Nathaniel Currier lithograph after a daguerreotype by John Plumb, 1848
(Library of Congress, Prints and Photographs Division, reproduction number
LC-USZC2-2415). This portrait was the first in the long-running Gallery of
Wonders series. The border panels feature eleven of Stratton's characters: top
to bottom (left) are Napoleon, Highlander, Cain, Gladiator, Hercules, Cupid,
and (right) American Tar, Yankee, Ajax, Romulus, Samson, and again, Cupid.

BARNUMS GALLERY OF WONDERS Nº 4.

THE LANCASHIRE BELL RINGERS.
The most talented and wonderful band of the kind in the world.
Performing under the auspices of P. T. BARNUM Proprietor of AMERICAN and CHINESE MUSEUMS New York and BARNUMS MUSEUM Philadelphia.

FIGURE 8

The Lancashire Bell Ringers, Nathaniel Currier lithograph, late 1840s (© Shelburne Museum, Shelburne, Vermont). After discovering these English musicians on tour in 1844, Barnum sent them back to the United States, often presenting them as the Swiss Bell Ringers. Invented stage names and biographies were standard components of the puffing system.

MISS SUSAN BARTON,
THE MAMMOTH LADY
as Exhibited at
BARNUM'S AMERICAN MUSEUM, NEW YORK 1860.
Weight 576 Pound's.

Height	5 feet		Calf	33½ inc.
Arms	33½ inches.		Bust	60
Waist	59		Hips	87

FIGURE 9

Miss Susan Barton, the Mammoth Lady, Nathaniel Currier lithograph, 1849
(Library of Congress, Prints and Photographs Division, reproduction number
LC-USZ62-13754). The conventional middle-class costume and domestic
interior are part of a formula for portraits of Barnum's "living curiosities":
an extraordinary body set against putatively normal surroundings.

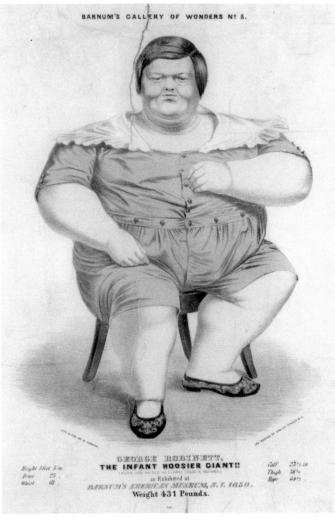

FIGURE 10

George Robinett, the Infant Hoosier Giant, Nathaniel Currier
lithograph, 1850 (© Collection of the New-York Historical
Society, neg. #74824). Robinett was one of Barnum's many
celebrity "fat boys."

WILLIAM CAMMELL,
THE PERSON OF THIS NEGRO IS NOW UNDERGOING A WONDERFUL CHANGE.
AS EXHIBITED AT BARNUMS AMERICAN MUSEUM NEW YORK 1850.
He was a slave in the South and it is said accidently discovered a weed which by
its juice, gradually Converts the skin of a Colored person into the hue of a white one

FIGURE 11

William Cammell, Nathaniel Currier lithograph, 1850 (© Collection
of the New-York Historical Society, neg. #67611). Cammell was one
of a broad group of racially ambiguous figures in Barnum's cultural
production. Cammell exhibits a depigmentation condition known as
vitiligo, but Barnum's caption suggests that he was turning white:
"He was a slave in the South and it is said accidentally discovered
a weed which by the juice gradually converts the skin of a
Colored person into the hue of a white one."

Orientalism
giving them a specific
identity

FIGURE 12

The Living Chinese Family, Currier colored lithograph, April 1850 (© Museum of the City of New York, Theater Collection, 41.419.11). This exhibition was part of Barnum's short-lived Chinese Museum in New York. At other points in his career, the showman exhibited Chinese magicians, acrobats, conjoined twins, giants, and dwarfs. Orientalist imagery was a common feature of the early culture industry.

THE SWISS BEARDED LADY,
The most remarkable case of the kind ever known; she has a very handsome
HEAVY BEARD and an unsurpassed PAIR OF WHISKERS,
which are the admiration and envy of many of the sterner sex,
SHE IS NOW ON EXHIBITION AT BARNUM'S AMERICAN MUSEUM, N.Y.
Where she is to be seen at all hours, day and evening, in connexion with the other won-
ders and curiosities, and the elegant Dramatic Performances at 3 and half past 7 O'Clock
P. M. and for the low price of 25 cts. Children under 10 years 15 cts.

FIGURE 13

Madame Josephine Clofullia, the Swiss Bearded Lady, Nathaniel Currier
colored lithograph, mid-1850s (© Museum of the City of New York,
Theater Collection, 41.419.2). An anomalous body is surrounded by the
conventional markers of domesticity: elegant clothing, fine jewelry, a
lace handkerchief, parlor furniture, and children. Clofullia is at once
mirror image and grotesque other to the Victorian woman.

THE ONLY LIVING RHINOCEROS, OR "UNICORN", IN AMERICA.
NOW ATTRACTING SUCH CROWDS OF WONDER LOVING PEOPLE.
AT BARNUM'S MUSEUM.

FIGURE 14

The Living Rhinoceros, Nathaniel Currier lithograph, mid-1850s (© Collection of the New-York Historical Society, neg. #23511). Well before the three-ring circuses, Barnum exhibited a wide range of exotic animals before American audiences. Although most of the animals were genuine, the showman had few scruples about adding promotional embellishments. In this case, he presents his rhinoceros as the fabled unicorn.

THE MAINE GIANTESS-MISS SILVA HARDY-NEARLY 8 FEET HIGH.
NOW EXHIBITING AT BARNUM'S AMERICAN MUSEUM, NEW YORK.

FIGURE 15

Barnum's Gallery of Wonders, No. 10, the Maine Giantess, Miss Silva Hardy, nearly 8 feet high, Nathaniel Currier colored lithograph, mid-1850s (© Museum of the City of New York, Theater Collection, 57.100.19). Along with Anna Swan and Routh Goshen, Hardy was one of Barnum's best-known giants. Hardy's first name was more commonly spelled Sylvia. In 1855, she appeared in conjunction with the Grand National Baby Show.

FIGURE 16

General Tom Thumb, Currier and Ives lithograph, late 1850s (© Collection
of the New-York Historical Society, neg. #41423). This portrait features a
number of interesting contrasts to figure 7. Stratton's face appears more
mature in this version, and the surrounding panels feature a number of
new characters, including one in English court dress and another in drag
("My Mary Ann"). This is also the first Currier lithograph to include Ives
(who became a full partner in 1857) in the credit line.

FIGURE 17

Old Neptune, the Great Black Sea Lion, Currier and Ives lithograph,
1860 (© Collection of the New-York Historical Society, neg. #74821).
The most surprising feature of this lithograph is the bilingual text.
One suspects it was produced for exhibition in Havana, a frequent stop
on Barnum's tours.

"CHANG" AND "ENG"
THE WORLD RENOWNED UNITED
SIAMESE TWINS.
NOW EXHIBITING AT BARNUM'S AMERICAN MUSEUM, NEW YORK.

FIGURE 18

Chang and Eng, Currier and Ives lithograph, 1860 (Harvard Theatre
Collection, Houghton Library). The era's most famous conjoined twins are
depicted as gentlemen farmers. Side panels show Chang and Eng hunting,
fishing, plowing fields, clearing forests, and driving a carriage in genteel
dress. Before their appearance at the American Museum, Chang and Eng ran
a working farm in North Carolina. The women depicted in the side panels
were their wives, sisters named Sarah and Adelaide Yates.

"WHAT IS IT"?

Is it a lower order of MAN! Or is it a higher order of MONKEY! None can tell! Perhaps it is a combination of both. It is beyond dispute THE MOST MARVELLOUS CREATURE LIVING. It was captured in a savage state in Central Africa, is probably about 20 years old, 4 feet high, intelligent, docile, active, sportive, and PLAYFUL AS A KITTEN. It has the skull, limbs and general anatomy of an ORANG OUTANG and the COUNTENANCE of a HUMAN BEING.

TO BE SEEN AT ALL HOURS AT BARNUM'S MUSEUM.

FIGURE 19

What Is It? Currier and Ives lithograph, early 1860s (Photography by Ken Burris; © The Shelburne Museum, Shelburne, Vermont). Three months after the publication of Charles Darwin's *Origin of Species,* Barnum introduced a possible "missing link" between man and brute creation. Billed as What Is It? this perpetually liminal figure (played by a short African American man) raised complex questions about racial identity, even as it insisted that those of African descent constituted a lower order of being.

FIGURE 20

The Wonderful Albino Family, Currier and Ives lithograph, early 1860s (Collection of James W. Cook). Barnum claimed that these albinos were "born of perfectly black parents" in Madagascar. In fact, Rudolph Lucasie and his family hailed from the Netherlands. Barnum discovered them in 1857 while on tour in Europe.

FIGURE 21

The Wonderful Albino Family with Two Children and Violin, Currier and
Ives lithograph, early 1860s (Collection of James W. Cook). It is not clear
why Barnum commissioned so many lithographs of the albino family, but
these images do reveal the showman's penchant for recycling images and
text. A fourth lithograph of the Lucasies, now held by the Library of Congress
(digital ID #cph 3b51176), contains the same artwork as figure 20 but
presents the text in both English and Spanish.

ALBINO CHILDREN,
WITH THEIR BLACK MOTHER AND BLACK SISTER.—
The most extraordinary case known, the Father and Mother being very black, and their Children
ALTERNATELY BLACK AND WHITE.
The white Children as well, as the black, having every indication of
PURE AFRICAN BLOOD.

NOW EXHIBITING AT _____

FIGURE 22

Albino Children with Their Black Mother and Black Sister, Currier and
Ives lithograph, early 1860s (Harvard Theatre Collection, Houghton
Library). Testing the limits of public credulity, this exhibition claimed
that a black mother had given birth to "alternately black and white"
children. The historical forces driving Barnum's display of racial
anomalies during the 1850s and 1860s are somewhat easier to fathom.
During this period, American debates about racial status and hierarchy
escalated into Civil War. Though careful not to offend any particular
constituency, Barnum was happy to offer a steady stream of racialized
"nondescripts" for public scrutiny.

{ 173 }

FIGURE 23

The Aztec Children, Currier and Ives lithograph, early 1860s (© Collection of the
New-York Historical Society, neg. #74823). The Aztec Children were prominent
figures on the international exhibition circuit before making their debut at the
American Museum. The artist's depiction of two well-dressed patrons interacting
with the Aztec Children results in a far more genteel and intimate representation
of American freakery than one finds two or three decades later.

FIGURE 24

What Is It? Shown with Patrons, Currier and Ives lithograph, early 1860s
(Collection of James W. Cook). This lithograph demonstrates some of the
flexibility of Barnum's approach to racial caricature. In stark contrast to the
menacing figure in figure 19, the caption here claims, "He is playful as a Kitten
and every way pleasing, interesting and amusing."

COMMODORE NUTT,
THE $ 30,000 NUT.
The Smallest man alive 18 years old, 29 inches high and weighs only 24 pounds.
On exhibition day and evening at
BARNUM'S MUSEUM, NEW YORK.
Commodore George W. M. Nutt

FIGURE 25

*Commodore Nutt, The $30,000 Nut, The Smallest man alive 18 years old, 29
inches high and weighs only 24 pounds, on exhibition day and evening at
Barnum's Museum, New York,* Currier and Ives colored lithograph, c. 1862
(© Museum of the City of New York, Theater Collection, 41.419.3). Barnum
presented George Washington Morrison Nutt as an updated version of Tom
Thumb. Nutt was even shorter than Stratton, standing only twenty-nine inches
tall. The signature by Nutt (bottom right) suggests that this lithograph was sold
at the exhibition.

WM TILLMAN, THE COLORED STEWARD,
of the Schooner S. J. WARING which was captured by the Piratical Brig JEFF DAVIS
and recaptured by TILLMAN and WM STEDDING the German Sailor after having killed three
of the Pirates in charge of her. He is receiving Visitors daily at
BARNUM'S MUSEUM, NEW YORK.

FIGURE 26

William Tillman, the Colored Steward, Currier and Ives lithograph,
early 1860s (© Collection of the New-York Historical Society, neg.
#74822). According to the African American abolitionist William Wells
Brown, Tillman's reception at the American Museum was enthusiastic:
"Unstinted praise from all parties, even those who are usually awkward in
any other vernacular than derision of the colored man, has been awarded
to this colored man. At Barnum's Museum he was the center of attractive
gaze to daily increasing thousands" (*The Negro in the American Rebellion*
[Boston: Lee & Shepard, 1867], 75).

FIGURE 27

General Tom Thumb and Wife, Commodore Nutt and Minnie Warren, Currier and Ives lithograph, 1863 (Library of Congress, Prints and Photographs Division, reproduction number LC-USZC2-2439). Few celebrity weddings generated more public attention than the 1863 union of Charles Stratton and Lavinia Warren in New York's Grace Episcopal Church.

FIGURE 28

Four Giants and Two Dwarfs, Currier and Ives lithograph, mid-
1860s (© Collection of the New-York Historical Society, neg. #43430).
The juxtaposition of physiological extremes–tall and short, fat and thin,
dark skin and albino–was a common formula in the show trade.

THE WONDERFUL ELIOPHOBUS FAMILY.
RUDOLPH LUCASIE WIFE AND SON FROM MADAGASAAR.
THEY HAVE PURE WHITE SKIN WHITE HAIR AND PINK EYES
TAKEN MARCH 1870.

FIGURE 29

The Wonderful Eliophobus Family, Currier and Ives lithograph, 1870 (Collection of
James W. Cook). Despite the name change, the family depicted here is still the Lucasies.
This seems to be the last Barnum lithograph produced by Currier and Ives.

Barnum's Public Reception

For many years, the question of public reception rarely surfaced in discussions of Barnum's career. When audiences were mentioned at all in the early biographies, it was usually to demonstrate their extreme gullibility. On the rare occasions when the public was allowed a degree of self-consciousness about Barnum's promotional tricks, no one seemed to mind. Genial crowds, we are told, gave "three cheers" for the clever impresario who had just fleeced them.[1]

This long-running manipulation myth made it harder to grasp one of the most important lessons from Barnum's career: even the era's most ingenious promoter never simply controlled public opinion. Some consumers embraced the pitch. Others rejected it outright. And in general, no two consumers embraced or rejected in exactly the same way. It was this dialectical, market-driven dance between restless promoter and fickle public that constituted the ongoing drama of the nineteenth-century culture industry.[2]

What, then, do we find when we actually dig into Barnum's press reviews? The quick answer is just about everything: race, class, gender, sexuality, sectionalism, imperialism–even a little natural history. Yet this rich body of popular opinion needs to be unpacked carefully. First, we need to remember that contemporary critics were sometimes only partially cognizant of the showman's promotional schemes. The Joice Heth campaign provides a useful example. Barnum's strategy here was to offer a series of competing interpretive possibilities: some ads described Heth as the 161-year-old nursemaid to George Washington; others presented her as an object of abolitionist charity; still others floated the possibility that she might be an India-rubber automaton. The goal was to get people talking, to stimulate debate. Yet only one antebellum commentator (writing well after the event) seems to have recognized that the debate itself boiled down to a bogus choice between equally specious claims. In this case, at least, the idea of unmediated consumer democracy was about as illusory as the story of "raising little George."

It is also important to be aware of the considerable gaps and elisions in Barnum's public reception. As far as possible, this gallery offers a broad spectrum of nineteenth-century viewpoints: celebratory and critical, male and female, bourgeois and working-class, northern and southern, domestic and foreign. Still, there are key voices missing from the conversations. Leading African American newspaper editors such as Samuel Cornish, Frederick Douglass, and Benjamin T. Tanner, for example, rarely said a word about Barnum's exhibitions.[3] One important exception to this rule was Barnum's Grand National Baby Show, which provoked a brief flurry of commentary in *Frederick Douglass' Paper* (reprinted below). More typically, though, the early black press chose to focus on higher-stakes issues such as slavery, segregation, and civil liber-

ties. Or perhaps they felt that Barnum's racialized caricatures were simply unworthy of their hard-won editorial columns.

It is worth noting that Barnum's reviewers had lots to say about the culture industry itself. We can see these early glimmers of consumer knowingness in the *New York Herald's* complaint about "unreasonable" doses of Feejee Mermaid puffery; or in Mike Walsh's description of the Hoboken Buffalo Hunt as the most "insulting humbug that ever took place even in Jersey"; or in the suggestion of the *Times* of London that Barnum employed a "police of puffery" to choreograph the Jenny Lind furor. Such isolated grumblings rarely put a stop to Barnum's promotional campaigns. But they do suggest an intriguing evolution in audience response patterns. By relentlessly drawing attention to his own working methods, Barnum sparked some of the first self-conscious debate about popular culture as a modern commodity system.[4]

ON JOICE HETH

NEW YORK EVENING STAR, AUGUST 7, 1835

Niblo, whose prolific genius for the invention of novelty to please the public, never fails—now has recourse to the antique, instead of modern discoveries—and has found a woman! Startle not reader—she is a woman of by-gone days! One hundred and sixty-one years of age! Niblo has engaged her for a few days only—and she will, no doubt, prove as great an object of attraction as the forthcoming comet itself. She will be a greater star than any other performer of the present day, and has no fear of rival—and having been the slave of Washington's Father, renders her an object of intense interest—and will, no doubt, receive the congratulations of every individual in New York.

LETTER TO THE *NEW YORK SUN*, AUGUST 20, 1835

To the Editors of the Sun.
Gentlemen—

Allow me to occupy a brief space in your columns, in reference to that relic of gone by days, the old colored woman, Joice Heth. It is the prevalent opinion that she is the original Joice Heth who was the nurse of Gen. George Washington; and my reasons for troubling you with this communication, is to ascertain why she who nursed the "father of our country," the man to whom we owe our present happy and prosperous condition, should at the close of her life be exhibited as "our rarer monsters are." Is there not philanthropy enough in the American people to take care of her, although her skin be black? She is the common property of our country—she is identified with the foundation, rise, and progress of our government—she is the sole remaining tie of mortality which connects us to him who was "first in war, first in peace, and first in the hearts of his countrymen"—and as such, we should protect and honor her, and not suffer her to be kept for a show, like a wild beast, to fill the coffers of mercenary men.

Henry Cole.

"BARNUM AND JOICE HETH," *THE SCALPEL*
3–4, NO. 9 (NOVEMBER 1850): 58–59.

We have always considered our fellow citizen of the Museum a man of decided genius; and now that he has placed us under obligations we shall never forget, we feel inclined to jot down, now and then, an instance of his claim to that title.

It is but a few years since, that Joice Heth departed this life, full of years and honors, and went to join the innumerable throng of servants that waited upon the illustrious Father of our country. Poor Joice, who was said to be some one hundred and thirty years old, was a smoke-dried wench of some seventy years, found by a traveling Yankee in a hut in the interior of Virginia, as guiltless of all knowledge of Washington, as she was of her own wonderful age and power of coining money. She would have gradually dried up into a mummy, had not the lynx-eyed Yankee come across her whilst selling his tins. After much persuasion, a few dollars and more whisky, she agreed to be lifted into a sedan-bed, and, mounted on an easy-wagon, was carried off, to make the grand tour. She looked for all the world like a large monkey. At seventy years, rheumatism and tobacco had abstracted all her juices, and left her to appearance as near a hundred and fifty as any other age. No sooner had she arrived, than Barnum seized upon her, and rigged her up for a show.

The scene was inimitable: lying on a bedstead, nicely trapped out with dimity and fine blankets, and placed in the middle of a large saloon for convenience of access and air, she was plied with small and comforting drinks and a pipe, whilst a well-smoked and antique-looking bill of sale from one of the Custis family, duly certified by Dicky Riker, was hung upon the wall. She was usually remarkably tractable, having received her religious education from a shrewd lawyer out of briefs at the time of her advent, and perfectly cognizant of the power of whisky and tobacco in producing compliance with the wishes of a legal adviser. She always uttered her pious exclamations in an ejaculatory manner, repeating a few short phrases, always the same, in a very edifying way, and reserving all answers to any general questions, unless the words whisky or tobacco fell upon her ear, when she would generally give an expressive grunt of assent.

One day, however, a Yankee friend, who was cognizant of the whole scheme, observing her with a little less steam on than was desirable to keep her in training, asked her in presence of her keeper, if she remembered Massa George, meaning her alleged illustrious owner. A ray of anger shot from the old woman's hitherto closed eyes, as she replied, "No! Debil take 'em all; don't know nutin bout him! Dey make me say dat all de time: gimme drink!" The ladies stared, and Joice speedily got her drink, with a soothing reproof for her impiety.

But the funniest part of the business was when the old wench died. Instead of finishing the process of embalming so happily begun by the whisky and tobacco and steeping her in a solution of corrosive muriate, and hanging her up alongside of his mermaid, in a corner of the Museum to dry, where she would have been a permanent investment till the day of judgment, she was given up to the philosophers for a post mortem.

The Magnus Apollo of surgery at that time, went to the Museum, duly heralded in the papers, with all his students, and what other verdant gentlemen he could collect, and held a great pow-wow over the old wench. We did not enjoy the honor of being present, but were informed that "the coronary and femoral arteries were ossified," and fully established her great age. Indeed, her anatomy would have given her a clean ticket for any period short of 200 years. What a spectacle it must have been! We are a great people, and there is but one Barnum.

ON THE FEEJEE MERMAID

PHILADELPHIA PUBLIC LEDGER AND
DAILY TRANSCRIPT, JULY 27, 1842

Important to Naturalists—A Mermaid Caught. The present age exceeds all others in the extent and variety of its discoveries, and the confirmation and establishment of facts in science and nature, which have always been questioned. This is undoubtedly the era of progress, and we should not be surprised if even in our own generation, the human mind has reached its highest acme of perfection. The discoveries in the great sciences of Phrenology and Animal Magnetism, discoveries made in our own day and generation, for the ancients were too stupid or lazy to carry out the few hints they had received, and left it for us to acquire all the glory of establishing the sublime principles of these sciences, are enough to adorn the reputation of any age, and warrant us in putting faith in Mr. Miller's predictions that the progress of humanity has got to the end of its reach, and the world is about to wind up in a catastrophe of fire. The greatest discovery yet made has still to be announced, and it is left for us to make the fact public. *We have seen a mermaid!!* Start not and curl your lips in scorn, though concerning a fish it is not a *fish story.* We have seen the tangible evidence exhibited to our senses, of the existence of that monster hitherto deemed fabulous by all the learned, though religiously believed by every salt water naturalist that ever crossed the Gulf Stream. A mermaid we have seen, not in the alluring garb and seductive form represented in the picture books, with an angel's face, which the Naiad beauty herself enamored of . . . the mermaid we saw has none of these attractions, but is as ugly a little monster as was ever seen, resembling more in appearance about the upper part of the body a mummified monkey than an angelic fish. Still the monster is one of the greatest curiosities of the day. It was caught near the Feejee Islands, and taken to Penambuco, where it was purchased by an English gentleman named Griffin, who is making a collection of rare and curious things for the British Museum, or some other cabinet of curiosities. This animal, fish, flesh or whatever it may be, is about three feet long, and the lower part of the body is a perfectly formed fish, but from the breast upwards this character is lost, and it then approaches human form—or rather that of the monkey. It has a pair of perfectly formed breasts, arms and hands; the latter resembling the human hand more than the monkey's, with white nails on the finger ends. The head is also larger than the monkey's head, though shaped somewhat like it, the top is bald, but the sides are covered with hair, which extends down upon the neck, like the well trained ringlets of some fair damsel. The cheeks, eyes, and lips all bear a semblance to humanity, except the chin, which is deficient. The animal is now in the charge of a gentleman at Jones' Hotel, who was about to leave for New York yesterday afternoon. It is worthy of the notice of the naturalists of this city, though the owner has refused to exhibit it publicly.

Now the question arises, is not this the mermaid so much talked of, and whose existence there is ample testimony to establish, though so generally doubted? Accounts of them state that one was fished up in England, in 1187, and kept six months alive, and finally escaped by plunging into the sea. One was caught in the mud, in the dykes of Holland, in 1430, after a tempest. It was found by some girls who were going in a boat to milk—they caught it, dressed it, and taught it to spin, and so great was its piety that it used to bow its head reverently whenever it passed a crucifix. Seven mermen and mermaids were caught together in one net, in 1560, at the island of Ceylon. One off the coast of Martinico used to be seen wiping its hair and blowing its nose. Not withstanding all the testimony, the existence of the creature was still doubted to the end of creation, if fortune had not thrown the Feejee beauty into the hands of the present proprietor, where all may satisfy themselves of its reality. It would be a curiosity in our Museum.

PHILADELPHIA SPIRIT OF THE TIMES,
AUGUST 2, 1842

That Mermaid—The mermaid which we noticed a day or so ago, and which our friends at the *Ledger* wrote a half column about in the way of a eulogy, turns out to be—the head of a monkey fastened to the tail of a fish!! That was too shabby,

NEW YORK TRIBUNE, AUGUST 2, 1842

That Mermaid. Has arrived in this City on its way to the British Museum, and we were yesterday gratified with a private view of it. We tried hard to determine where or how some cute Yankee had joined a monkey's head to a fish's body, but had to give it up, though our incredulity still lingers. If such an animal ever *did* exist, it is surely the most extraordinary fact in Natural History. Believe it we can hardly; but how to account otherwise for what our eyes have seen staggers us. We should like to hear the opinion of better judges, after a rigid scrutiny.

PHILADELPHIA PUBLIC LEDGER
AND DAILY TRANSCRIPT, AUGUST 8, 1842

• • • The specimen of the mermaid now in this country is said to have been brought from the Feejee Islands, a group in the South Pacific Ocean. This may or may not be true. But if it be true, how, we ask, got the *crittur* there? It was probably carried there from Java, or it might have been prepared there by some Javanese, or even a native. The Chinese, and the natives of the islands in the Indian Ocean, who, with the islanders of the Pacific Ocean, constitute one race, are exceedingly ingenious in preparing such fabrications as the mermaid, and have plenty of monkeys and fishes for raw material; and the "English gentleman" who has imported this specimen, has been duped by some clever Malay, or purchased the *article* with full knowledge of its properties, for the creditable purpose of defrauding the public, or rather of living upon its credulity. We trust that the people of this country will be wise enough to discourage this impudent fraud, by *letting it alone*. If they pay their money for such a sight, they will deserve to be imposed upon by every pretender who comes along. One of these specimens of Malay ingenuity was brought to this country in 1824 or 1825, and exhibited first in Boston. It was not very popular there, the people believing that it was the head and body of a monkey united to the tail of a fish. We have not heard of it since, and should not be surprised in learning that this new specimen were the old affair revived. It appeared first in Montgomery, in Alabama; the wrong quarter for the first appearance of an importation from the East Indies. It is said to be the property of an "English gentleman"; and he is probably some *cute* Yankee, intent on a "Joice Heth" scheme.

NEW YORK HERALD, AUGUST 11, 1842

Humbug–The Mermaid–and no mistake. We can swallow a reasonable dose, but we can't swallow this.

CHARLESTON COURIER, MARCH 20, 1843

The Mermaid again. It will be seen from the following extract, clipped from a northern paper, that Mr. Barnum, of N.Y., disclaims the imputed ownership but attests the genuineness of the Mermaid; and intimates the question of genuineness will probably be submitted by the real owner to the arbitrament of a jury. We understand that the owner of the Feejee is Mr. Moses Kimball of the Boston Museum. Mr. Barnum paid $1000 for the privilege of exhibiting it at the American Museum, New York:

> To the Editor of the Sun:
> Sir–the Sun of yesterday contained an article in relation to the Feejee Mermaid with reference to the Pretended examination of a clergyman and committee of physicians* (*These men only saw the animal through the glass case, as thousands and thousands saw it in this city–and they neither handled it, nor "cut it up" as has been erroneously reported) of Charleston, which concludes with the following paragraph–"Barnum threatens to prosecute for $20,000 damages for calling his Mermaid a monkey." Now sir, I am not nor ever was the owner of the Feejee

or any other mermaid, but whenever that animal was exhibited at this Museum, I hired it at a high price; believing then, (and I have seen no good reason since for changing my opinion) THAT IT WAS PRECISELY WHAT IT REPRESENTED. The story, probably originated from the fact that the owner, who does not reside in this city, has, or is about to commence an action for damages, which will give an opportunity to the gentlemen IF ABLE, to substantiate their assertions, and unless I greatly err, the result of that trial will discomfit a number of two-penny self dubbed "scientific" wiseacres, whose optics, like those mentioned by the poet, can discover "things not to be seen."

I imagine further, that the sage and sagacious Charleston D.D. and M.D.'s must each possess a pair of Sam Weller's "patent double million has microscopes of hextra power" instead of EYES, to enable them to see the pretended "seams," through a glass case, which many men in this city could discover by handling the animal, though aided by strong magnifying glasses. It is an easy thing to LOOK WISE, and raise learned "doubts" without examination of the thing criticized, but in this instance I opine that it will require something more than senseless innuendoes to prove the falsity of what no naturalist dare swear is not genuine, and I may add which no man can give a reason for believing false, except the general notion of the non-existence of mermaids.

P. T. Barnum

American Museum, Feb. 27, 1843

[handwritten marginalia: Barnum defending his claims]

THEODORE ROOSEVELT, "A LAYMAN'S VIEWS OF AN ART EXHIBITION," *THE OUTLOOK*, MARCH 22, 1913

Probably we err in treating most of these pictures seriously. It is likely that many of them represent in the painters the astute appreciation of the power to make folly lucrative which the late P. T. Barnum showed with his fake mermaid. There are thousands of people who will pay small sums to look at a faked mermaid; and now and then one of this kind with enough money will buy a Cubist picture, a picture of a misshapen nude woman, repellant from every standpoint. . . .[5]

ON THE HOBOKEN BUFFALO HUNT

MIKE WALSH, *THE SUBTERRANEAN*, SEPTEMBER 2, 1843

Grand Buffalo Hunt–This affair, which took place on the afternoon of Thursday last, was the most superlative and insulting humbug that ever took place even in Jersey.[6] The public will recollect that for the last week or ten days their attention has been unremittingly called by show-bills and advertisements, to the fact that a herd of wild buffaloes were to be hunted at Hoboken in a spacious enclosure, by western hunters skilled in throwing the lasso, and that all this was to be seen, free gratis, for nothing. They will also probably recollect that they indulged in no small amount of surprise that any individual should be found so generous and self-sacrificing as to afford this public a treat at his own private expense; and that they bestowed upon him, in consequence, no small degree of grateful compliment in anticipation. But we who saw matters in a truer light, expected nothing more than a piece of the most contemptible deception. We expected this; firstly, because we knew the whole affair to be got up by Barnaby Diddleum, a professional and professed swindler, who had hired all the ferries for the day on the speculation; and secondly, because the scene of its operation was to take place in Jersey. With this view of the matter, and expecting to see a grand row and hunt of humbuggery, rather than buffaloes, we crossed in one of the crowded ferry boats, and after struggling through some half mile of marsh, arrived on the ground at four o'clock. There we found assembled about ten thousand spectators of all classes, sexes and degrees, sweltering under the fierceness of a torrid sun and dodging about in vain attempts to catch a glimpse of three tottering, mis-shapen calves, who were *shoved* up and down the sides of the hill, by a Jerseyman on horseback, in the costume of an Indian. Never before did we see a sight so painful and so ridiculous. The poor tortured animals, who were in the first place but little larger than good sized hogs, had been kept on starvation allowance for the previous fortnight, and had also been bled the day before, for the purpose of reducing them to a state of perfect helplessness. They staggered first one way and then another to escape the torment of the crowd, and now and then managed to crawl into a clump of bushes for a moment's respite from the annoyances of the shameless blackguard who kept lashing them about the head with a thong, on pretence of casting the lasso. Here, through mixed sensations of humanity and disgust, the crowd interfered with his operations, and were about kicking him off the ground, when they were induced by the earnestness of the protestations to let him try his skill on a cow to prove his skill as a wild hunter. A cow was accordingly driven from the swamp, when caroling his horse to her side, the impudent scoundrel actually *dropped* the noose upon her horns–The cow however not relishing this amusement, made a sudden plunge which jerked the mountebank from his saddle and dragged him several feet through the mud and slime of the marsh. As this trial did not prove very satisfactory to the spectators, it was insisted that he should essay his dexterity upon a Jerseyman, upon which a sandy-faced, blear eyed fellow, who is Justice of the Peace for the Hoboken district, volunteered his services, and mounting on a broken-winded nag, taken from one of the road hacks, started off with a lead of about twenty yards–the mock Indian following in chase. The display in this case was much the same as the cow, with the exception of the Jersey Justice wearing the halter more naturally and kindly than the indignant quadruped. It was now approaching six o'clock, and absolutely sickened with disgust at the whole spectacle, we prepared to withdraw, but paused a moment on the ascent near the road to see an apple woman, who had been paid a shilling by a humane bystander for the service, get down on her hands and knees and catch two of the buffaloes in her arms in succession, and carry them into the stable. The third fell down with exhaustion, and was carried in and laid down in her stall by the crowd, where she was left in a dying state. Thus ended the great buffalo hunt, the last and most bare-faced swindle of the most unprincipled swindler in the community. . . .

ON TOM THUMB

NEW YORK HERALD, DECEMBER 1, 1843

General Tom Thumb–This extraordinary and beautiful man in miniature has determined to set sail for London in the packet of the first of January. Our transatlantic friends can form some idea of this charming Lilliputian, when we state, that although he long since got his growth, he now stands but twenty-five inches high and weighs only fifteen pounds. He is very handsome, perfect in his proportions, has bright blue eyes, rosy cheeks, is hearty, manly and graceful, and the happiest little fellow we ever saw. He has been visited by nearly half a million persons in America, and has been *feted* by many families of the first distinction. He is so graceful, so pert, so intelligent, and withal, so wonderfully diminutive, that all who see him are charmed with him at once, and his visits to all our cities, have necessarily been so many signal triumphs. He will undoubtedly visit Queen Victoria and be received with marked attention by all the nobility of Europe. He intends visiting Paris, Edinburgh, &c. before his return, and particularly Dublin, where he means to challenge O'Connell and do justice to Ireland. He will also call upon the Queen at Buckingham Palace.

TIMES OF LONDON, FEBRUARY 21, 1844

Princess's Theatre–The extraordinary little dwarf, surnamed General Tom Thumb, of whom the American papers have recently given such incredible accounts, made his first public appearance last night at this house, turning out to be no creature of Kentucky imagination, but certainly the most minute specimen of walking and talking humanity it is possible to conceive. On his first entrance, as he toddled down to the foot-lights, the reflectors of which must have hidden a good portion of him from the pit, he was greeted with shouts of laughter and surprise. He is perfectly symmetrical; his dimensions and proportions being those of a child of six months old, and the contrast of his infantine form with the firmness and strength developed in his motions had a most whimsical and striking effect. In answer to the questions of his exhibitor, he stated his age to be 12 years, his height 25 inches, and his weight 15 lbs., his voice and articulation being quite childish. In the course of the evening, he parodied walk and manner of Napoleon, danced a hornpipe, and went through what are commonly called "the Grecian Statues." The latter were by far the most interesting part of the exhibition, as they showed his actual proportions in a most distinct manner, and gave a proof of his advanced age, in the spirit and intelligence with which he assumed the several attitudes. A rather painful sensation was created by the evidence that the little fellow in his latter performance was suffering from the cold; this might easily be remedied by the use of a screen thrown round him. At the close of his exertions he was loudly summoned before the curtain, where he returned a series of graceful bows to the applause of the audience.

PORTLAND (MAINE) ADVERTISER, APRIL 25, 1845

Mr. Barnum, of the American Museum, says the New York Express, has sent home $14,000, as the proceeds of but six weeks exhibition of Tom Thumb. The aggregate of profits made by him out of that unfortunate little monstrosity, is not far from a hundred thousand dollars.

"TOM THUMB ON KISSES," LIVING AGE 12, NO. 138 (JANUARY 2, 1847)

An American as I am—a free citizen of the smartest nation in creation, 't isn't for me to find fault with the gals of free Columbia.[7] Nevertheless, truth is mighty, and with fair play will whip her weight in wild-cats. Therefore, I cannot say much for the kissing of America. Governor Barnum tells me that I ought n't to give any 'pinion of the matter till I get back again, with all my snuff-boxes and tooth-picks, and pencil-cases of crowned heads about me; when the kisses will be a different matter, as the royalty of Europe will be saluted through me. But this I must say; the kissing of America, of my own countrywomen, was terrible cautious; nothing more than what you might call respect with the chill off. But, then, Barnum says I was a nobody; and gals don't kiss nobodies like somebodies. For all that, I am a little riled when I think of it. For I remember, how at New York they used to look at me, and mince round and round me, and put their hands under my chin, as if I warn't a human cretur, but a gooseberry bush, and they were afraid of their fingers. And then the boldest on 'em kissed me short and not at all satisfactory; for all the world as if they thought they was doing me a service, and not themselves an honor. They'll find me rayther different when I get back, I calculate; so they'd better practice a little afore I come among 'em.

Now in England kissing is mighty hearty. The gals aren't a bit ashamed on it. I shall say no more here about the maids-of-honor as kissed me a million times in the palace, but speak of the 'Gyptian Hall, where I was kissed four thousand times a day, which is only allowing eight kisses a piece for every female: some on 'em took more–some less, but I'm striking the averages. I had when I first showed here, tarnation pretty dimples; and in a month, my cheeks was as smooth as an apple. The dimples was kissed out; run away with the lips of the ladies. I often said to Barnum, "Governor, this is by no means the Cheshire. I feel my face is wasting away with so much kissing; melting slick like a sugar-plum in a baby's mouth. Tell you what it is; if I'm to lose my cheeks, I ought to be making something by 'em. Therefore, it is my opinion that you should alter the price, in this way. 'Them as only looks, a shilling; them as kisses, eighteen pence.'" Once or twice–for to be kissed eight different ways by five hundred females is tarnation hard work–one or twice, I thought I'd have a notice writ, and hung about my neck; sich a one as I seed at a flower show, with these words–"Admire, but touch not." I confess it: now and then I used to be riled; used to say to myself, "Have you nobody at home to kiss; that you will put your bonnets and patterns to come and kiss a little gentleman in public?" But as I said afore; take the people altogether, English kissing is mighty pleasant. . . .

PAWTUCKET (RHODE ISLAND) GAZETTE AND CHRONICLE, MARCH 5, 1847

Tom Thumb–The little "general"–the most remarkable specimen of infinitissimal humanity that has ever traversed the Old or the New World, came home in the steamship Cambria. He has appeared, says a Liverpool paper, before more crowned heads than any person living *in the exhibition line!* The same paper in summing up his mental and pecuniary profits makes the following statements: "He has been absent from America between three and four years, and weighs no more now than the day he left his native shore; but his intellectual faculties have improved immensely. He speaks French fluently–plays the piano–is learning the violin and other instruments. He played in a French piece in Paris; has played Hop o' my Thumb and Bombastes Furioso, with great *eclat,* in London and elsewhere. He has received many valuable presents from the principal sovereigns of Europe; has kissed more than a million and a half of ladies; has exhibited before 3,000,000 of persons, and the gross receipts of his exhibitions, including his theatrical performances, and his private levees at various palaces, and at the houses of the nobility of England, France, Spain, &, exceed £ 150,000. . . .

"GOSSIP OF THE MONTH," *UNITED STATES DEMOCRATIC REVIEW*, APRIL 1847

General Tom Thumb, the traveled Thumb, having been announced by the newspapers, and by graceful though immodest sketches of himself upon the walls, that he received at the American Museum, we hastened to pay our quarter and our respects to the remarkable being who had been visited by all England and France, feted by nobility, fondled and kissed by princesses and queens; after passing in review of Barnum's curious glass cases, where the five-legged calf vies with the razor with which Thomas Nokes "slit his wife's weasand," we reached a long, low platform–or rather, we reached three hundred women, of all descriptions, from the Fifth Avenue down to Orange-street, pressing upon a long, low platform, which upheld a miniature rostrum, containing a Lilliputian sofa and infinitesimal chairs. Presently a shrill, elf-scream rang through the room: "How do you *do,* la*dies* and gen-*tel*-men?" This came from Thumb, who, attired in irreproachable black, was borne in by his faithful and fortunate Barnum. We had seen this minimum exponent of humanity before his triumphs abroad, and remembered him as a hydrocephalus infant, dressed in coat and trousers. His present appearance is not prepossessing; the head is too large for the body, and the features puffy, without much expression. In fact, the General looks like a preparation withdrawn from its antiseptic alcohol, costumed and galvanized. Having mounted the rostrum, Mr. Thumb waved and kissed both hands to the public, and addressed them with "Yankee Doodle." But at this moment all the mothers, like so many opossums[,] produced innumerable youngsters hitherto invisible, and elevated them upon the platform, effectually shutting out both sight and sound of his Littleness. The other females, if less parturient, were equally anxious to see the show, and became so unruly that the General was obliged to adjourn to the theater. Here he underwent several contortions, which Barnum called dancing, and gave utterances to fife-like noises, which Barnum informed us were French songs. And this, we thought, as we scrambled down stairs to the street, this is the mannikin who has commanded more attention from the transatlantic Great and Small, than any full-grown man or properly-developed General has ever received, or can ever expect to receive. Wonderful little fellow! Who would have thought it? How true the old proverb: "One can never tell by looking at a toad how far he will jump!"

TAIT'S EDINBURGH MAGAZINE 22 (1855)

We now come to the grandest of all the impostures of this genius of delusion and deceit–which, as it was the most outrageously impudent and mendacious, was also the most profitable.[8] It was at Bridgeport, Albany, and in the year 1842, that Barnum fell in with a babe not five years of age and under two feet in height, the son of a Mr. Stratton, resident in that town. We are not under the necessity of recounting the history of the notorious fraud practised upon the people of America, of England and of the Continent, by means of this unfortunate infant. All the world knows by this time of day, that in this as in all previous emergencies Barnum lied audaciously–that he more than doubled the age of the infant in order to transform a baby into a dwarf–that by dint of constant drilling he got the pot-bellied little brat to assume the airs and consequence of manhood–that having showed him off in New York for a month, he started with him for England, where bringing him first, "by way of advertisement," upon the stage of the Princess's Theater, he played off his humbug among the ranks of the nobility; by dint of bribery and intrigue succeeded in forcing his way into Buckingham Palace, where in the presence of the Queen, her family and her court, he abused the royal ear by lies and for ever lies, which he had not even the condescension to transmit through the usual courtly medium of the Lord-in-Waiting, but bounced to Her Majesty face to face–that having thus secured the patronage of the highest personage in the realm, he opened the Egyptian Hall to receive the golden shower which he knew, judging from the influence of courtly example here, would inevitably follow. . . .

From London, backed by the *prestige* of queenly patronage in England, Barnum and his brat proceeded on a continental tour. Wherever they went the golden shower continued to fall upon their path, and after a successful foray they returned again to London by way of Brussels. The farce was now repeated in London and again in Scotland; and finally the party of impudent hoaxers returned to America in 1847. The Tom Thumb speculation proved to be a literal coinage of money. . . .

———————

ON THE AMERICAN MUSEUM "LECTURE ROOM"

NEW YORK TRIBUNE, JUNE 19, 1850

The opening of the American Museum, after being closed nine weeks, was the signal for a rush, which crowded the new hall to its utmost capacity. About three thousand persons were present, who witnessed the performance of the moral Drama of the Drunkard with repeated bursts of applause.[9] After the performance, Mr. Barnum was loudly called for, and responded to the call as follows:

Ladies and Gentlemen: I can scarcely command language to express my thanks for this unexpected compliment. I confess to you during a somewhat eventful life, this is the proudest moment I have yet experienced.

During the last nine years it has been my pleasure, on this spot, to cater for the amusement of this community, as well as the vast numbers of strangers from the country, who visit our great metropolis, and *here* is the place where permanent prosperity for the first time attended me. I feel, therefore, no small degree of pride and satisfaction in presenting you with this beautiful temple, on which Art has lavished all her powers, and it is you, my patrons, whom I may and do most sincerely thank for giving me the *ability* to erect a place of amusement, which all who have seen it acknowledge is an honor to our City, and to the refined taste and artistic skill of this country.

I trust that you will believe me, when I pledge my honor, that the thought of *gain* was but a *secondary* consideration with me in making the valuable improvements just completed in this establishment. I was doing well pecuniarily, and had been already blessed by fortune far beyond my expectations, and fully equal to my desires. Indeed, I had seriously thought of retiring from public life, and transferring my interests in all public exhibitions, to my valuable assistants; to whose integrity, energy, and good habits, I am indebted for much of my success; but knowing that amusements and relaxation from the business and cares of life are absolutely required and will be had, in every civilized land, I felt that this community needed and demanded at least more place of amusement where we might take our children, and secure much rational enjoyment, as well as valuable instruction, without the risk of imbibing moral poisons in the chalice presented to our lips.

This reflection induced me to take the necessary steps for erecting and perfecting what is acknowledged to be the most beautiful, commodious, comfortable, and best contrived Saloon in this country, and I verily believe in the world, and so long as a discerning public shall prefer pure enjoyments, pleasing exhibitions, and wholesome specimens of Comedy and Drama, upholding virtue, portraying its beautiful and certainly happy consequences, and as vividly painting the positive and inevitable evil consequences of vice, in whatsoever form—just so long during the continuance of my life and health, will I cater for public gratification; but, unless, some unforeseen calamity overtakes me, I pledge myself to withdraw into private life, if ever the moment arrives that the great mass of citizens prefer immoral and vicious, to moral and reformatory entertainments. But I know the American public too well to fear any such result. I have studied too long, and too thoroughly, the habits and tastes of my countrymen and women, to mistake their wholesome instincts upon this subject.

I do not wish to be understood, in making these remarks, as reflecting in the slightest degree upon other places of public amusement. Their managers pursue, no doubt, the course that their particular views dictate, and it is not for me to challenge either their judgment or their policy. The Bee, we are told by naturalists, contrives to gather honey from even the most poisonous of Nature's productions. I conceive it possible, after a somewhat similar fashion, to distill for the great Public every species of popular drama, and present them all so completely divested of mental impurity,

{ 195 }

so perfectly racked off the lees of verbal pollution, that the most inexperienced may imbibe them without apprehension, and the most cautious prescribe them with a confident hope of intellectual advantage. It remains for *you* to say whether the effort to effect such a reform is not worthy of encouragement; it is for *you*, ladies and gentlemen, to decide whether or not I fall short in my endeavor thus felicitously to combine innocence with pleasure, rational amusement with a proper sense of virtue and morality.

his goals

BROOKLYN DAILY EAGLE,
SEPTEMBER 11, 1850

American Museum—This place of amusement was last night crowded from pit to dome with an assemblage of beauty and fashion. We were altogether unprepared for a sight so brilliant. The ladies in point of number predominated three to one. The moral drama of the Drunkard was admirably performed, and presented a fearful picture of the inebriate's course. The tendency of such representations cannot but be productive of beneficial effects, not only on the young, but on the practiced Bacchanalian. The mass of the public journals sneer at the idea of teaching virtue through such a medium as that of a museum theater, but for our own part, so that the good result is attained, we do not object to the means employed, even though it be a Spartan one. . . . *art form as a way of teaching lessons*

ON JENNY LIND

"JENNY LIND AT THE CASTLE AMPHITHEATER,"
INTERNATIONAL MAGAZINE OF LITERATURE,
***ART, AND SCIENCE,* OCTOBER 1, 1850**

The arrival of Jenny Lind is the most memorable event thus far in our musical history. The note of preparation had been sounding for half a year; her name, through all the country, had become a household word; and every incident in her life, and every judgment of her capacities, had been made familiar, by the admirable tactician who had hazarded so much of his fortune in her engagement. The general interest was increased by the accounts of the chief foreign journals of her triumphal progress through England, and when at length she reached New York, her reception resembled the ovations that are offered to heroes. Her first concert was given at the Castle Amphitheater, on the 11th September, to the largest audience ever assembled for any such occasion in America. There was an apprehension among the more judicious that the performances would fall below the common expectations; but the most sanguine were surprised by the completeness of her triumph. She surpassed all that they had ever heard, or dreamed, or imagined. It was, as the *Christian Inquirer* happily observes, as if all the birds of Eden had melted their voices into one, to rise in gushing song upon the streaming light to salute the sun. Her later concerts have increased rather than diminished the enthusiasm produced by her first appearance. Mlle. Lind is accompanied by M. Benedict, the well known composer, and by Signor Belletti, whose voice is the finest *baritone* probably ever heard in New York, and whose style is described by the *Albion* as "near perfection." The orchestral arrangements for her concerts have never been surpassed here. Many were deterred from being present at her first appearance by a fear of crowds and tumults, but so perfect were Mr. Barnum's appointments that all the vast assemblies at the Castle have been as orderly as the most quiet evening parties in private houses.

The personal interest in Mlle. Lind is almost as great as the interest in the singer. Her charities in New York have already reached more than $15,000, and it is understood that all the profits of her engagement in America, not thus dispensed here, are appropriated by her for the establishment of free schools in Sweden.

Mlle. Lind has given to the Fire Department Fund, $3,000; Musical Fund Society, $2,000; Home for the Friendless, Society for the Relief of Indigent Females, Dramatic Fund Association, Home for Colored and Aged Persons, Colored and Orphan Association, Lying-in Asylum for Destitute Females, New York Orphan Asylum, Protestant Half-Orphan Asylum, Roman Catholic Half-Orphan Asylum, and Old Ladies' Asylum, each $500. Total, $10,000. The lives of Mr. Barnum, Jenny Lind, M. Benedict, and Signor Belletti, with all the details of the concerts, have been issued in a pamphlet displaying the usual typographical richness and elegance of Van Norden & Leslie, Fulton-street.

NEW YORK DAILY TRIBUNE,
SEPTEMBER 14, 1850

JENNY LIND'S SECOND CONCERT AT CASTLE GARDEN—Jenny Lind has already won a hold on the American public, such as no other vocalist ever obtained. She will do more—she will keep it. Her second Concert last night was in every respect as complete a triumph as the first. Leaving out the glorious welcome with which she was received, and which could not be repeated, the applause awarded to her was as warm, as heartfelt and as tumultuous as it was possible to give. The audience for which she sang was the greatest ever assembled at a Concert in this city. It numbered upward of *seven thousand,* filling the vast amphitheater to the topmost circles of the gallery. The sight of that dense sea of heads, from either extremity of the balcony, reminded us of one of Martin's grand, gloomy pictures, and the resemblance was further increased by the semi-oriental appearance of the Hall, with its long, light pillars dropping from the center, as well as by the dimness of the illumination, the lamps, many and bright as they were, being lost in the immense area of the building.

The audience did not gather so early by an hour as on Wednesday night, the admirable arrangements outside and inside obviating the necessity of taking the seats two hours in advance. The crowd about the outer gate was very small, and no disturbance of any kind occurred. Carriages did not enter the Battery grounds, as on the former occasion, and much trouble was avoided in consequence. Inside, there was quite a rush to take possession of the forfeited seats, when 8 o'clock arrived. The movement was too soon, however, and a number who arrived two or three minutes before the hour, claimed their places. One of the ushers then announced that holders of tickets would retain their right to the seats till the close of the first overture, and those who had taken them would be obliged to give way. But it was too late for that night. The plan is a good one, nevertheless, and should be adopted for succeeding concerts. . . .

In Jenny Lind, we still feel that it is not easy to separate the singer from the person. She sings herself. She does not, like many skillful vocalists, merely recite her musical studies, and dazzle you with splendid feats unnaturally acquired; her singing, through all her versatile range of parts and styles, is her own spontaneous activity–integral, and whole. Her magnificent voice, always true and firm, and as far beyond any instrument as humanity is beyond nature, seems like the audible beauty of her nature and her character. That she is an artist in the highest sense is a question long settled, and any little incidental variation from the bold and perfect outline of success in any special effort, as the faltering of her voice from natural embarrassment in the commencing of *Casta Diva* that first night, could not to a true listener at all impede the recognition of the wonderful art which could afford a little humanity on so trying an occasion. For she was as it were beginning her career anew; literally to her was this a new world; and she felt for a moment as if in her first blushing maidenhood of song. This second time the hesitation of the voice in that commencement was not felt. The note began soft and timid and scarce audible, as the prayer of Norma might have done; but how it gradually swelled with the influx of divine strength into the soul. . . .

BOSTON EVENING TRANSCRIPT,
SEPTEMBER 28, 1850

Notwithstanding the rain last evening and the muddy conditions of the streets, every seat at the Tremont Temple was occupied before eight o'clock; and, thanks to the provident arrangements of Mr. Barnum, the audience went to their places without confusion or delay. In the front of the building there was an immense assemblage; and the police were obliged to keep the sidewalk clear by extending ropes which none but those having tickets were allowed to pass. The gas burners in front of the Tremont House were thrown into the shape of stars and presented a very ornamental appearance; while a brilliant Drummond light, set in a conspicuous place in the upper story of the Temple by Mr. Whipple, shed its strong rays through the mist.

The outside arrangements were as efficient as those of the interior; and great credit is due to the police for their firm and, at the same time, courteous discharge of their duties. We regret to say, however, that some "barren quantity of spectators," principally boys, in the early part of the concert disturbed it greatly by their incessant shoutings. We hope that this annoyance will not be repeated. A number of persons climbed by means of ladders to the windows, and there surreptitiously "snatched a fearful joy." We are sure that Jenny would have invited them in, if she could have done so consistently with her regard to the audience and to her engagement with Mr. Barnum.

Some twenty ushers were stationed on the steps of the hall and in the aisles to receive the audience and conduct them to their seats, to which the color of their tickets already afforded them a partial guidance. A few minutes before eight o'clock, a commotion among the ushers in the isle near us indicated that something extraordinary was about to happen. We heard one of them whisper something to another, who replied aloud, "Certainly!" and then exclaimed in a still louder tone of voice, "This way Mr. Dodge!" At once a very decided sensation was created in our neighborhood, and spread immediately throughout the entire audience. Ladies rose on all sides and lifted their opera glasses. A buzz of curiosity, followed by applause from the gentlemen, succeeded. In the midst of it all, a modest looking gentleman, with quite an intellectual cast of features, made his way politely to his seat, where he stood a moment bowing to the audience, and then took his seat amid reiterated applause. This was Mr. Dodge, the comic vocalist, who bought the $625 ticket, and, as he placed his hand on his heart, his smile seemed to say, "Ladies and gentlemen, this is the proudest moment of my life!"

TIMES OF LONDON, OCTOBER 31, 1850

It is the boast of the modern Republic that the public opinion of her free and enlightened citizens reigns with undisputed and absolute sway. Eschewing the enormous faith of many made for one, she has adopted for herself the creed that the few are made for the many. On every subject, in every township throughout the States, the opinion of the majority is final, conclusive, and indisputable. . . .

Any one impressed with these reflections must have perused with a painful interest the accounts which have from time to time appeared in this journal of the

Lindomania in New York. It is humiliating to see a nation which boasts that it leads the van of human improvement so little capable of appreciating the relative dignity and merit of human talents and employments as to bow down in prostrate adoration at the feet of a woman who, after all, is merely a first-rate vocalist. . . .

But what is stranger still than this moral obliquity is, that the possession of this much-prized faculty by Jenny Lind was entirely taken for granted by this acute and calculating people, who were so enraptured by her musical powers before they had heard a single note of her voice that we verily believe if at her first concert she had croaked like a raven or howled like a hyena, public opinion would have pronounced her performance a little superior to the music of the spheres. We were totally unable to account for this palpable surrender to all common sense on the part of the American public till we fell in with an article in the *New York Herald*, in which that journal, justly solicitous for the dignity of its calling, vindicates the American press from the charge of having excited the American public to so outrageous a pitch of folly and self-abasement. It appears from the article of our able contemporary, which bears on its face the stamp of truth, that Mr. Barnum, the great showman of the age, the exhibitor of the living skeleton, General Tom Thumb, the woolly horse, and the nurse of General Washington, had struck out, for the express benefit of Jenny Lind and himself, a new idea which the blacking of Warren and the waistcoats of Moses have never inspired their poets withal. He invented what we must call for want of a better name the police of puffery. He had actually, for months before Jenny Lind's arrival, a number of provocative agents, as the French call them, in his pay, whose business was to "get up a *furore*" for Jenny Lind. This *furore* once excited, was chronicled by the newspapers, and thus infinitely multiplied, as heat and light are increased by being reflected. The whole susceptibility of the country was soon in a blaze, and long before Jenny Lind had placed her foot on the American continent, public opinion had pronounced in her favor, and she was peerless. . . .

GODEY'S LADY'S BOOK, NOVEMBER 1850, 312

THE age of music has come for America.[10] The national enthusiasm which has greeted and welcomed the sweet nightingale of Europe to our shores proves that our people have souls to appreciate the highest kind of this heavenly art, namely, vocal music. The perfection of this melody can only be reached by the female voice; hence we find another reason besides personal beauty why woman should be called angelic. Jenny Lind adds the third and holiest requisite to this claim on our hearts–excellence of character. She is a woman who brings honor to her sex and glory to humanity; so gifted and so good; so rich and so bounteous; seemingly so far removed from care and sorrow, and yet so ready to sympathize with the poor and the afflicted. The melody of her voice seems but the natural expression of her sweet, earnest desire to confer happiness on the world. And this is the secret of her great popularity. This deep swell of benevolent love for humanity (which her heart, by its overflowings in charity of deeds, as well as her lips, by kind words and pleasant smiles, testifies) brings home to almost every person the ideal hopes of making earth a paradise, which, at some time in our lives, we all cherish. "I'd sow the earth with flowers, had I the seed," is the spontaneous feeling of almost every heart; but few, probably, would fulfill these ideal fantasies were they entrusted with the power. Prosperity corrupts; success dazzles; the false is magnified by glitter and tumult, and those who are thus surrounded soon cease to search in the shade for humble merit, or listen for the still small voice of truth. But Jenny Lind has never suffered the love of the false to enter into her heart. Simple in her tastes, and true to the moral instincts of her woman's nature, she keeps her beautiful soul open to the influences that enkindle hope and strengthen genius. While her nature moves thus in harmony with the music of her voice, she must—she will draw the hearts of people to love and honor her more and more. Some complain of the enthusiasm created by her presence, and denounce it as folly or madness. We do not thus consider it. We are glad to see this warmth of popular sentiment manifested, when it is done towards a woman who merits the homage. Jenny Lind has received from Heaven one of the richest gifts of genius; she employs this gift nobly. We thank her for the lesson she reads to all gifted women, that virtue is their highest glory; we thank her for the example she gives to our daughters, that the highest genius can be simple and natural as a village school-girl; we thank her for the sweet pleasure, without meretricious arts, which she confers on the guardians of our country's weal, and on the youth who are our country's hope. May her progress through our land be to her as pleasant as the tones of her sweet voice in the song are to all who hear them!

CINCINNATI DAILY ENQUIRER, APRIL 16, 1851

At an early hour on Monday evening, a large crowd of outsiders, those who had not the means of purchasing tickets but yet were possessed of the desire to see the delightful songstress, gathered around the [National] Theater, and watched each carriage as it drew up, and as its occupants stepped out there would arise a shout that "made the welkin ring." At length came a splendid vehicle out of which alighted a single lady and gentleman. Hurrah for Jenny Lind, was then shouted again and again, the crowd forming around the pair so as almost to prevent their progress to the entrance of the house. One of the officers of the night succeeded in convincing them that it was not Jenny but only a visitor at the concert. Off they went again to await the arrival of other carriages, determined if possible, to have a sight at the woman who had gained all hearts. She had, however, arrived two hours before, and the crowd, disappointed, actually proceeded to commit acts, we regret to say, that would disgrace the greatest blackguards of any community.

They scaled the fences on Third street and climbed upon the houses adjoining the Theater, and went so far as to attempt the opening of the blinds to the windows of the Theater, but they were compelled desist by the interference of the police. Even brickbats were thrown at the windows, and pistols fired, which considerably frightened the fascinating cantatrice as a matter of course. Under these circumstances Jenny Lind must form rather an humble estimate of the character of a portion of our citizens, the portion which all good people look upon as the rabble only—the same that migrates from the cities of the South.

Such scenes should be deprecated, and we lift our voice against them as strong as anybody can, and we hope they will not be re-enacted. For shame sake they should not; but if there are any who still wish to continue in their blackguard tricks, it is to be hoped that Marshal Ruffin and his posse will succeed in arresting and imposing upon them their just desserts.

**WALT WHITMAN, *NEW YORK EVENING POST*,
AUGUST 14, 1851**

The Swedish Swan, with all her blandishments, never touched my heart in the least. I wondered at so much vocal dexterity; and indeed they were all very pretty, those leaps and double somersets. But even in the grandest religious airs, genuine masterpieces as they are, of the German composers, executed by this strangely overpraised woman in perfect scientific style, let critics say what they like, it was a failure; for there was a vacuum in the head of the performer. Beauty pervaded it no doubt, and that of a high order. It was the beauty of Adam before God breathed into his nostrils.

ON THE GRAND NATIONAL BABY SHOW

**"DIAPERS AND DIMPLES," *UNITED STATES
DEMOCRATIC REVIEW*, APRIL 1855**

This is the age of novelties—of the prostration of old ideas—of the introduction of new, and the development of physical as well as moral progress. Of all the nations of the earth, this country claims to take the lead in pioneering out the march of intellect; and, as an humble fugleman to the grand advance, we propose to ourselves to indite a prose paean in honor of and to commemorate the last decisive stage at which the progress of humanity has arrived. . . .

[W]e speak of babydom in general, and of Barnum's baby-show in particular. It is the latest, the greatest, the wildest, the mildest, and likely to be the most successful of all Phinny Feegee's exploits. If not absolutely a new thing under the sun, it is, at least, a novelty in this civilized metropolis; and we know that many interested mothers, and many who are as yet only interesting, look forward to it with the most unbounded hope. Their bosoms swell as they think of the pride a certificate for the fattest baby would give them, and their "needles, once a shining store," are now more assiduous than ever in the making of microscopic shirts and Lilliputian linen night-caps. . . .

Often as Barnum has outraged decency and patriotism–played, as he has, with our veneration for our country's father by the dwindling representation of a filthy and decrepit negress, lied, as he has, about the woolly horse, which Colonel Freemont never DID catch among the Rocky Mountains–forged, as he has, the horrible abortion of a mermaid, and vouched it by perjurious witnesses, traduced us, as he has, in that thing he calls a book, whose aim and object is to elevate his own peddling cuteness at the expense of the common sense of our national character–this Baby-show we do not hesitate to denounce as the meanest, vilest, most degraded and degrading of all his dollar-getting schemes. Let him be successful in this, and we shall soon have the exhibition of wives, of husbands, of brawny sinews and finely rounded limbs! Where dollars can be made, what cares the chucking panderer to human gullibility. . . .

LETTER TO THE *NEW YORK TRIBUNE*, MAY 2, 1855

SIR: Rejoicing in the fact that our patriotic and enterprising fellow citizen, Mr. Barnum, is approaching, by his unmitigated zeal and indefatigable industry, to the full fruition of a scheme for the promoting of a proper spirit of emulation, among the baby producing matrons of this "land of the free and home of the brave." I say, Sir, that it is rejoicing in this philanthropic offspring of Mr. B's imagination, that I now address a line to him through the columns of your respected paper, hoping that a cloud of gloom that has hovered over the frost work of bliss, may be wafted away, and that we may look forward to the sunny days of the baby-show, as to a scene of unalloyed enjoyment and boundless edification. I wish to inquire whether, on this coming contest between the infantile members of the community, those to whom nature has given a dark exterior will be admitted to the arena, as combatants for the proffered rewards of merit. Resting in the disinterestedness of my esteemed friend, I trust that as my inquiry was advanced sincerely, it will merit a passing notice and elicit that shall cause solid satisfaction to take the place of doubt. I pause for a reply.
New York, May 1, 1855
WALLACE

*The above is a pertinent inquiry. We believe, however, that the advertisement of the Baby Show does not specify any particular complexion or requisite in the infant prodigies. That being the case Negro babies and mothers, complying with the conditions of entrance, will certainly be entitled to compete for the premiums.–ED.

LETTER TO THE *NEW YORK TRIBUNE*, MAY 4, 1855

Sir: When I first announced that I would distribute eleven hundred dollars in premiums at the Baby Show to be held in my Museum from the 5th to the 8th of June next, you expressed some disapprobation of the scheme, and seemed to doubt its success. I replied that I believed the Exhibition to be a legitimate thing, and that it would present one of the most agreeable and interesting scenes ever witnessed in this country. I added my conviction that one hundred of the finest babies in America would be presented for competition on that occasion. I now assure you that fifty-one certificates have already been issued; and as these include the certificates for twins, triplets, and one quatern, the number at this moment engaged may be said to exceed sixty. Hence the strong probability that the full number of "one hundred cradles" will be occupied during the event in question.

But I find an article in your journal this morning, purporting to emanate from an anonymous correspondent, and derisively asking me if colored children are to participate in this exhibition. To the communication is appended an editorial remark to the effect that such may be the case. Now, lest some person, unaccustomed to the discovery of jokes in the Tribune, might misapprehend the facts in the case, allow me to admit that when the public sanctions without exception the promiscuous assemblage and close companionship of black and white, in churches, schools, theaters, courts of justice, railroad cars, Italian Opera houses, editorial sanctums, and printing offices, as well as among bank directors, merchants on change, and in the social circle, I shall not be found backward in pronouncing your correspondent's inquiry "pertinent" and answering it accordingly. As society is as present constituted, however, and as it seems likely to remain during our day and generation, I regard his question as *im*-pertinent, and merely state that I shall manage the Baby Show, as I manage all other enterprises in which I engage, with a respectful deference for the social usages of the community I seek to please.

Permit me to add in conclusion that after exhibiting (as I certainly shall in June next) from sixty to one hundred of the finest white babies on the continent, I shall have no objection to offer the same amount of cash premiums for a similar exhibition of the finest colored ones, providing your anxious correspondent will guarantee, under good security, that an equal number will be brought into the competition, at

such a suitable places as I may select, as well as at such a time within six months
as I may designate.
Truly yours,
P. T. Barnum

*It really strikes us that Mr. Barnum's exclusion of "dark complected" babies and
matrons comes rather too late. The Courts have decided that colored persons have a
right to travel on public conveyances as well as whites; and why have they not equal
right to compete at a National Baby Show. Or can there be any truly National Baby
Show from which so large a part of the nation are excluded?–ED.

NEW YORK DAILY TIMES, JUNE 7, 1855

THE SECOND DAY.
Once before we have seen as great a crowd. It was when Bishop Hughes was
consecrated Archbishop–and St. Patrick's Cathedral was only large enough to hold
the little link end of the crowd that reached from the street, in through one door of
that Church and out the other. That was a great crowd, and from that day to this, we
are not cognizant of as great a one until that yesterday which pervaded, and rolled
up against, and squeezed in at, and was turned away from Barnum's. From 11 o'clock
until 3, the Museum was jammed full. The sidewalks were entirely blocked up. A sick
friend got into the omnibus at Trinity Church, and it took him just half an hour to
reach Astor House, so great was the crush and crowd in the street consequent upon
the rush to Barnum's. The flags stretched across the street did much, the picture of
the babies that is mounted over the entrance did more; but that perpetual crowd at
the door obliged every leisurely passer-by to stop and try his luck at forcing an entrance. The ticket office at the Museum was compulsorily closed at 1 P.M., the building
being full to repletion. For nearly one and a half hours afterward a constant throng
of ladies and gentlemen was flowing into the doorway and out, but none could be
admitted. Meanwhile a door had been opened on Ann-street, out of which flowed
perpetually such of the crowd as had arrived at the conclusion that it were better
to go than risk being squeezed to death. "Now," said a lady that evidently was fat in
the morning–"now I've seen the babies, and been standing for an hour, I want to see
Barnum, and then I'm ready to go back to old Kentuck."

But Barnum was not to be seen–in more than one place at a time. At the door he
was waving back the multitude that held back their quarters–"Back, back, gentlemen," said he, "it ain't no use a-tryin–you can't come in–the old Museum will burst
if I let in another one." . . .

NEW YORK HERALD, JUNE 10, 1855

The show was open yesterday at the Museum, but the attendance was not so good as before. The following conversation took place between a lady of this city and one of the exhibitors of fat babies at Barnum's show on Friday, on board one of the Brooklyn ferry boats:

LADY: That is a very fine fat baby you have, madam.

EXHIBITOR: Yes, ma'am, but fine and fat as it is, it was not sufficiently so to get a prize at Barnum's show.

LADY: Have you exhibited it there?

EXHIBITOR: Yes, ma'am, for two days.

LADY: Has it not been there to-day?

EXHIBITOR: No, indeed, my baby and myself have been in that hot furnace long enough, and she has got sick in consequence. That old humbug Barnum shall not make any more money with my assistance.

LADY: How did it happen that you did not get a premium?

EXHIBITOR: Had it not been for Mrs. Barnum my baby would have got a prize. She is far superior to any Mrs. Barnum ever had, or ever will have.

LADY: What were the arrangements for awarding the premiums?

EXHIBITOR: The babies and their mothers were all placed in a hot room, where a number of questions were put to us. Mrs. Barnum asked me what country I was from. That was none of her business, as my baby was born here in New York. What difference did it make if I come from Ireland? She asked me what kind of looking man my husband was, and I told she might go to him if she liked, and see for herself. Only for her I would have got a prize. She thought I was poor, because my child and myself were not dressed as fine as some who were there, and that is another reason why my baby was rejected. But I can tell Mrs. Barnum I am not as poor as she might think me. My husband owns four houses and lots up town.

LADY: Do you think your baby was surpassed by any that were there?

EXHIBITOR: No, ma'am. My baby was the finest in the exhibition; but Mrs. Barnum favored the doctors and the big bugs, and I was turned off.

LADY: That was too bad.

EXHIBITOR: Yes, ma'am, it was. And I can tell you, ma'am, that this baby show is the biggest humbug old Barnum ever got up.

(Exit, indignant)

FREDERICK DOUGLASS' PAPER, JUNE 15, 1855

Black Eyes Versus Blue–The baby who received the prize at Barnum's "baby show," we understand had, "black, lustrous eyes." Colored people, generally, have black eyes, the whites, blue. "Blue eyes" will, hereafter, probably, be at a discount. Nothing is stated about the complexion of the handsome and fortunate baby.

But as "black, lustrous eyes" are not a usual accompaniment of a fair complexion, we infer the color to be something bordering on that rich hue, for which some of "our people" are noted, a soft, delicate yellow.

"FROM OUR BOSTON CORRESPONDENT," *FREDERICK DOUGLASS' PAPER*, SEPTEMBER 28, 1855

Barnum's white baby show "came off" as advertised. The number of children competing for prizes was made up several days before the exhibition, and many "brats" were refused. It was successful so far as money and attendance goes. Barnum brags of its success and says that 103,000 persons visited the exhibition. It is generally believed that he cleared about twenty thousand dollars. A good week's work that but nothing extra for that humbug.

Bateman's colored baby show, was held at the same time as Barnum's, and it is generally believed that Barnum was at the bottom of it.[11] The colored babies looked well. Some 25,000 persons visited the exhibition, and he cleared about $5,000. At the close of the exhibition he gave a benefit for the mothers of the unsuccessful competitors for prizes, which must have amounted to the neat little sum of one or two dollars each,* for their trouble of sitting there a week dandling their babies and answering all kinds of questions that an inquiring visitor or an insulting loafer, chose to propound on them. WE saw more than one mother insulted. There were some curiosities there in the shape of "human natures" and "urchins" of all shades, from the pure virgin black, to the pale and lifeless color. We did not notice any mulatto colored children with dark mothers, though we saw some half dozen or more white mothers with colored children. As many as 8,000 marriageable white young ladies were at the exhibition, and we were surprised at the inexhaustible encomiums bestowed upon the mulattos. We shall see if this exhibition does not have a tendency to increase amalgamation. The exhibition was by no means popular among the colored people, though many very respectable colored persons visited it, and many took part in the exhibition, who would not be likely to take part in another. The whole affair was a farce played at the expense of the colored people. Bateman advertised to give away nine hundred and fifty dollars in premiums; instead of that he only gave away one hundred and ninety-six dollars. One of the judges, a very aristocratic lady who had the good fortune to have at least one colored relation, was very indignant at white women having colored children, and tried to exclude them from the prizes. An illegitimate child who was admitted by all to be deserving of the first prize was excluded because it never had a father. . . .

*Since writing the above, one of the victims of this humbugging affair told me that he only gave her fifty cents!

ON "WHAT IS IT?"

NEW YORK HERALD, FEBRUARY 28, 1860

"What is It?"—They have added to the list of curiosities at Barnum's Museum a most extraordinary freak of nature, consisting of a creature supposed to belong to the ourang outang species, but having all the appearance of a human being. It was said to have been captured in the interior of Africa, on the border of the river Gambia, by a party who were in search of the famous gorilla. It stands about four feet high, and it weighs some fifty pounds; its age cannot be correctly ascertained, but it is supposed to be over twenty years. The formation of its hands, arms and head are those of an ourang outang, but its movements are those of a human being. Those who are fond of looking at the freaks nature frequently indulges in, should stop in, and form for themselves an opinion as to, "What is It?" After viewing the creature above described, about which hangs a cloud of doubt and uncertainty, we turned into the "lecture room," where the "Octoroon" was being performed. This play having had the run of two of our theaters, has been taken up and placed upon the stage at Barnum's, where for the last four weeks it has attracted crowds. It is very well put upon the stage, and the acting is highly creditable to the managers. The novelty of the Museum appears never to wear off, and with its endless variety of strange things—its bears, seals, and lecture room—will always draw full houses, despite the hard times and the season of Lent, which affects nearly all places of amusement.

NEW YORK TRIBUNE, FEBRUARY 29, 1860

Barnum's Museum—The new curiosities that have just been added to the collection are well worthy of the attention of those interested in Natural History. They consist of a huge California Bear, weighing over 2,000 pounds, a Sea Lion, which on this occasion is not an ordinary Seal, and a nondescript, which has not as yet been named. The grizzly bear is truly a monster of the most formidable description, to conquer which, in fair fight, would be an exploit worthy of the hardest pioneer. The Sea Lion, is a black vicious looking monster, weighing about 700 pounds, with powerful jaws and teeth, which had better be avoided. The nondescript animal, is about three feet and a half high, and is as lively and playful as a kitten. It seems to be neither a deformed or imbecile negro, as some insist, nor yet a curious specimen of the ape species, but, if such a description can be comprehended, a sort of cross between the two. The brightness of its eye, and its intelligent responses to the words and motions of the person in charge, at once relieve it from the imputation of imbecility. It is a curiosity certainly, no matter what position in the scale of animal life may be allotted it by the Naturalists.

NEW YORK TIMES, MARCH 5, 1860

For some days past, all the brick piles in the City—which, by the way are neither few nor far between—have been postered with a pertinacious query, printed in extremely interrogative type and to the effect: "What is It?" The public [knew] by long experience that an answer would be vouchsafed in due time, and on Monday received light from Barnum's Museum. The proprietors of that establishment, it seems, have secured what they are pleased to term a nondescript—a bipedal creature, with traits of animalism that seem to confound it with the brutes, and hence—seeking knowledge—they demand from the philosophical, "What is It?" We are not, of course, vain enough to reply, but may state briefly and superficially that, to the eye, the nondescript bears a striking resemblance to a malformed African and a curious approximation to an ourang-outang. The exhibitors state that he was caught by a party of Gorilla hunters; that there were five in a tree; that three were captured and two escaped; that of the three but this solitary one remains—all of which sounds very probable, and if true, would indicate the existence of a new species. The little creature is sadly attenuated in body, and presents the cerebral peculiarities of an idiot. It is not at all vicious, although enjoying a distinguished reputation for ferocity. It seems indeed to be playful as a kitten. Singular facts about him—for he is obviously of the male species—are, that he can laugh with thorough heartiness, and occasionally mutter a few words of unintelligible gibberish. The "nondescript" is already enjoying the consideration of the public, and will prove a profitable addition to the many excellent items provided by the liberal management of the establishment.

FRANK LESLIE'S ILLUSTRATED NEWSPAPER,
MARCH 24, 1860

Barnum's Museum—The "irrepressible conflict" still rages in the Zoological world as to what the "What is It?" is. Some people think it has too much intelligence for a nigger, and not enough for a monkey. In addition to this *lusus naturae* there is a capital burlesque of a "Poor Young Man," and an inexhaustible collection of natural curiosities. Our friend Greenwood's Museum is their best place to pass an afternoon in all New York.

Barnum's Museum has been closed for repairs and "renovations," which it was much in need of. This novelty in the career of the Museum commenced on Saturday night, the 24th inst., on which occasion Barnum made his appearance on the stage, and announced that he had resumed his old position as proprietor of the establishment, "and although," said he, "there was a time when I felt as if Othello's occupation was gone, I am happy to say to you all tonight, that Richard is himself again!" The fact is, Barnum has never been as great a sufferer as the public were led to suspect from his clock speculation. He lost considerably by it, but he has saved a little out of the fire, and he has managed with consummate skill and energy to come forth again anything but a poor man. However, he is again at the head of affairs at the Museum, and the first act of the reign of the "King of Humbugs" is the imposing on the public credulity by the exhibition of a *lusus naturae* in the form of an idiot negro boy, as a species of "animal found in Africa, that forms the connecting link between the monkey tribe and the Negro." This last humbug is decidedly one of Barnum's best, as it is a plausible one. The individual who exhibits this mental and physical deformity, alludes to the fact of the critter's "having only recently learned to stand erect," whereas it is almost impossible for it to walk on all fours. Besides, it understands English remarkably well, and, when the keeper is not on the *qui vive*, indulges in many sly maneuvers that let in the light of the humbug terribly. In fact, the evidence of the falsity of the statements made in reference to its capture &c., is sufficient to expose the imposture at once to any person of common sense. The dramatic entertainments are far from being *bad*, except the orchestra which is very poor indeed. Hadaway remarked on Saturday evening that the Dramas had declined considerably; in fact, said he, even the Sensation Dramas don't draw, and we have to resort to Ourang Outangs and What Is Its to fill the house. We may look for some new humbug soon, for Barnum promised it when he said that Richard was himself again, which he would not do unless he could impose on the credulity of the dear people. The Museum will remain where it is for some time yet, unless it should tumble down some day like the Pemberton Mills.

ON THE VISIT OF THE PRINCE OF WALES
TO THE AMERICAN MUSEUM

NEW YORK MERCURY, DECEMBER 8, 1860

A comparison of our places of public amusement in New York with those of London, shows a large balance in our favor, and seems to indicate that with all our proverbial haste to be rich, and slavish devotion to business, we are far more liberal in our patronage of artistic and healthful public entertainments than our boastful British cousins. Of the many theaters in London, only the Adelphi and Haymarket are doing well, and even those owe their prosperity to what we may term American influences. The Boucicaults are the cynosures of the former, while at the latter, our friend, John Brougham, has been earning golden opinions and receipts.

On the other hand, four of our New York temples of the drama are making fortunes for their managers, while the Museum, with its drama and curiosities combined, is fairly eclipsing its palmiest precedents. And it is of the Museum that we would speak principally, for we consider it one of the great specialties of the city and worthy of particular attention, as a result of most salient characteristics as a nation. Its fame is patent to the world, and despite the spirit of envy and spleen that would perpetually connect the odor of humbug with the name of Barnum, there is not an operatic director, a theatrical manager, or a public caterer of any description in this country, so widely or favorably known abroad as the great showman. The Museum was the only place of amusement in America voluntarily visited by the Prince of Wales during his late visit to our shores, and the cordial manner in which he inquired after Mr. Barnum—who was absent at the time—proved that royalty, at least, can appreciate the sterling abilities of a representative man in a representative nation. It is not our present purpose, however, to indulge in a eulogy on Mr. Barnum; but rather to notice some of the more quaint and curious things peculiar to this famous conservatory of curiosities.

The celebrated and mysterious Aztec Children may take the first rank among the latter, as the most remarkable phenomena of the age. Emperors, presidents, kings, queens, and *savants* of all degrees have visited these strange little creatures at various times; and the late Baron Von Humboldt made them a subject of profound study and research; but still they are an unsolved enigma of Nature, and we only know them as "the Aztecs." Next we have the waggish and irrepressible specimen of dubious creation known as the "What Is It," whose humiliating likeness to mankind has led certain muddled philosophers to insinuate that he is an idiotic negro. Only a single glance from the bright and very intelligent eyes of the creature is necessary to disprove this absurd guess, while it adds to our bewilderment when we would trace a brute genealogy for him. Following this nondescript are a number of rare animals, monster serpents, the "Happy Family," or cats, rats, dogs, rabbits, birds, monkeys, etc.; all living together in domestic bliss; that most instructive and beautiful of all new pleasures–the Aquaria; and two millions of strange and curious things from all parts of the habitable globe. Nearly every vessel that arrives from foreign lands brings additions to this countless store of wonders; and should the Museum be destroyed by fire, the world would never again see such a concentration of the wonderful, the grotesque, and the indescribable.

In its dramatic department, the Museum has achieved one of the greatest theatrical successes ever known in this country. The singularly picturesque play of "Joseph and His Brethren" enjoyed over one hundred successive presentations there, and the drama now in progress bids fair to have a great run.

Taken altogether, in fact, the Museum may be regarded as the most successful place of amusement in the world; and it is in view of this fact that we have here given it such special attention. Year after year, from the first of January to the last of December, day and night, its doors stand open to the public, and "no such word as fail" is to be found in its venerable records.

⟶➤●◄⟵

ON THE FIRE AT BARNUM'S FIRST AMERICAN MUSEUM

NEW YORK TIMES, JULY 14, 1865

The fire which yesterday destroyed Barnum's American Museum, while greatly injuring and materially impoverishing its enterprising and public-spirited proprietor, did a damage to this and the adjacent communities, which neither time nor money can replace. Granting the innumerable sensations with which the intelligent public were disgusted and the innocent public deluded, and the ever patent humbuggery with which the adroit manager coddled and cajoled a credulous people, the Museum still deserved an honorable place in the front rank of the rare and curious collections of the world.

Beside it, there was none in this country worthy of the name. Boston and Philadelphia, Baltimore, New Orleans, and some one of the western cities have buildings called "museums," but their features are rather the theatrical attractions than the curiosities on their shelves. A better geological cabinet than the one which Mr. Barnum had, by patient and consecutive exertion gathered, we have never seen; so far as the peculiarities of this continent are concerned, a faithful and singularly detailed representation was made, while from every quarter of the earth his agents had sent or brought material interesting to the amateur and most valuable to the cultured man of science. Collectors in the interest of colleges, men monomaniacally inclined in speciarities dreaded the competition of the museum at auction or private sales, for wherever and whenever money could secure the curious or rare, there and then they were certain of defeat. We believe we are correct in stating that no public institution in the country pretended even to rival the geological collection of the museum either in extent or value.

The conchological and ornithological departments were likewise extended in range, infinite in variety, and full of interest. Those of our citizens who thronged to the Lecture-room of the Museum to the neglect of the well-filled shelves in the many rooms, knew nothing of the capacities of the place for instruction and genuine edification. Birds of rarest plumage, fish of most exquisite tint, animals peculiar to every section, minerals characteristic of every region, and peculiarities of all portions of the earth, costly, beautiful, curious and strange, were crowded on the dusty shelves of room after room, where they attracted the earnest attention and studious regard of the scholar and the connoisseur.

All this has gone.

Almost in the twinkling of an eye, the dirty, ill-shaped structure, filled with specimens so full of suggestion and of merit, passed from our gaze, and its like cannot soon be seen again. Considering that for many years the Museum has been a landmark of the city; has afforded us in childhood the fullest vision of the wonderful and miraculous; has opened to us the secrets of the earth, and revealed to us the mysteries of the past; has preserved intact relics of days and ages long since gone, and carefully saved from the ravages of time and gnawing tooth of decay the garments and utensils of men of note long since moldered, and afforded men of learning and of science opportunities for investigation and research, which their limited means and cramped resources relentlessly refused them, we deem it but right to the public, but meager justice to the hard-earned success of Mr. Barnum, that we place on record a CATALOGUE OF THE CONTENTS of the building when at noon yesterday the fierce tooth of fire pierced and destroyed it. . . .[12]

NEW YORK TRIBUNE, JULY 14, 1865

The destruction of no public building in this city could have caused so much excitement and so much regret as that of Barnum's Museum. The collection of curiosities was very large, and though many of them may not have had much intrinsic or memorial value, a considerable portion was certainly of great worth for any Museum. But aside from this, pleasant memories clustered about the place, which for so many years has been the chief resort for amusement to the common people who cannot afford to treat themselves to a night at the more expensive theaters, while to the children of the city Barnum's has been a fountain of delight, ever offering new attractions as captivating and as implicitly believed in as the Arabian Nights' Entertainments. Theater, Menagerie, and Museum, it amused, instructed and astonished. If its thousands and tens of thousands of annual visitors were bewildered sometimes by a Woolly Horse, a What is It? or a Mermaid, they found repose and certainty in a Giraffe, a Whale, or a Rhinoceros. If wax effigies of pirates and murderers made them shudder lest those dreadful figures should start out of their glass cases and repeat their horrid deeds, they were reassured by the mildest and most amiable of giants, and the fattest of mortal women, whose dead weight alone could crush all the wax figures into their original cakes. It was a source of unfailing interest to all country visitors, and New York to many of them was only the place that held Barnum's Museum. It was the first thing–often the only thing–they visited when they came among us, and nothing that could have been contrived out of our present resources, could have offered so many attractions unless some more ingenious showman had undertaken to rival Barnum's collection of waxen criminals by putting in a cage the live Boards of the Common Council. We mourn its loss, but not as without consolation. Barnum's Museum is gone, but Barnum himself, happily, did not share the fate of the rattlesnakes and his at last most unhappy Family. There are fishes in the seas and beasts in the forests; birds still fly in the air and strange creatures still roam in the deserts; giants and pigmies still wander up and down the earth; the oldest man, the fattest woman and smallest baby are still living, and Barnum will find them. Or even if none of these things or creatures existed, we could trust to Barnum to make them out of hand. The Museum, then, is only a temporary loss, and much as we sympathize with the proprietor, the public may trust to his well-known ability and energy to soon renew a place of amusement which was a source of so much innocent pleasure, and had in it so many elements of solid excellence. . . .

THE NATION, JULY 27, 1865

Barnum's Museum is gone at last. It has fallen before that conflagration with which it has often been threatened, and which it has more than once barely escaped. The children will miss an accustomed place of amusement for their Saturday vacations. The occasional visitors to the city from the "rural districts" will no longer yield to its irresistible attractions. The worst and most corrupt classes of our people must seek some new place of resort, and other opportunities of meeting each other. A most dangerous man-trap is removed, and without loss of human life. These four considerations make the sober citizen of New York hesitate whether to regret this burning and destruction or not.

But there is another consideration. Were the lovers of curiosities–whether of natural history or human ingenuity or historical association—the more pleased by the existence which are now destroyed, or more insulted by their insufficiency, disorder, neglected condition, and obviously secondary importance? It is one thing to love shells and minerals, and to enjoy collections of them, but quite another to enjoy *every* collection of them. The more truly one loves a good collection well arranged, the more he will be offended by a chaotic, dusty, dishonored collection. The more one loves the order and system of scientific enquiry, the more he will feel personally injured by disorder and lack of system among the minerals of scientific enquiry. The more one aspires to neatness, exactness, and care in his own private "cabinet," the more he will revolt at slovenliness in a larger and more public museum. And it is probable that no class of the community was less satisfied with the museum of Mr. Barnum than that class for which it would seem to have been originally intended.

This class is not an unimportant or even a small one. The host of readers whose favorite reading is natural science, the armies of listeners to lecturers on geology, that large portion of our boys and young men who collect and study "specimens" of minerals, all belong to it. The profoundly scientific are not those who care for public museums, unless containing this or that unique treasure. The frequenters of museums are those who cannot themselves give much time or means to the collection, classification, and study of specimens, but who read in the evenings, and would gladly see by day a larger number and a greater variety of helps to understand than their own limited time has sufficed to discover—than their own limited means have sufficed to procure. There are thousands of these amateur students, whose amateur studies are not to be despised even by the profounder scholar. These would visit the lost museum rarely, early in the morning when no disreputable crowd was thronging it, looking along the crammed and disordered shelves in the hope of lighting on something which they wished to see, finding it or not as the blind deities of chance might order. Without scientific arrangement, without a catalogue, without attendants, without even labels, in very many instances, the heterogeneous heap of "curiosities," valuable and worthless well mixed up together, could not attract our students very often or detain them long.

This class of visitors was never wholly ignored in the advertisements which announced to the world the charms of Barnum's Museum. The "million of curiosities" were mentioned, and their scientific value hinted at. These curiosities were never, so far as we are aware, turned out of the building to make room for fat women, giants, glass-blowers, mermaids, learned seals, and dog-shows. The *aquaria* had a certain attraction for the intelligent, and, in almost any other place, would have been worth frequent visits. Dog-shows in themselves are harmless and not without interest. We desire to give the late "American Museum" all the credit it deserves. For it needs it all. Its memory is not pleasant. It pandered to the most foolish curiosity and to the most morbid appetite for the marvelous. The most gross deceptions were shamelessly resorted to cause a week's wonder and to swell the week's receipts. The "Lecture Room"–once a sort of "lyceum hall," latterly a minor theater in look and character–furnished for the entertainment of its patrons the most vulgar sensation dramas of the day. Its patrons were suitably entertained. It has been many years since a citizen could take his wife or daughter to see a play on that stage.

That respectable people never went to this so-called museum we do not assert. There were hours in the day when the halls were nearly empty; and, where certain shells, stuffed birds, and Indian relics are, there is always something to see. But we hold that this class of students of whom we have spoken deserve better mental fare than this dreary refectory could afford.

It is in behalf of this class that we ask for a real museum. It is in behalf of all classes of the community, except that vicious and degraded one by which the late "American Museum" was largely monopolized, that we ask the community for a building and for collections that shall be worthy of the name so sadly misapplied. Μουσεῖον, *museum, musée;* the word seems full of honorable meaning in every language but our own, and with reason. Home of the Muses, it means, and is akin to "music" and "musing," and to "amusement," too, which is a good word with a good meaning. Collections of animals belong to it, indeed, both living and prepared, collections of minerals and shells, of historical and personal relics, and not only these, but collections representative of all the arts, both industrial and decorative, fine art and artisanship. All those valuable things which men do not consume but keep, (money, of course, as it has no value except to represent value, is not in itself a valuable thing, and it is not included in our statement) have a home in a museum. And "American," "The American Museum!" when that name is again written across the front of a building, let it be a building worthy in itself and in its contents of the honorable and responsible rank which, by taking that name, it assumes.

The British Museum is a national institution, founded and supported by the revenues and the government of an empire. The American Museum of the future will be such another, and even more worthily lodged. It would be good taste if all local institutions, whether belonging to individuals, to companies, to cities, or to States, would adopt names less inappropriate to their natures. But as long as we have American institutes of various kinds, and American companies of many sorts, all incorporated under State laws and limited in their spheres of action by State boundaries, such observance of fitness as we might desire we certainly cannot hope for. Let New York City, then, create for itself an "American Museum." And let the thing itself not be unworthy of the name it rashly assumes.

By the perseverance and the intelligence of some, aided by a series of happy accidents, New York obtained a park, which was put into the hands of good managers and ingenious and conscientious artists, and was carried on by them to such a point of *quasi* completion that it can hardly be spoiled now, and is likely to remain for ever, to cause posterity to doubt the truth of the future historian's account of misgov-ernment and corruption in New York in the nineteenth century. Let us try to make our descendants still more incredulous on this point. Let us have a place of public instruction as well as a place of public enjoyment. Perhaps in the neighborhood of the Central Park itself would be the best place for it; let us establish it there, and try to draw encouragement and a stimulus to exertion from our beautiful neighbor. . . .

There is talk of a joint stock company which proposes to have a museum and to pay a large profit in money to stockholders. It may be doubted whether a joint stock company can best do such work; whether the sum of three hundred thousand dol-lars is enough money to do it with; whether this particular enterprise, if successful, will give us what we want, or not rather another undertaking like Mr. Barnum's of yore, which Mr. Barnum himself, also in the field, will delve one yard below and blow to the moon—and then buy out. There is money enough to be had which will not seek pecuniary interest, intellect enough to be had, and experience enough to establish such a museum as we need, if only these three—money, intelligence, and experience—will come together and understand each other. Let New York beware lest Philadelphia and Boston should each step in before her and use the intelligence, experience, the opportunity, the well stocked markets, and some part of the money which she should secure. . . .

But of one thing let us be certain. No individual or stock company which may be undertaken to form and manage a museum as a way of making money will be of any great or permanent service to the community. Let those who are disposed to aid any of these movements remember this, that the efforts of an ingenious showman to attract popular attention and make money rapidly are not likely to accrue popular enlightenment. It would not seem well to such a showman to spend money, time, and thought to make valuable antiquarian and scientific collections, classify and cata-logue them accurately, and build a fitting and permanent building to contain them. Perhaps the British Museum, charging twenty-five cents admission fee, would take in less money in a year than did Mr. Barnum's old museum at the same price. Let the would-be stockholder invest his money in a proper enterprise, properly guarded, and take dividends for his reward. Of his abundance let him give to the foundation of a real museum for his own enlightenment, the good of his children, and the honor and benefit of the community.[13]

LONDON SATURDAY REVIEW, AUGUST 13, 1865

It is impossible to hear without a sigh of the destruction of Barnum's Museum. Many of the inestimable treasures collected by the proprietor had already passed into oblivion. The new wonders which still appealed to the curiosity of New York were mere remainder biscuits after the feast. They were to those great strokes of genius by which Barnum won his fame what *Paradise Regained* was to *Paradise Lost*, or what *Our Mutual Friend* is to *Pickwick.* The giantess who was nearly smothered in the flames may have had great intrinsic merits; but it is not the vulgar height or weight which makes the merit of a giantess, but the poetic halo of puffery with which her proprietor surrounds her. . . . The essential merit of Barnum was that he showed things utterly worthless in themselves. He is like a man who is proud of catching his fish by artificial flies, and who would never condescend to offer the substantial attractions of a worm. Any one can produce an impression by means of a real live ghost; it requires the skill of a genuine artist to make a ghost out of a turnip and an old sheet. The Feejee mermaid, which was in Barnum's earlier style, was intrinsically valueless; it was knocked together out of a few old fish skins and a stuffed monkey. In other hands, they would have remained mere raw material; in his they became a most excellent monster of the deep. So, too, Washington's nurse was a mere dirty old negro woman, such as may be found by hundreds in the United States; it was Barnum's special glory to appeal to patriotic sight-seers by that touch about Washington, and to make an old negress as attractive as Jenny Lind. The highest poetry is that which finds new meaning in the commonest things; and the true showman is the man whose wonders are the vilest objects invested with charming associations by the mere force of his imagination. . . .

ON BARNUM'S SECOND AMERICAN MUSEUM

SAMUEL CLEMENS (MARK TWAIN), *ALTA CALIFORNIA*, APRIL 9, 1867

Now that Barnum is running for Congress, anything connected with him is imbued with a new interest.[14] Therefore I went to his Museum yesterday, along with the other children. There is little or nothing in the place worth seeing, and yet how it draws! It is crammed with both sexes and all ages. One could keep going up stairs from floor to floor, and scarcely find room to turn. There are numerous trifling attractions there, but if there was one grand, absorbing feature, I failed to find it. There is a prodigious woman, eight feet high, and well proportioned, but there was no one to stir her up and make her show her points, so she sat down all the time. And there is a giant, also, just her own size; but he appeared to be sick with love for her, and so he sat morosely on his platform, in his astonishing military uniform, and wrought no wonders. If I was the impresario of that menagerie, I would make that couple prance around some, or I would dock their rations. Two dwarfs, unknown to fame, and a speckled negro, complete the list of human curiosities. They profess to have a Circassian girl there, but I could not find her. I think they have moved her out, to make room for another peanut stand. In fact, Barnum's Museum is one vast peanut stand now, with a few cases of dried frogs and other wonders scattered here and there, to give variety to the thing. You can't go anywhere without finding a peanut stand, and an impudent negro sweeping hulls. When peanuts and candy are slow, they sell newspapers and photographs of the dwarfs and giants.

There are some cages of ferocious lions, and other wild beasts, but they sleep all the time. And also an automaton card writer; but something about it is broken, and it don't go now. Also, a good many bugs, with pins stuck through them; but the people don't seem to enjoy the bugs any more. There is a photograph gallery in one room and an oyster saloon in another, and some news depots and soda fountains, a pistol gallery, and a raffling department for cheap jewelry, but not any barber shop. A plaster of Paris statue of Venus, with little stacks of dust on her nose and eyebrows, stands neglected in a corner, and in some large glass cases are some atrocious waxen images, done in the worst style of the art. Queen Victoria is dressed in faded red velvet and glass jewelry, and has a bloated countenance and a drunken leer in her eye, that remind one of convivial Mary Holt, when she used to come in from a spree to get her ticket for the County Jail. And that accursed eye-sore to me, Tom Thumb's wedding party, which airs its smirking imbecility in every photograph album in America, is not only set forth here in ghastly wax, but repeated. Why does not some philanthropist burn the Museum again? . . .

━━━━◆━━━━

ON BARNUM'S CIRCUSES AND JUMBO

NEW YORK DAILY STANDARD,
DECEMBER 28, 1871

Mr. P. T. Barnum is the only man in show business who thoroughly comprehends the demands of the public, and is willing to satisfy them at any expenditure of time and means. His projects are conceived on a gigantic scale, very far in advance of the conservatism so characteristic of even liberal managers. . . .

In the spring of 1871, when the great show was about to enter upon its first campaign, complete as it seemed to the manager and to other experts, Mr. Barnum thought a most valuable feature might be added. He telegraphed to the whaling ports of New England, and sent messages to San Francisco and Alaska, to know if a group of sea lions and other specimens of the phocine tribe could be secured. Finally, through his agents in San Francisco, he organized an expedition to Alaska. By the first of July, several fine specimens of seals and sea lions, some of the latter weighing more than

1,000 pounds each, were brought in tanks over the Union Pacific Railway, were safely landed in Bridgeport, and, thereafter, were forwarded to the show, then on its travels through New England. As these delicate animals are likely to die, arrangements have been made to keep good the supply, and December 16, 1871, Mr. Barnum received a telegram from San Francisco that six more sea lions had just arrived at the port for him. Two of these will be sent, by arrangement, to the Zoological Gardens, in Regent's Park, London, and the rest, with several seals captured in the same expedition, will be added to Barnum's show next spring.

Mr. Barnum's active and enterprising agents are in Europe, Asia, Africa, South America, and elsewhere in the world, wherever anything rare and valuable—bird, beast, reptile, or other animate or inanimate curiosity—can be secured, which will add to the interest of the exhibition. In the menagerie, and the hippodrome also, experts are constantly engaged in training elephants, camels, performing horses, and other animals, and are thus preparing new and attractive features, some of which will be as novel to the show profession as they will be new and attractive to the public.

"BARNUM ON THE TENTED FIELD," NEW YORK CLIPPER, JULY 6, 1872

With every spring commences a vigorous campaign in the tented field. In this instance the invading army is on a mission of peace and is heartily welcomed by the people who pay tribute to the stranger without a murmur. The march of a circus company with its host [of people] and the moving of baggage vans from town to town is similar to the progress of an army. No conqueror ever entered a city half so welcome or [was] greeted by so many smiling faces as the glittering pageant threads its way to the inspiring strains of martial music.

Adam Forepaugh made an innovation when he exhibited his aggregation under two tents for one price of admission, where those who had been brought up in a straight-lace school could contemplate the wonders of the animal kingdom without contaminating themselves with the tights and spangles of the arena.

When P. T. Barnum and manager Coup placed their Mastodon on the road, the jovial Dan Castello and his circus were given the principal tent, a second being used for the menagerie, and a third for a museum of living and inanimate curiosities.[15] The success of the great showman's latest venture was without parallel. The seating capacity of the tents was again increased and still found to be inadequate. Wherever they went, the populace turned out en masse and every train and by-road running into the cities added their contributions by the thousands. A greater portion of the season, three performances were given daily, causing the fat woman and the giant to lose flesh and the living skeleton, if possible, to grow thinner than ever.

Phineas was ubiquitous, "here, there, and everywhere," now ahead of the com-

pany, giving gratuitous lectures on "How to Make Money," not forgetting to always say a good word for the "greatest show on earth," to which he would hasten back to publicly present some employee with a gold badge, medal, or other valuable gift as a token of his regard and esteem, an extra attraction that would cram the three canvases to overflowing. . . .

NEW YORK TIMES, APRIL 28, 1874

Mr. Barnum's Great Roman Hippodrome was opened last night and was crowded by a truly Metropolitan audience of vast numbers. Every entrance to the building on Madison and Fourth avenues and Twenty-seventh street was rendered unapproachable by those persons who had not had the good fortune to arrive before 7:30 o'clock; all who had to purchase tickets managed, however, with few exceptions, to effect an entrance in time for the first feature of the entertainment, "The Great Congress of Nations," representing European and Eastern countries. But the holders of admissions bought in advance were obliged to invoke the aid of the Police to reach the building before 8 o'clock. This could only be done through the Fourth avenue doorway. Promptly at 8 o'clock the show began, the display of the pageant above named occupying more than an hour. Each addition thereto and change therein elicited hearty applause. But the features of this highly entertaining programme which appeared to afford the most gratification to the spectators were the flat race by six ladies on English thoroughbreds; a Roman chariot race between three ladies driving two horses each, and one between two driving four horses each; an exciting scene of lassooing Texas cattle, in which a Comanche Chief and three Mexicans participated; a flat race between six English horses ridden by English jockeys, and a hurdle race between six ladies on fast horses. There was such an air of reality about these contests, into which the riders entered with great spirit, that the audience soon shared the excitement, and rising to their feet towards the close of each race, shouted and acted as people do on the grand stands and quarter stretches of Monmouth and Jerome Parks at the Spring and Fall meetings. The contestants, though trained and experienced performers, ran considerable risk, especially in the chariot and hurdle races, on account of the restive dispositions of their steeds. Indeed, it was only by a tremendous effort and the exercise of great skill that Miss Mattie Lewis, in the two-horse chariot competition[,] succeeded in saving herself from injury by the threatened overthrow of her vehicle; in the hurdle race Miss Cateyrena was tossed violently from the bay mare she rode, and was unable to take part in any of the latter sports of the evening. The lassooing of the Texas cattle was a very savage scene, but although it was an exhibition of genuine skill and had its admirers, it seemed to be distasteful to a portion of the assemblage because of the rough usage of the poor steers at the hands of a *ranchero,* who rode down on one now and then, seized it by the tail, and dexterously rolled it over and over on the ground. A stag hunt, participated in by all of the riders and a pack of hounds, concluded the evening's amusements, which proceeded with marvelous smoothness for a first night.

APPLETON'S JOURNAL, JUNE 20, 1874

Mr. P. T. Barnum has recently opened a hippodrome. It is said to be the largest establishment of the kind in the world. In addition to the usual circus performances, there are chariot-races, steeple-chases, and races of other varieties, all of which are said to be genuine contests. Proof of this is given by the fact, in the eagerness of the struggle, the racers are often thrown or hurt. But there is better proof in the circumstance that young men resort to the place as to a horse-race, get intensely excited in watching the sport, and are as free in offering and taking bets as at Jerome Park or the Fashion Course. And, for all this, Mr. Barnum, according to one of our religious papers, "is entitled to the thanks of every Christian"; while another rejoices in "an amusement that is free from the vices that pertain to the theater!!"

NEW YORK TIMES, MAY 5, 1878

P. T. Barnum has had constructed, at a cost of $10,000, a railway vehicle, to be used as an "advertising coach," which is pronounced the most complete structure of the kind in existence. Yesterday afternoon this car departed from the New Jersey Southern Depot at Communipaw, for a trip through the New England States. The body of the coach is 62 feet in length, supported by a number of heavy springs, resting upon two six-wheeled tracks. The outside is gaily decorated with striking designs. Covering one entire side is a group representing the kingdom of wild animals. The opposite side is ornamented with a panoramic representation of the daily street procession preceding each exhibition.

LONDON TELEGRAPH, FEBRUARY 22, 1882

Jumbo's fate is sealed. The disappointing answer from his new American proprietor, which we published yesterday, proves too clearly that there is nothing to expect delicacy or remorse in that quarter. Moved by the universal emotion which the approaching departure of London's gigantic friend had aroused, we communicated with Mr. Barnum, indicating that "money was no object" if he would only listen to the entreaties of the English children, and let the Royal Zoological Council off their foolish bargain. The famous showman replied—as all the world now knows—in tones of polite but implacable decision. He has bought Jumbo, and Jumbo he means to have, nor would "a hundred thousand pounds" be any inducement to cancel the purchase. If innumerable children are grieving here over the loss of a creature so gentle, vast and sensible, "fifty millions of American citizens," Mr. Barnum says, are anxiously waiting to see the great elephant arrive in the States. Then, to increase the general regret, the message depicts the sort of life which poor Jumbo has before him. No more quiet garden strolls, no shady trees, green lawns, and flowery thickets, peopled with tropical beasts, bright birds, and snakes, making it all quite homely. Our amiable monster must dwell in a tent, take part in the routines of a circus, and, instead of his by-gone friendly trots with British girls and boys, and perpetual luncheon on buns and oranges, must amuse a Yankee mob, and put up with peanuts and waffles. Worse things even than all this are foreshadowed in the message. Mr. Barnum announces the intention of taking his "mammoth combination of seven shows" round the world, via California, Australia, and the Suez Canal. Elephants hate the sea. They love a quiet bath as much as any Christians; but the indignity and terror of being slung on board a ship and tossed about in the agony of sea-sickness, which is probably on a scale with the size of their stomachs, would appear to them worse than death. Yet to this doom the children's "dear old Jumbo" is condemned, and it is enough, if he knew of it, to precipitate that insanity which his guardians have pretended to fear. It is true Mr. Barnum holds out hopes that we may some day see again the colossal form of the public favorite. In the summer of 1883 he proposes to bring the good beast back to England, exhibiting him in "every prominent city"; and the message adds, "I may afterwards return Jumbo to his old position in the Royal Zoological Gardens." There is a gleam of consolation in this, which we would not darken by any remarks upon the great showman's ironclad inflexibility; but what will be the mental and physical condition of our immense friend when bereavement, seasickness, and American diet shall have ruined his temper and digestion, and abolished his self-respect? There will be a Yankee twang in his trumpeting; he will roll about on his "sea-legs," with a gait sadly changed from the substantial swing so well known, and Alice herself will hardly know him. . . .

NEW YORK TIMES, MARCH 25, 1883

There was more excitement in this City last than there would be in London if Queen Victoria's imperial knee was swelled to twice its royal size, and the cause of all the commotion was that the Barnum and London shows were to parade through the streets in all their variegated glory. At 7 o'clock the populace began to throng the streets along the lines of the March, and at 8, if anybody was at home, they were invalids, for, according to a hasty census, the 1,200,000 population of the City were in the streets, with the exception of about 208 individuals. Broadway was thronged from Forty-second street to Canal, and the crowd embraced all the heterogeneous elements of the City, and they occupied so much space that pedestrians were obliged to go around to side streets, while cars and stages had to have a passage forced for them by the Police. The "tone" of the crowd ranged from the Bowery tough and East Side villain to aristocrats and the nobility of Fifth avenue, who observed the parade from carriages, and were shocked when the rabble resorted to profanity to express the profundity of their admiration. There were ladies and gentlemen in the throng who anticipated the dawn of Easter in their attire; mechanics, with their wives, from the better class of the tenement districts; gilded youth in gorgeous raiment; pampered infants in charge of nurses and footmen; young women who came unattended and went home with young gentlemen; young gentlemen who ventured forth alone and came back not quite so much so; the inebriate of both sexes from the slums, children of all ages from the East Side, who ranged in villainy from toddling infants who were just learning to swear, to their bigger brothers and sisters, who were beginning to figure in the police courts. There were "crooks" of all descriptions and both sexes, and detectives and Police officers who were on the alert with watchful eyes and vigorous clubs.

Mr. P. T. Barnum, with several brother showmen and a number of grandchildren, reviewed the procession from a balcony of the Metropolitan Hotel. The hand of time was grasping the coat-tail of 8:30 when the vanguard of the great cavalcade approached this point. There was a sound of a hundred musical instruments–the psalter, the fife, the drum, the bassoon, the calliope, the hand-organ, the jews-harp, the viol, the French horn, the flute, the tin whistle, the harmonicom, the accordion, and every other instrument of torture known to science or religion, accompanied by a glare of electric light, blue, green, yellow, pink, red and purple fire, Roman candles, rockets, pinwheels, gunpowder, dynamite, nitroglycerine, and other explosives as the mighty procession loomed up in the dim distance. Nearer they came; louder sounded the music; more gloriously flared the pyrotechnics; more fiercely growled the lions; bass-profundo chorused the tigers; more merrily jogged the elephants; blithely bobbed the camels; grandly rolled the chariots, and the multitude burst into a roar of applause, which almost shook the City to its foundations, and caused the cobblestones to grind against each other in the streets. First a number of gorgeously caparisoned heralds mounted upon prancing steeds burst upon the vision, winding flashing trumpets; a gilded and glorious band wagon came next, and from the musical instruments "The Girl I Left Behind Me" pealed forth in inspiring strains; a quartet of beautiful women on horseback cavorted gaily after, followed by a score of mounted warriors in armor; wagons enclosing raging tigers, lions, hyenas, leopards, panthers, bears, and numerous other beasts next rolled by. Knights in armor, ladies in flashing tinsel and glittering spangles, the old woman who lived in a shoe, Santa

Claus and other allegorical figures burst upon the spectators. Wagons drawn by every species of quadruped from giraffes to zebras, racing elephants, chariots and horsemen, wheeled past in a blaze of fire and glory. Half an hour it took the gorgeous cavalcade to pass a given point. The wondering crowd closed in behind it and followed it to the bitter end. Then the enterprising burglar began again to burgle, the policemen and detectives cast their prisoners they had gathered into their respective dungeons, the respectable portion of the crowd went home, and the rest dispersed over the City.

WASHINGTON POST, APRIL 3, 1883

New York—An agent of the Society for the Prevention of the Cruelty to Children applied to a police magistrate this morning for a warrant for the arrest of Phineas T. Barnum, the showman, and his managers, James L. Hutchinson and J. A. Bailey, and James Elliott, the father of the Elliott children, on the ground that they had violated the provisions of section 292 of the penal code in permitting the Elliott children to perform feats during the exhibition that are calculated to injure them. The warrants were issued and made returnable this afternoon. It was stated that the children performed only on the bicycle, and their performances consisted only of riding it. In the correspondence that passed between President Gerry, of the society, and Mr. Barnum, the latter stated that he had been a showman long enough to know what was injurious to a child, and that he was human enough to prevent children injuring themselves.

P. T. Barnum, James L. Hutchinson, and James A. Bailey, the showmen, and James Elliott, father of the children, were later arrested. In the police court the defendants were held for trial in $300 bail each, Mr. Barnum becoming surety for all. Late in the afternoon the children gave a private exhibition before 400 guests, among them many physicians, Judges Brady and Gildersleeve, Assistant District Attorney O'Byrne and all the police justices. The physicians present united in declaring the performance harmless and healthful.[16]

LOS ANGELES TIMES, JUNE 8, 1883

Chicago—There was almost a panic at the afternoon performance of Barnum's circus. The place was packed with over 15,000 people. The grand entry was being made, when one of the elephants attached to a chariot became frightened, went bellowing around, and dashing into the procession, smashing one or two lighter chariots. To add to the confusion one of the lady charioteers abandoned her horses, and they went dashing around the ring. The wild beasts were frightened at the uproar and began bellowing and beating about their cages. The rest of the elephants became frightened and unmanageable. The vast audience, composed largely of women and children, was greatly terrified, rose upon the seats and those near the exit made a rush and the jam for a few moments was general. A panic seemed inevitable but continued playing by the band reassured the frightened multitudes somewhat, and the employees succeeded in getting the unruly animals out and restoring quiet. No one was seriously hurt.

NEW YORK TIMES, FEBRUARY 20, 1884

The controversy about Mr. Barnum's sacred white elephant—if it is sacred and white—promises at least to serve as an object lesson in natural history, if the controversy is ever decided.[17] A London newspaper correspondent calls the brute pink, and says it is no more white than an alligator. A gentleman who has just returned from Siam declares that it is the color of Jersey mud. The Siamese minister at the court of St. James's says there is no such thing as a white elephant, and the Rev. Wilbur F. Crafts told his congregation Sunday evening that Mr. Barnum is trying to palm off on an outraged community for a white one. In regard to the sanctity of the beast a Burmese gentleman residing in London writes that there are no religious rites performed in honor of the white elephant, and a scholar versed in the lore of Buddhism corroborates him. On the other hand, Mr. Barnum strenuously asserts that the prize is white and sacred, and proves the latter with a couple of priests that King Theebaw, of whom he made the purchase, threw in with the white elephant to close the bargain. Thus the doctors disagree. It is within the bounds of possibility that Mr. Barnum has stirred up all this discussion in order that the public will find it necessary to go and see the elephant personally and decide the momentous questions for themselves.

NEW YORK WORLD, APRIL 1, 1884

About two hundred gentlemen, clergymen, doctors and scientists gathered before Toung Taloung, the sacred white elephant, yesterday in Madison Square Garden and showed by diverse ways why Toung was born with white toes and a pink trunk. The children of Burma, dressed in their Sunday clothes and with their faces washed and hair combed for the occasion, sat around the elephant on Oriental rugs and kept small boys away who attempted to feed Toung on apples. Yesterday Toung ate peanuts and when the Burmese discovered it they were indignant. Toung Taloung contains the souls of five kings, and the Burmese chief expects to eventually inhabit him, hence the idea of having their souls mixed up with peanuts makes them angry. . . .

CHICAGO TRIBUNE, SEPTEMBER 2, 1884

Barnum is a smarter man than the King of Siam, who is said to be the "Lord of Many Elephants," for, though it costs just as much to feed and clothe an elephant in Siam as America, the great American showman makes his stable of those quite expensive beasts pay him a profit. "It pays better to have the genuine article," said Mr. Thomas, the press agent, yesterday, while escorting a reporter for The Tribune through the acres of canvas on the Lake Front. "For instance, there are those Nubian Arabs. Nobody doubts they are genuine. Of course we could hire darkies in New York to dress, look, and act like them, but they would want $6 or $8 every week, while these fellows are satisfied with half of that. . . .

WASHINGTON POST, JANUARY 14, 1889

Mr. Starr, P. T. Barnum's agent, who has been scouring Europe for two months, has secured many animals and curiosities, which he shipped to America by the steamer Werra yesterday. Mr. Starr himself sailed on the Werra. He will return soon to arrange for the coming visits of Barnum's show in England.[18]

TIMES OF LONDON, NOVEMBER 12, 1889

The world-renowned exhibition associated with the name of Mr. Barnum—a combination of circus, wild beast show, and curiosity museum—has at length been transferred from its headquarters in New York to the Olympia building at Addison-road, where, as we interpret the announcements, it now invites the admiration, not merely of London or Great Britain, but of Europe and, indeed, the Old World generally. Of the inception and progress of the great undertaking which has thus been crowned with success the public of both hemispheres have been kept sufficiently well informed, for Mr. Barnum is not one of those who do not let their right hand know what their left hand doeth. The result of the experiment is already more than promising. High as expectations may have been raised as to the merits of the "greatest show on earth," the public are not likely to experience any sense of disappointment when they come to inspect it, especially as the whole galaxy of natural and artificial wonders is on view for the modest charge of 1s. or 2s., according to the day of the week. Mr. Barnum contends that his show has not been and never will be beaten. In point of extent and cheapness combined he is probably right. He certainly offers a marvelous—we may fairly say as far as London is concerned an unexampled—shilling's worth. Under one roof he has brought together not one entertainment, but half-a-dozen, of more than respectable proportions individually, and collectively of a magnitude that enables us to understand even the grandiloquent phraseology of the advertisements. The spacious arena of Olympia has been so laid out as to include three rings of the usual hippodromic measurement–that is to say, more than 40 ft. in diameter. Between these[,] two stages or platforms for acrobatic and other variety shows have been laid down; and at all these points performances are given simultaneously. With everything in full swing from one end of the huge hall to the other, a novel sensation of wonderment creeps over the observer, who is distantly reminded of the great "machinery in motion" gallery of the Paris Exhibition. That it is impossible for the most lynx-eyed onlooker to follow all these performances at one and the same time Mr. Barnum has not to be told. In truth the shilling charge is an amiable delusion, and a snare to boot. It is precisely in the immensity, the complexity, the kaleidoscopic variety, and, to use the word in its strict etymological sense, the incomprehensibility of the show that Mr. Barnum's genius is displayed; for, unlike the ordinary showman, who would be disposed to make a separate charge for each particular sight, he throws all his marvels into one bewildering heap, thereby not only dazzling and delighting the visitor, but laying him, in spite of himself, under the necessity of coming again and again. This generalization, we ought to add, applies to but one phase of the whole entertainment. The three simultaneous circuses, together with the variety shows, give way to one culminating historical spectacle in which the full strength of the *personnel* is employed–a series of tableaux called "Nero, or the Destruction of Rome"; while by way of prelude to the grandiose operations in the arena, a large menagerie, and a host of museum curiosities, monstrosities, and other sights such as only America can produce, including Jumbo stuffed and Jumbo in skeleton form, invite inspection in various annexes to the main building. The low rate of admission implies that Mr. Barnum has a democratic belief in numbers. As a matter of fact sitting room has been provided for 5,000 more people than Olympia has ever held before. By taking in some space beneath the galleries the actual number of seats has been raised to 12,000, and last night, when the show was thrown open for the first time, the whole of the vast area was filled to overflowing. Things being ordered upon such a scale, one reads without surprise in the programme that the establishment comprises no fewer than 1,200 "people" and 380 horses. In all its branches the great enterprise, which is mainly directed by Mr. J. A. Bailey, Mr. Barnum's partner, works with a smoothness implying a high degree of departmental organization and efficiency. It consists of almost as many departments as the United States Government itself, including a "Press bureau," which is ably administered by Mr. Thomas Burnside.

The stuffed figure and the skeleton of Jumbo, who, it will be remembered, was killed by a railway train, soon after his arrival in America, are the first objects that catch the eye of the visitor to Olympia. They are very typical of American enterprise. Many persons, perhaps, would have had the idea of preserving the bones of the famous elephant, but it needed a Barnum to perceive that, to borrow the language of the profession, there was money also in his hide. In Mr. Barnum's hands Jumbo dead has in fact become an even more profitable speculation than Jumbo alive. . . . From the two Jumbos one passes to an annex filled with curiosities of the class which secured Mr. Barnum his reputation in the first instance, for the great showman was a "museum" man before he took up the circus business. Here we find a dwarf of absurdly Lilliputian proportions in evening dress, chatting freely with all comers in a tiny piping voice. He gives his name as Master Dudley Foster, and is said to be 18 years of age, to weigh only 8 lb., and to stand 31 in. in height. Perfectly proportioned and intelligent enough, or more than enough for his size, he could be stowed away comfortably in the capacious pocket of an overcoat. By the side of the dwarf are two Kentucky giants, who are wonderful rather by contrast with their near neighbor than with humanity at large. They are tall fellows of a pronounced American aspect, and appear to be free from the physical weakness of their class. Next comes the bearded lady, who but for Barnum's well known professional rectitude might be taken for a young man of a somewhat effeminate cast. The fat woman and the man who writes with his toes are obviously genuine. So are the skeleton "dude," or American "masher," whose legs are hardly any thicker than a barnyard fowl's, the two-headed child, and the man with no legs, whose feet appear to be attached to his hip-bones. The tattooed lady may be taken on trust, and the two Aztecs—man and wife—are old friends of admitted respectability. It is in his scientific gallery, where the subtle aid of reflecting mirrors is probably invoked, where Mr. Barnum tries our credulity. For here with a beautifully curved fish-tail is a living, breathing, smiling mermaid of prepossessing appearance. She lies doubled up in a vase with her head and tail projecting, and gracefully acknowledges the attention of the crowd. Other wonders are also on view in the shape of living trunkless heads and breathing truncated busts. This is the science of the great show, and thence the visitor passes to its natural history. The menagerie may not greatly impress a public accustomed to the "Zoo," but it is tolerably complete in what be called the staple features of such collections—lions, tigers, and other "cat animals," bears, wolves, seals, monkeys, and above all, elephants, of which there are no fewer than 17 of all sizes. The rarities of the collection are a double-horned rhinoceros, an ostrich, which happens at present to be molting, a cassowary, and an emu. The elephants are all of the Asiatic bread, and are, of course, able to "perform." Not the least interesting section of this department is the vast stable of horses, of which nearly half take part in the operations of the ring. Among them are a beautiful zebra and a few zebra-like animals, which are said to be half-breeds.

Those side-shows, however, though numerous and interesting, are, properly speaking, but the *hors d'oeuvre* of the entertainment which Mr. Barnum spreads before his patrons. His energies and his great administrative faculties are concentrated upon the equestrian, acrobatic, variety and spectacular feats of the arena; and it is here that he easily distances all competitors. The surpassing greatness of the show is no vain boast. Multiplying circuses and platforms and entertainments, each of which can directly appeal only to some particular sections of the mass of spectators, may appear at first sight to be a waste of energy and talent, but there is no denying the impressiveness that it lends to the show as a whole. The spectator feels himself oppressed by the variety of the efforts made for his entertainment. If he has not been to the "machinery in motion" section of the Paris Exhibition, he will perhaps be constrained to imagine himself in some vast factory, with its endless spindles and revolving shafts and pulleys. At a given moment, he may note here the exercises of the *haute école,* there a group of performing elephants, bears or seals, elsewhere clowns, acrobats, trapezists, contortionists, bicyclists, skaters, all in bewildering medley. If he cares to confine his attention to his own immediate circus or platform, he will find plenty to absorb his attention unless the outlying entertainments are temporarily suspended for some grand central feat of wire-walking or equestrianism. Space fails us to note all of the striking features of a programme which is almost as complicated as a railway timetable, but a word is due to the bare-back riding and to a thrilling five-horse tandem hurdle race, in which the animals, running at full speed, seem to pour over the various obstructions in a living stream. In the equestrian "acts" one or two slight accidents occurred last night, the most alarming of which consisted in a lady rider being thrown beyond the ring. There was no harm done, however, in any case, the unhorsed performer, whose fall attracted most attention, being able to rise and walk off without assistance. To the variety business of the platforms and the operations of the different rings succeed horse and dog races around the entire arena. In one instance Shetland ponies have for their riders tiny monkeys in jockey colors, who hold on grimly to their saddles while the animals fly at their highest speed. The "Destruction of Rome" furnishes a fitting climax to the programme. After some stirring views of Roman life—encounters between the people and the Praetorian Guards and public homage to the tyrant Nero—there is a great consumption of red fire typifying not only the ravages of the "devouring element," but also, according to the programme, the "dawn of Christianity" in the center of civilization. This spectacle is organized on a grander scale than anything of the kind that has ever been seen in London, and the ringing cheers with which it was received as the crowning feature of Mr. Barnum's enterprise, prove that the "greatest show on earth" has not traversed the Atlantic in vain.

NEW YORK TRIBUNE, MARCH 28, 1890

The safe return of Phineas T. Barnum to the land of his birth is something of which all rejoice to hear—his triumphs in the British capital are a matter of National congratulation. The cable has told us much of these triumphs, but the cable is cold and distant—nothing so formal, haughty and expensive as your cable message. We knew that the Royal family visited the Great Show, but we did not know that they fed the elephant peanuts—the bumptious cable would not unbend and tell us that. We knew that Gladstone, too, saw it, but we did not know that the Grand Old Man was pleased with the monkeys and punched the little fellows in the ribs with his stick. We knew that the Show's morality was approved of in a general way, but we did not know that the Bishop of Rochester gave Barnum a personal letter vouching for it, and recommending the Show as a proper study for youth in all parts of the world. The cable has many mistakes of omission for which it must answer. Americans were proud of the success of Buffalo Bill in England. But it was nothing compared to Mr. Barnum's. There was a vast difference in the treatment of our two distinguished citizens. True, royalty hobnobbed with Bill, but when the Prince of Wales gave him a cigar he did it in much the same spirit in which he handed a peanut to Mr. Barnum's biggest elephant. Bill became at home in the greatest London drawing-rooms, but he was regarded in much the same light as were Mr. Barnum's animals when being fed immediately after the close of the performance. Curiosity was expressed as to what Bill would probably do if he should get a taste of blood or happen to see a wild buffalo. But with Mr. Barnum it was different—his was a great personal triumph—he was looked on as a man, not a curiosity, and a man who, but for the base ingratitude of republics, would be occupying the place which is the highest gift of the people. Mr. Barnum was fairly smothered in honors while in London. His Moral Show was visited by everybody. . . .

Barnum's Legacy

When Barnum died in Bridgeport, Connecticut, on April 7, 1891, virtually every newspaper in the United States (as well as many leading newspapers in Europe) ran lengthy obituaries. Some of these simply reported the facts: cause of death, funeral arrangements, and so on. More often, though, contemporary journalists used the occasion to comment on Barnum's long professional résumé. For a life spent largely in public, the showman's obituaries served as the final reviews.

NEW YORK TIMES, APRIL 8, 1891

THE GREAT SHOWMAN DEAD

Bridgeport, Conn., April 7—At 6:22 o'clock to-night the long sickness of P. T. Barnum came to an end by his quietly passing away at Marina, his residence in this city.

Shortly after midnight there came an alarming change for the worse. Drs. Hubbard and Godfrey, who were in attendance, saw at once that the change was such as to indicate that the patient could not long survive. The weakened pulse, more difficult respiration, and lower temperature showed that the action of the heart had become so feeble as to presage the collapse which was the beginning of the end. Mr. Barnum seemed to realize that he could not live much longer, and spoke of his approaching end with calmness. Through the night he suffered much pain. Mrs. Barnum remained at the bedside during the night. . . .

When it became certain that the end was but a few hours distant, telegrams to relatives were sent out, and among the sorrowing group in the sick room this evening when the final moments came were Mrs. Barnum, the Rev. L. B. Fisher, of the Universalist church of this city, of which Mr. Barnum was a member; Mrs. D. W. Thompson, Mr. Barnum's daughter; Mrs. W. H. Buchtelle of New-York, another daughter; C. Barnum Seeley, his grandson; Drs. Hubbard and Godfrey, his physicians; C. B. Olcott, a trained nurse from Bellevue Hospital, and W. D. Roberts, his faithful colored valet. The scene at his deathbed was deeply pathetic. All were in tears. Although Mrs. Barnum has stood up bravely under the strain, the closing moments were too much for her and she gave way at times. For an hour or two before his death those at the bedside watched for some sign of recognition or a word from the dying man, but in vain. His end was peaceful and apparently perfectly painless.

Although no arrangements have as yet been made for the funeral it is known that it will take place Friday. The Rev. Mr. Collyer of New-York, a lifelong friend of Mr. Barnum, will assist the Rev. Mr. Fisher in the services, which will be private. In accordance with the expressed wish of the deceased he will be buried in Mountain Grove Cemetery, where he recently had erected a massive granite monument.

As has been repeatedly published, Mr. Barnum makes provision in his will for the continuance as a permanent institution of the great show with which his name is associated. For his wife, his daughters, and other relatives, he has made handsome provision, but the bulk of his property goes to C. Barnum Seeley, his only grandson. Mr. Seeley lives in New-York. He is a member of the Stock Exchange, Mr. Barnum having purchased a seat for him a short time ago. . . .

Mr. Barnum's solicitude that no business cares should devolve upon his wife at his death had led him to make and publish his will in 1883. He had three physicians with him at the time, who subscribed to affidavits that he was of sound and disposing mind and memory. His estate was then valued at $10,000,000. The will named twenty-seven heirs and was generous in charitable bequests. He valued his share in the show at $3,500,000. His executors were empowered to renew contracts to carry on the show for the estate at the expiration of the present contract in 1899. The Children's Aid Society was specifically named as a beneficiary of a certain percentage of each season's profits.

"I don't know anybody connected with that society," the great showman explained, "but I believe in the society. To me there is no picture so beautiful as smiling, bright-eyed, happy children; no music so sweet as their clear and ringing laughter. That I have had power to provide innocent amusement for the little ones, to create such pictures, to evoke such music, is my proudest reflection. I believe this society to be the most practical Christian institution in America. I have catered to four generations of children. I want children to remember me."

Other codicils were afterwards added to the will to include the Tufts and Bridge-port institutions within its provisions. In April, 1889, he arranged that the management of his interests in the show after his death should devolve upon his grandson, Clinton Barnum Seeley. Mr. Barnum's latest great personal triumph was won during his visit to England in the Fall of 1889 and Winter of 1890. The feat of carrying across the ocean his enormous show compelled the admiration of the English people. They forgot the Jumbo incident and received him with popular enthusiasm. All classes extended to him every possible honor, and his London season was a most wonderful and satisfying success. . . .

Phineas Taylor Barnum was a good father, a faithful husband, a true friend, and a faithful public servant. He was a shrewd manager, and in his business made money when he could. From the humblest beginnings he won notoriety, if not fame, in two continents. His life was filled with the most striking examples of what might be accomplished by that peculiar quality known as "Yankee push." His name will long be remembered in his native land. He was twice married, his second wife being an English lady. He engaged in live stock enterprises with Vanderbilt, the Eastmans, and others.

WASHINGTON POST, APRIL 8, 1891

Yesterday, as with the silent folding of the tents, died the most widely known American that ever lived. He held no exalted official station, neither was he eminent in the world of politics, literature, science, or art. He possessed no marvelous wealth. He was only a showman. Yet his name has been borne to a greater multitude than that of any other man of his time.

Such was the singular and remarkable achievement of Phineas Taylor Barnum. He could not have existed in any other age, and he was in some respects the most representative as he was one of the most unique products of this age. He was denounced as a charlatan; he proclaimed himself as "the great humbug." Yet few men have lived more worthy, useful, or beneficent lives.

For fifty years he was never lost to view. Through his search for curiosities his name became familiar to strange people and in far parts of the earth. No man was so well known to the youth and adults of America. His "Greatest Show in Earth," merely a money-making institution, was a collection of the wonderful, the curious and pleasing. It grew from Barnum's brain alone.

This was his eulogy, that he was a public-spirited citizen, he furnished delights to millions, he added to the sum of childhood's and of human joy.

OBITUARY EXCERPTS REPRINTED IN THE
WASHINGTON POST, APRIL 10, 1891

The Great Showman's Exit.

New York World: The story of his long and busy career makes an average Arabian Nights' tale seem like a very plain bit of prosy fact.

New York Times: It may be said of Barnum as truly as it was said of Garrick that his death "eclipsed the gaiety of nations and diminished the public stock of human pleasure."

Pittsburgh Dispatch: His varied career before entering the show business illustrates the indomitable pluck of the man. Failure only spurred him to renewed effort, and in that characteristic at least he is worthy of emulation by the youth of today.

Pittsburgh Chronicle-Telegraph: There is a great deal of philosophy in Barnum's remark that it required three adults to take a child to the circus to see the animals; and this remark shows the clear understanding of human nature which led to his success.

Boston Herald: In his way he must be ranked as a great man, for he was the foremost showman, not only of his day, but of all time. Endowed with wonderful powers of organization, and an instinctive perception of what would take with the public, he engaged in many enterprises covering the widest possible range, and in all of those he was, at least, measurably successful, while in some of them he achieved a triumph which won acknowledgement from the world.

TIMES OF LONDON, APRIL 8, 1891

The great men are dying fast, and now among them Barnum is gone. That fine flower of Western civilization, that *arbiter elegantarium* to Demos, has lived. At the age of eighty, after a life of restless energy and incessant publicity, the great showman has lain down to rest, with what we may be sure was more than the unwillingness of all old soldiers to leave the battlefield. He gave, in the eyes of the seekers after amusement, a luster to America; he gave a new word to various European languages, where "un Barnum," is a phrase as intelligible as it is, we regret to say, unflattering. But that need not disturb the last slumber of the great man. He may have reflected that it was one thing to be *a* Barnum, an imitator, a humble member of a class, and therefore very likely conspicuous for all the less excellent qualities of the original, and quite another to be Barnum, one and unapproachable. He belongs, we must remember, rather to the America of the date before the Civil War than to that of the last thirty years. It was then that he made his name and his first fortune; it was then that he created the *métier* of showman on a grandiose scale, worthy to be professed by a man of genius. He early realized that essential feature of a modern democracy, its readiness to be led to what will amuse and instruct it. He knew that "the people" means crowds, paying crowds; that crowds love the fashion and will follow it; and the business of the great man is to make and control the fashion. To live on, by, and before the public was his ideal. For their sake and his own, he loved to bring the public to see, to applaud, and to pay. His immense activity, covering all those years, marked him out as one of the most typical and conspicuous Yankees of the old sort. He had his eye and his hand everywhere, retaining meanwhile an accurate touch upon the pulse of his patron, the public. He had tried everything—newspapers, shows, lectures, real property speculations, and even such public life as is provided by the Connecticut Legislature. From Jenny Lind to Jumbo, no occasions of a public "sensation" came amiss to him. In his eightieth year he organized the "greatest show on earth" at Olympia in London, bringing over his elephants, his Roman chariots and all his company in a special steamer for the purpose. And—what few people know—he made this venture pay, though for his purposes he caused it to be believed that London had not treated him so well as he had treated London.

We give elsewhere the principal facts of Phineas Taylor Barnum's career. Born in 1810 in Bethel, Connecticut—how serious and puritanical it sounds!—he was a man of business by the age when most boys are learning grammar at school. From 1834 to 1841 he was in New York, trying various ventures; and in the latter year he became the owner of the American Museum. His destiny was thenceforward fixed. He became the showman *par excellence;* the type upon which Artemus Wards of the next generation were modeled; the *impresario,* the expounder, the humorist—shall we add, the humbug? Later in his life he wrote a book on "The Humbugs of the World"; and no one was more conscious or more proud of the extent to which he resembled the people he was describing. But he would have died with a merely local reputation unless chance had favored him by putting in his way something to make a hit with. He stumbled across Charles H. Stratton, the famous, the immortal "General Tom Thumb" of our childhood, the first and the best of the dwarfs who entertained the public with their talk and their attitudes. The little creature suited Barnum exactly and Barnum suited him. Together they came to Europe and held "receptions" everywhere. It was the moment when the Queen's eldest children were in the nursery, and Barnum saw that a fortune depended on his bringing them into friendly relations with Tom

Thumb. He succeeded; and the silly British public flocked to see the amusing little person who had shown off his mature yet miniature dimensions by the side of the baby Heir Apparent. Then came the Jenny Lind *furore;* and Barnum persuaded her to come out in America under his guidance. She gave 93 concerts there, at which the astonishing sum of 140,000 pounds is said to have been received; the proportion that fell to Barnum's share is unknown to the world at large, which he did not always take into his confidence on points of this nature. Then came a divagation into publicity of a different sort. Mr. Barnum became a legislator for his State, and even, in 1875, Mayor of Bridgeport. Why not? The man who can organize the amusements of the people may very well be trusted to organize a few of their laws for them; and as to the mayoralty, have we not, in historic London, the example of an eminent *impresario* becoming Sheriff amid general applause? But Barnum's greatness was not allowed to die down in the latitude of Bridgeport. He had a fine country house, to which he gave the characteristic name of Iranistan, as though he were the Shah at least. Unluckily it was burnt; nor was this the only misfortune that checkered the great man's career. A bankruptcy or two came to him as the penalty of speculating in real property; and two or three times his show was burnt out. "These losses," we are told, "he bore with great equanimity." We wonder whether the insurance companies did the same. But equanimity and a fair front to the world were always characteristics of his, as was the ready wit which gave him half his success. "Well, Mr. Barnum," said an Illustrious Personage to him at the Agricultural Hall, as the Household troops went by in a musical ride, "would you not like to run the Life Guards in the States?" "Sir," he answered, "I have no desire to run the Life Guards; but I will give good terms to be allowed to run your Royal Highness."

When, in 1889, the veteran brought over his shipload of giants and dwarfs, chariots and waxworks, spangles and circus-riders, to entertain the people of London, one wanted a Carlyle to come forward with a discourse upon "the Hero as Showman." It was the *ne plus ultra* of publicity; that is, of superficiality; that is, of sham. Barnum knew it as well as any one, or better. He reveled in it. "The world," he said in effect, "likes to be tickled and talked into a momentary belief in what it well knows to be a delusion. I am here to do it for them." There was thus a threefold show—the things in the stalls and cages, the showman, and the world itself. Each was unreal, and of the three perhaps Barnum was not the most hollow, for he at least was conscious of his own good-natured, innocent imposture. At all events, he was the most interesting feature of the show at Olympia. The chariot races and the monstrosities we can get anywhere, but the octogenarian showman was unique. His death removes a noteworthy figure from this amusing and crowded panorama of the nineteenth century; an almost classical figure, indeed, and a typical representative of the age of transparent puffing through which modern democracies are passing. His name is proverb already, and a proverb it will continue until mankind has ceased to find comedy in the showman and his patrons—the comedy of the harmless deceiver and the willingly deceived.

NEW YORK CLIPPER, APRIL 18, 1891

In this city the news of Mr. Barnum's death caused sincere regret in all circles. There were no performances of the Barnum & Bailey Show at Madison Square Garden on Friday, the day of the funeral, but otherwise there was no interruption to the circus. . . . The announcement is now made by the sole surviving partner, J. A. Bailey, that the shows will continue, and that in nothing in the future will the public be able to discover the slightest change, either in the policy or the character of the "Greatest Show on Earth."

Notes

INTRODUCTION

1. P. T. Barnum, *Funny Stories Told by Phineas T. Barnum* (New York: George Routledge and Sons, 1890), 361.

2. The term "culture industry" comes from Max Horkheimer and Theodor Adorno's landmark study, *Dialectic of Enlightenment*, first published in 1947. See also Adorno's later essays on the subject, reprinted in *The Culture Industry* (New York: Routledge, 1991). My choice of terms is not intended to revive the hegemonic specter of mass deception sometimes associated with Adorno and his Frankfurt School colleagues. Rather, I prefer "culture industry" because it captures the historical specificity of Barnum's working methods far better than do more generic labels such as "popular culture" (which includes front-porch quilting as well as Hollywood blockbusters) or "commercial entertainment" (which begins well before 1835). Adorno's critical language forces us to grapple with the complex socioeconomic processes at the heart of this anthology: promotion, distribution, mass production, corporate combination, and so forth.

3. I offer this list merely as a starting point for assembling a more rigorous genealogy of the U.S. culture industry. Peale assembled the nation's first major museum, in Philadelphia. Maelzel was the most prominent itinerant showman of the early national period. T. D. Rice was the first international blackface star. Catlin exhibited Native American people and artifacts in London. Van Amburgh was a leading lion tamer and circus manager. Niblo ran one of the most successful pleasure gardens and theaters in New York City. Kimball achieved similar success with his museum/theater in Boston. As "Buffalo Bill," Cody created the modern Wild West show. Keith and Albee built the first national vaudeville syndicate. For background on these figures, see Charles Coleman Sellers, *Mr. Peale's Museum* (New York: Norton, 1980); David R. Brigham, *Public Culture in the Early Republic* (Washington, D.C.: Smithsonian Institution Press, 1995); James W. Cook, *The Arts of Deception: Playing with Fraud in the Age of Barnum* (Cambridge, Mass.: Harvard University Press, 2001); Robert Toll, *Blacking Up: The Minstrel Show in Nineteenth-Century America* (New York: Oxford University Press, 1974); Eric Lott, *Love and Theft: Blackface Minstrelsy and the American Working Class* (New York: Oxford University Press, 1993); W. T. Lhamon Jr., *Jump Jim Crow: Lost Plays, Lyrics, and Street Prose of the First Atlantic Popular Culture* (Cambridge, Mass.: Harvard University Press, 2003); Richard Altick, *The Shows of London* (Cambridge, Mass.: Harvard University Press, 1978); Bruce McConachie, *Melodramatic Formations: American Theatre and Society, 1820–1890* (Iowa City: University of Iowa Press, 1992); Robert Allen, *Horrible Prettiness: Burlesque and American Culture* (Chapel Hill: University of

North Carolina Press, 1991); Joy Kasson, *Buffalo Bill's Wild West: Celebrity, Memory, and Popular History* (New York: Hill and Wang, 2000); Robert Snyder, *Voice of the City: Vaudeville and Popular Culture in New York* (New York: Oxford University Press, 1989); M. Alison Kibler, *Rank Ladies* (Chapel Hill: University of North Carolina Press, 1999); and Marybeth Hamilton, *"When I'm Bad, I'm Better": Mae West, Sex, and American Entertainment* (Berkeley: University of California Press, 1997).

4. The body of historical writing on Barnum is vast and diverse. Biographical studies include Irving Wallace, *The Fabulous Showman: The Life and Times of P. T. Barnum* (New York: Knopf, 1959); A. H. Saxon, *P. T. Barnum: The Legend and the Man* (New York: Columbia University Press, 1989); and Philip B. Kunhardt Jr., Philip B. Kunhardt III, and Peter W. Kunhardt, *P. T. Barnum: America's Greatest Showman* (New York: Knopf, 1995). For more-scholarly treatments, see Constance Rourke, *Trumpets of Jubilee* (New York: Harcourt, Brace, 1927); Neil Harris, *Humbug: The Art of P. T. Barnum* (Chicago: University of Chicago Press, 1973); Peter George Buckley, "To the Opera House: Culture and Society in New York City, 1820–1860" (Ph.D. diss., State University of New York, Stoney Brook, 1984); Bluford Adams, *E Pluribus Barnum: The Great Showman and the Making of U.S. Popular Culture* (Minneapolis: University of Minnesota Press, 1997); Andrea Stulman Dennett, *Weird and Wonderful: The Dime Museum in America* (New York: New York University Press, 1997); Cook, *Arts of Deception;* Benjamin Reiss, *The Showman and the Slave: Race, Death, and Memory in Barnum's America* (Cambridge, Mass.: Harvard University Press, 2001); and Janet Davis, *The Circus Age: Culture and Society under the American Big Top* (Chapel Hill: University of North Carolina Press, 2002). For a critical survey of Barnum scholarship, see my review essay "Mass Marketing and Cultural History: The Case of P. T. Barnum," *American Quarterly* 51, no. 1 (March 1999): 175–86.

5. *The Life of P. T. Barnum, Written by Himself* is now available in a reprint edition from the University of Illinois Press (2000). This volume includes a fine critical introduction by Terence Whalen, "P. T. Barnum and the Birth of Capitalist Irony."

6. The most glaring omission involves Barnum's "living curiosities" (e.g., conjoined twins, bearded ladies, missing links), many of which are rarely mentioned in his memoirs. Recent scholarship has done a great deal to correct this. In addition to the Barnum-focused studies cited in note 4, see Leslie Fiedler, *Freaks* (New York: Simon and Schuster, 1978); Robert Bogdan, *Freak Show: Presenting Human Oddities for Amusement and Profit* (Chicago: University of Chicago Press, 1988); Susan Stewart, *On Longing: Narratives of the Miniature, the Gigantic, the Souvenir, the Collection* (Durham: Duke University Press, 1993); Rosemarie Garland Thomson, ed., *Freakery: Cultural Spectacles of the Extraordinary Body* (New York: New York University Press, 1996); Rosemarie Garland Thomson, *Extraordinary Bodies: Figuring Physical Disability in American Culture and Literature* (New York: Columbia University Press, 1997); John Kuo-Wei Tchen, *New York before Chinatown: Orientalism and the Shaping of American Culture, 1776–1882* (Baltimore: Johns Hopkins University Press, 1999); Rachel Adams, *Sideshow U.S.A.: Freaks and the American Cultural Imagination* (Chicago: University of Chicago Press, 2001); and Charles D. Martin, *The White African American Body: A Cultural and Literary Exploration* (New Brunswick, N.J.: Rutgers University Press, 2002).

7. *New York Atlas,* June 14, 1840; Barnum, *Struggles and Triumphs* (Buffalo: Warren, Johnson, 1872), 73. For further analysis of the Heth episode, see Saxon, *P. T. Barnum;* Adams, *E Pluribus Barnum;* Cook, *Arts of Deception;* and especially Reiss, *Showman and the Slave.*

8. On the shifting contours of Barnum's audience, see Adams, *E Pluribus Barnum,* and Cook, "Mass Marketing and Cultural History." For a pioneering analysis of class categories and promotional rhetorics, see Michael Denning, *Mechanic Accents: Dime Novels and Working-Class Culture in America* (London: Verso, 1987).

9. See Michael Kammen, *American Culture, American Tastes* (New York: Knopf, 1999). See also William R. Taylor, *In Pursuit of Gotham: Culture and Commerce in New York* (New York: Oxford University Press, 1992), and Richard Butsch, *The Making of American Audiences: From Stage to Television, 1750–1990* (New York: Cambridge University Press, 2000).

10. Kammen, *American Culture,* 9–17. The term "massification" is often used in studies of twentieth-century consumer culture. See, for example, James B. Twitchell, *AdcultUSA: The Triumph of Advertising in American Culture* (New York: Columbia University Press, 1996).

11. A. H. Saxon has noted that between 1841 and 1868, Barnum's American Museum attracted more customers (relative to U.S. population) than did Disneyland during its initial twenty-seven years of operation. Saxon estimates the total number of tickets sold for the American Museum at forty-two million. U.S. population during the 1860s was roughly thirty-five million. Saxon, *P. T. Barnum,* 107–8.

12. Barnum, *Struggles and Triumphs,* 130.

13. For the origins of this argument, see Harris, *Humbug.* Over the past quarter century, Harris's framework has influenced much of the scholarly discussion of nineteenth-century cultural consumption. See, for example, Lawrence W. Levine, *Highbrow/Lowbrow: The Emergence of Cultural Hierarchy in America* (Cambridge, Mass.: Harvard University Press, 1988); Miles Orvell, *The Real Thing: Imitation and Authenticity in American Culture, 1880–1940* (Chapel Hill: University of North Carolina Press, 1989); Allen, *Horrible Prettiness;* Kammen, *American Culture;* and Butsch, *The Making of American Audiences.*

14. For more detailed analysis of these issues, see Cook, *Arts of Deception,* 1–118, and Michael Warner, *Publics and Counterpublics* (New York: Zone Books, 2002), 7–124.

15. Kammen discusses the history of "spectatoritis" in *American Culture,* chapter 8.

16. As we shall see, late nineteenth-century reviews for the Greatest Show on Earth noted both of these patterns, quoting verbal exchanges overheard in the sideshow even as they made it clear that Barnum's spectacles represented a radical departure. The best analysis of structural changes in circus production is Davis, *Circus Age.*

17. One might reasonably ask what twenty-first-century promoters mean by "everywhere." Consider the film *Matrix Revolutions,* which in 2003 had the largest commercial debut in motion picture history. According to the *New York Times* (op-ed section, November 11, 2003), the film opened simultaneously in "43 languages and on more than 10,000 screens." One suspects, though, that this record will not last very long. As film distribution moves to the Internet, "everywhere" will quickly come to signify an even larger number of venues and consumers.

18. These comparisons are based on Consumer Price Index calculators available on the Internet. See, for example, the Economic History Service's CPI calculator at http://eh.net/hmit/compare/.

19. See, for example, his 1855 dedication page in *The Life of P. T. Barnum:* "To the Universal Yankee Nation, of which I am proud to be one."

20. On this point, see Barnum's February 5, 1862, letter to Robert Bonner, the proprietor of the *New York Ledger.* Along with a "season ticket" to the American Museum, Barnum offered reassurances about what Bonner's family might encounter: "We sell no rum nor segars there; we long since excluded improper characters; we keep it nice & genteel & are patronized by the *best class* of society. . . . If you venture into the lecture room you will hear nothing vulgar nor profane." Robert Bonner Papers, New York Public Library Rare Books and Manuscripts Division.

21. Barnum's invitation to "persons of color" appeared in at least two different newspapers: the *New York Atlas* (February 25, 1849) and the *New York Tribune* (February 27, 1849). On Barnum's "baby shows," see Adams, *E Pluribus Barnum,* 97–111. For rare evidence of black women as American Museum consumers during the 1860s, see Farah Jasmine Griffin, ed., *Beloved Sisters and Loving Friends: Letters from Rebecca Primus of Royal Oak, Maryland, and Addie Brown of Hartford, Connecticut, 1854–1868* (New York: One World, 1999), 56–57.

22. See Barnum's June 11, 1864, essay for the *New York Mercury,* reprinted in gallery 1.

23. I am referring here to the famous but apocryphal thesis often attributed to Barnum: "there's a sucker born every minute." For more on the phrase's long-running history, see Saxon's appendix in *P. T. Barnum.* On the issue of consumer agency in popular culture, see the "AHR Forum" in the *American Historical Review* 97, no. 5 (December 1992): 1369–1430, with essays by Lawrence W. Levine, "The Folklore

of Industrial Society: Popular Culture and Its Audiences"; Robin D. G. Kelley, "Notes on Deconstructing the Folk"; Natalie Zemon Davis, "Towards Mixtures and Margins"; and Jackson Lears, "Making Fun of Popular Culture." Other key interventions in this long-running debate include Stuart Hall, "Notes on Deconstructing 'the Popular,'" in *People's History and Socialist Theory,* ed. Ralph Samuel (London: Routledge and Kegan Paul, 1980), 227–40; and George Lipsitz, *Time Passages: Collective Memory and American Popular Culture* (Minneapolis: University of Minnesota Press, 1990).

24. The transnational scope of the nineteenth-century culture industry has received surprisingly little attention by modern scholars. Recent exceptions to this rule include: John G. Blair, "First Steps toward Globalization: Nineteenth-Century Exports of American Entertainment Forms," in *"Here, There and Everywhere": The Foreign Politics of American Popular Culture,* ed. Reinhold Wagnleitner and Elaine Tyler May (Hanover, N.H.: University Press of New England, 2000), 17–33; Richard Waterhouse, *From Minstrel Show to Vaudeville: The Australian Popular Stage, 1788–1914* (Kensington, NSW, Aust.: New South Wales University Press, 1990); Roslyn Poignant, *Professional Savages: Captive Lives and Western Spectacle* (New Haven: Yale University Press, 2004); and the document collections cited in gallery 1, note 54. Barnum's international aspirations are chronicled throughout this volume. The showman's final press interviews frequently mentioned plans to take the Barnum and Bailey Circus to the Continent and beyond.

25. One good illustration of these changes is the short-lived Barnum Universal Exposition Company, a "million-dollar public corporation with a business plan ultimately to open as many as a dozen separate exhibitions in America and Europe" (Kunhardt et al., *P. T. Barnum: America's Greatest Showman,* 243). The company failed in 1875 due to a series of freak accidents. But a nineteen-page auction catalog (an example of which is now owned by the William Clements Library, University of Michigan) provides vivid evidence of Barnum's ongoing capital accumulation. Items for sale included more than 250 circus animals, 13 railroad cars, and 48 boxes of costumes, as well as dozens of chariots, saddles, cages, tents, chandeliers, and advertising posters. On this issue, see also Davis, *Circus Age,* 1–81.

26. *London Times,* November 12, 1889.

27. *London Times,* April 8, 1891.

GALLERY I
BARNUM'S SERIALIZED WRITINGS

1. Many of these letters have been reproduced in A. H. Saxon, ed., *Selected Letters of P. T. Barnum* (New York: Columbia University Press, 1983).

2. A. H. Saxon, *P. T. Barnum: The Legend and the Man* (New York: Columbia University Press, 1989), 88.

3. Analyses of the novella can be found in Bluford Adams, *E Pluribus Barnum: The Great Showman and the Making of U.S. Popular Culture* (Minneapolis: University of Minnesota Press, 1997), 2–10, 197–98; James W. Cook, *The Arts of Deception: Playing with Fraud in the Age of Barnum* (Cambridge, Mass.: Harvard University Press, 2001), 96–100; and Benjamin Reiss, *The Showman and the Slave: Race, Death, and Memory in Barnum's America* (Cambridge, Mass.: Harvard University Press, 2001), 4, 171–78, 227.

4. These include chapters 11–15, which ran in the *Atlas* from June 6 to July 4, 1841.

5. *New York Atlas,* December 30, 1838, January 6, 1839. Two years later, James Gordon Bennett made a similar claim, describing the *Atlas* as the largest among the "Sunday prints." *New York Herald,* August 9, 1841. The nineteenth-century historian of American journalism Frederic Hudson offered a more modest appraisal. By his calculation, the *Atlas* was the second-largest of the five Sunday papers in 1842, with a circulation of 3,500. *Journalism in the United States, from 1690 to 1872* (New York: Harper, 1873), 525. Regardless of the exact circulation numbers, one larger point seems clear: the *Atlas* was a prominent periodical in antebellum New York.

6. See, for example, the *New York Mercury* of January 3, 1864.

7. This slogan appeared in *Mercury* promotional materials during the early 1860s.

8. A later exception to this rule was Samuel Clemens (Mark Twain), who published briefly in the *New York Mercury* after Barnum's association with the paper.

9. Even with the best electronic search engines, the numbers of extant copies are difficult to gauge accurately because the editors and titles of the two papers changed frequently. Many library holdings, moreover, are incomplete for the periods when Barnum published his series; in some cases, the catalog records claim issues not actually on the shelves or included in the microfilm prints. The Library of Congress catalog, for example, asserts that the library holds a microfilm copy of the *New York Mercury* for 1864, the period during which Barnum published the bulk of his "humbug essays." But on the first frame of the microfilm, one discovers a hand-typed catalog card listing the 1864 run as missing.

10. *New York Atlas,* June 21, 1840. There is some indication that the project had been in the works for at least a year. See, for example, the *Atlas* of June 2, 1839, which promised a forthcoming "exposé of the literary and theatrical humbugs of this city." This anonymous notice probably came from Barnum, who was then living in the city and looking for new employment opportunities.

11. P. T. Barnum, *The Life of P. T. Barnum* (New York: Redfield, 1855), 210–11. The first Vauxhall Gardens ad signed by Barnum appeared in the *Atlas* on June 21, 1841.

12. On the 1837 Panic and its aftermath, see Edwin G. Burrows and Mike Wallace, *Gotham: A History of New York City to 1898* (New York: Oxford University Press, 1999), 603–45. Contemporary press coverage suggests a significant lingering impact on New York's entertainment industry. See, for example, the *Atlas* of March 15, 1840, which described the theatrical market as "flat, stale, and unprofitable."

13. P. T. Barnum to Fogg, Stickney, Ludlow, and Smith, Mobile, Alabama, February 27, 1841, Missouri Historical Society.

14. Barnum, *Life of P. T. Barnum,* 212–13.

15. Years later, Barnum offered specific dates for both the start of the Pittsburgh episode (March 30, 1841) and his arrival in New York

(April 23, 1841). See Barnum, *Life of P. T. Barnum,* 212–13. If correct, this chronology suggests that Barnum probably worked on *Adventures* while traveling between the two cities.

16. *New York Atlas,* April 25, 1841.

17. *Oxford English Dictionary,* Compact Edition (1991), s.v. "Diddle." Edgar Allen Poe later used the term in his essay "Diddling. Considered as One of the Exact Sciences" (1850).

18. For helpful discussion of this long-running cultural cycle, see William M. Hynes and William G. Doty, eds., *Mythical Trickster Figures* (Tuscaloosa: University of Alabama Press, 1997); and Lewis Hyde, *Trickster Makes This World* (New York: North Point Press, 1998).

19. In this respect, *Adventures* was part of a much larger cultural phenomenon. As one recent scholar has noted, "anecdotes and jokes about trade and its tricks" appeared regularly in "northern newspapers, almanacs, and journals." *Adventures* was also typical of the genre's "double-edged" character: "On the one hand, many stories depicted individuals being duped by the tricks of trade, or getting their own back on merchants, peddlers, dealers who had sought to pull a fast one on them; much of the humor in these jokes and tales bespoke an absence of sympathy with their victims and exemplified the dangers, anxieties, and fearfulness of making transactions on which livelihoods would depend. On the other hand, there was also an undercurrent of indignation and moral repulsion at these circumstances, suggesting sympathy among tellers and listeners for the dilemmas that trade imposed." Christopher Clark, "The Consequences of the Market Revolution in the American North," in *The Market Revolution in America: Social, Political, and Religious Expressions,* ed. Melvyn Stokes and Stephen Conway (Charlottesville: University of Virginia Press, 1996), 31–32.

20. This is a thinly veiled reference to Barnum's newspaper, the *Herald of Freedom,* which was launched on October 19, 1831. In October 1832, Barnum was fined and sentenced to sixty days in jail for libel against a local deacon.

21. On Barnum's disdain for scientific experts, see Neil Harris, *Humbug: The Art of P. T. Barnum* (Chicago: University of Chicago Press, 1973).

22. The origin of the fictional "monkey" character remains somewhat unclear. Besides Heth, Barnum's only other regular attraction during the 1835–36 season was Signor Antonio Vivalla, an acrobat and plate-spinner. In his later autobiographies, Barnum never expressed much contempt for Vivalla. The more likely satirical target is Master John Diamond, the young black-face dancer who caused Barnum much grief between 1839 and 1841.

23. The journal that Barnum refers to here has never been located, but we know that it did exist. He mentions it more than once in *The Life of P. T. Barnum*.

24. Barnum probably concocted the tooth extraction as a brutal allegory of the "puffing system" (in which antebellum managers regularly fabricated new names, images, and biographies for their performers). But it is hard to be certain. After all, he *did* sell tickets to Heth's autopsy.

25. In the original text, Barnum pokes fun here at Anne Royal, author of the *Black Book* and *Paul Pry*.

26. Part of this sentence is illegible in the original. The ellipsis stands in for a brief comment about the orchestra.

27. This may refer to a religious lecture that Barnum delivered in Tiffin, Ohio. In *The Life of P. T. Barnum*, he offers early September 1837 as the probable date (204).

28. The "half horse half alligator" was one of the standard Jacksonian metaphors for the Kentucky "backwoodsman." See Constance Rourke, *American Humor: A Study of the National Character* (New York: Harcourt Brace, 1931). For a discussion of the image in relation to Jacksonian gender roles, see Carroll Smith-Rosenberg, *Disorderly Conduct: Visions of Gender in Victorian America* (New York: Knopf, 1985).

29. For helpful analyses of these racial stereotypes, see George Frederickson, *The Black Image in the White Mind* (Middletown, Conn.: Wesleyan University Press, 1971); Reginald Horseman, *Race and Manifest Destiny* (Cambridge, Mass.: Harvard University Press, 1981); Deborah Gray White, *Ar'nt I a Woman?* (New York: Norton, 1985); and Alexander Saxton, *The Rise and Fall of the White Republic* (New York: Verso, 1990).

30. On the complex issue of Heth as "property," see Reiss, *Showman and the Slave*.

31. This is not the story that Barnum told in his later autobiographies, where he claimed to have purchased the rights to exhibit Heth in Philadelphia. The real exhibition opened in New York in early August 1835.

32. Here we can see Barnum beginning to think about the category of "living curiosities." See Robert Bogdan, *Freak Show: Presenting Human Oddities for Amusement and Profit* (Chicago: University of Chicago Press, 1988); Rosemarie Garland Thomson, ed., *Freakery: Cultural Spectacles of the Extraordinary Body* (New York: New York University Press, 1996); Adams, *E Pluribus Barnum;* Cook, *Arts of Deception;* Reiss, *Showman and the Slave;* and Janet Davis, *The Circus Age: Culture and Society under the American Big Top* (Chapel Hill: University of North Carolina Press, 2002).

33. By the mid-1830s, older "antitheatrical" prejudices were yielding to a rapidly expanding middle-class entertainment industry. But not all theatricals were acceptable to middle-class tastes shaped by the Second Great Awakening. William Niblo was a leader in mapping this new middle-class cultural landscape because he provided "theatricals" mostly free of rowdy behavior, drunkenness, prostitution, and gambling. Barnum would soon follow suit.

34. Barnum is referring here to his associate Levi Lyman, a lawyer from Penn Yan, New York. Lyman was Barnum's partner in crime for both the Joice Heth and Feejee Mermaid hoaxes.

35. Except for a few minor changes, these are the same reviews reproduced in *The Life of P. T. Barnum*. The one major exception is the "N.Y. Sunday M. News" review, which Barnum chose not to include in 1855. This pattern of recycling leads to two larger conclusions. First, it demonstrates that Barnum was indeed the anonymous author of *Adventures*. Second, it suggests that he worked closely from notes, diaries, and scrapbooks. No one, after all, could have reproduced this much textual detail entirely from memory.

36. Lawrie Todd was the pen name of Grant Thorburn, a Scottish-born travel writer known for his literary irreverence.

37. Barnum is referring here to *The Life of Joice Heth* (New York: Printed for the Publisher, 1835), reprinted in gallery 2 of this volume.

38. This may be the origin of the one surviv-

ing playbill for the Heth exhibition (dated December 11 and 12, 1835, and now housed at the Somers Historical Society, Somers, New York). The SHS playbill lists Bridgeport, Connecticut, as the location for the exhibition but also mentions previous shows in the Boston area, which may explain Barnum's reference to printing in Hingham. A reproduction of the playbill can be found in Reiss, *Showman and the Slave*, 34.

39. Barnum is referring to what eventually became the American Antiquarian Society in Worcester, Massachusetts. According to the society's staff, there is no surviving petition in its holdings. If the transaction did in fact take place, both the petition and Heth's hair have been lost.

40. For a description of the libel scandal on which this passage is based, see Saxon, *P. T. Barnum*, chapter 2.

41. The references here are to Edmund Kean, Thomas Hamblin, and Edwin Forrest, all leading dramatic actors on the early American stage.

42. On the antebellum market for corpses, see Michael Sappol, *A Traffic of Dead Bodies* (Princeton: Princeton University Press, 2002).

43. This account stands in striking contrast to Barnum's earlier claims that Heth had an "easy life" as a slave.

44. Here (and in the following pages) Barnum seems to have transcribed actual newspaper documents. See, for example, the *New York Sun*, February 26, 1836.

45. This was not the end of Barnum's European enterprises, however. By late June, he was on his way back to England. An August 18 letter to Moses Kimball laid out his next move: the debut of What Is It? at Egyptian Hall. See Saxon, *Selected Letters of P. T. Barnum*, 35–36, and *New York Atlas*, June 28, 1846.

46. Barnum, *Life of P. T. Barnum*, 214–15. Barnum published at least three "Barnaby Diddleum" essays beyond the final chapter of *Adventures of an Adventurer*. See, for example, the *New York Atlas* of October 10, November 28, and December 26, 1841. All three essays are short on substance and seem to reflect Barnum's chaotic professional situation during the fall of 1841. At this same moment, he was also writing press notices for the Bowery Amphitheater and working feverishly to acquire the American Museum.

47. See Barnum, *Life of P. T. Barnum*, chap-

ter 9. For more detailed discussion of the mermaid campaign and its place within Barnum's career, see Cook, *Arts of Deception*.

48. Barnum, *Life of P. T. Barnum*, 243.

49. Ibid., 243–45. On the long history of the exhibition, see also Alice Curtis Desmond, *Barnum Presents General Tom Thumb* (New York: Macmillan, 1954); Raymond Fitzsimmons, *Barnum in London* (New York: St. Martin's, 1970); Harris, *Humbug;* Mertie E. Romaine, *General Tom Thumb and His Lady* (Taunton, Mass.: William S. Sullwood, 1976); Richard D. Altick, *The Shows of London* (Cambridge, Mass.: Harvard University Press, 1978); Saxon, *P. T. Barnum;* and Adams, *E Pluribus Barnum*.

50. Barnum, *Life of P. T. Barnum*, 252.

51. See, for example, the installments of the *European Correspondence* from May 5 and June 9, 1844.

52. *New York Atlas*, June 2, 1844.

53. Throughout the early modern period, Europe's numerous annual fairs served as major sites of popular revelry and commerce, despite the efforts of local authorities to regulate cultural practices perceived as excessively vulgar or threatening. During the first half of the nineteenth century, however, these ancient institutions were largely supplanted by a plethora of new entertainment industries catering more specifically to middle-class tastes. By the time Barnum wrote this essay, virtually all of the older fairs were dying or gone, although some of his ads for the American Museum acknowledge the lineage. See, for example, the ad in the *New York Daily Plebian*, July 13, 1844, which describes the museum as a "Perpetual Fair." On the evolution of European carnival culture, see Mikhail Bakhtin, *Rabelais and His World* (Cambridge, Mass.: MIT Press, 1968); R. W. Malcolmson, *Popular Recreations in English Society 1700–1850* (Cambridge: Cambridge University Press, 1973); Peter Burke, *Popular Culture in Early Modern Europe* (New York: Harper and Row, 1978); Antony Hippisley Coxe, *A Seat at the Circus* (London: Macmillan, 1980); and especially, Peter Stallybrass and Allon White, *The Politics and Poetics of Transgression* (Ithaca: Cornell University Press, 1986).

54. *New York Atlas*, December 14, 1845, and April 26, 1846. For many years, scholars emphasized the young republic's early dependence on European cultural products, a portrait that

(although partially accurate) enabled a master narrative of an American "renaissance" during the 1840s. More recently, we have begun to acknowledge that the United States was a major exporter of popular entertainment during the very same period. Two recent document collections help to map the process and serve as useful counterparts to this volume: Dale Cockrell, ed., *Excelsior: Journals of the Hutchinson Family Singers, 1842–1846* (Stuyvesant, N.Y.: Pendragon Press, 1989); and W. T. Lhamon Jr., ed., *Jump Jim Crow: Lost Plays, Lyrics, and Street Prose of the First Atlantic Popular Culture* (Cambridge, Mass.: Harvard University Press, 2003).

55. Emile Guillaudeu was a French naturalist. He worked at the American Museum even before Barnum became manager.

56. Barnum's major acquisitions during this period included the Lancashire Bell Ringers (renamed the Swiss Bell Ringers), Herr Faber's talking machine, the Happy Family, and an automaton writer built by Jean-Eugene Robert-Houdin. Barnum also attempted to purchase the home where Shakespeare was born. A group of British preservationists narrowly beat him to it.

57. For background on these exhibitions and venues, see Altick, *The Shows of London.*

58. Barnum's "friend" here was the popular English writer Alfred Smith. For Smith's side of the story, see "A Go-A-Head Day with Barnum," *Bentley's Miscellany* 21, 1847.

59. The nasty passage that follows here was relatively typical of Barnum's racial views during the 1840s. On black Britons during the Victorian era see Douglas Lorimer, *Colour, Class, and the Victorians: English Attitudes towards the Negro in the Mid-Nineteenth Century* (Leicester, Eng.: Holmes and Meier Publishers, 1978); Peter Fryer, *Staying Power: The History of Black People in Britain* (London: Pluto Press, 1984); and Gretschen Holbrook Gerzina, ed., *Black Victorians/Black Victoriana* (New Brunswick, N.J.: Rutgers University Press, 2003).

60. "Lucy Long," "Dandy Jim," and "Miss Dinah" are all blackface minstrel show characters from the 1840s.

61. Eugene Sue was one of the pioneers of nineteenth-century urban sketch literature. Barnum is referring here to his best-known work, *The Mysteries of Paris,* published in serial form starting in 1842.

62. The Palais Royal was a crucial site in the development of European middle-class culture. It included a number of entertainment venues and some of the first restaurants in France. See Robert Isherwood, *Farce and Fantasy: Popular Entertainment in Eighteenth-Century Paris* (Chicago: University of Chicago Press, 1986).

63. Henri Franconi was one of the era's leading equestrians and circus showmen. He opened a hippodrome in New York City in 1853.

64. H. G. Sherman came to France in June 1844 to help Barnum manage the Tom Thumb tour.

65. Barnum is referring here to the millenarian teachings of William Miller, whose New York–based religious sect received widespread attention during the 1830s and 1840s.

66. "Codfish aristocracy" was a derisive early nineteenth-century phrase often used to describe the Northeast's nouveau riche, many of whom became wealthy from the fishing trade.

67. Recent scholarship has examined Barnum's shifting views on slavery in some detail. See Saxon, *P. T. Barnum;* Adams, *E Pluribus Barnum;* Cook, *Arts of Deception;* and Reiss, *Showman and the Slave.* For broader analysis of northern attitudes towards slavery and racial distinction, see Saxton, *Rise and Fall of the White Republic.*

68. On George Catlin's European exhibitions, see Harold McCracken, *George Catlin and the Old Frontier* (New York: Bonanza Books, 1959); Altick, *Shows of London;* and Joy Kasson, *Buffalo Bill's Wild West: Celebrity, Memory, and Popular History* (New York: Hill and Wang, 2000).

69. Dion Boucicault was a popular Irish actor and playwright. Boucicault's controversial slavery drama *The Octoroon* appeared in Barnum's Lecture Room theater during the early 1860s.

70. George Sand was one of nineteenth-century France's best-known writers and women's rights activists.

71. Barnum is referring to one of the major events of the antebellum culture wars: the transformation of Boston's Tremont Theater into an evangelical stronghold. Renamed Tremont Temple, the building served as one of the nation's centers of Protestant moral reform.

72. The individuals mentioned in this section were key figures in the development of the nineteenth-century circus. "Major" Lewis

B. Titus was one of the first American showmen to exhibit in Britain (1838). Rufus Welch's company traveled widely, too, including a trip to Cuba in 1829. James "Yankee" Carter, a lion tamer, became a celebrity at Astley's London Amphitheatre in 1839. Carter's chief rival, Isaac Van Amburgh, toured extensively in Britain between 1838 and 1845. Barnum later partnered with Van Amburgh during the early 1860s. For biographical sketches of these and other circus celebrities, see William L. Sloat, ed., *Olympians of the Sawdust Circle: A Biographical Dictionary of the Nineteenth-Century American Circus* (San Bernardino, Calif.: Borgo Press, 1998).

73. Barnum's old friend Fordyce Hitchcock served as manager of the American Museum during the 1844–46 tour.

74. This list includes some of the most prominent entertainers of the mid-1840s. The "Misses Cushman" refers to Charlotte and Susan Cushman, who sailed to England in the fall of 1844. Charlotte was the chief attraction and ultimately became perhaps the most successful American actress of the mid-nineteenth century. Edwin Forrest was a dramatic actor known for his bombastic style. His heated rivalry with Charles Macready sparked the Astor Place Riot in 1849. The Hutchinson Family was an enormously popular singing group from New Hampshire. Their concerts included temperance and abolitionist themes. Dumbolton's Ethiopian Serenaders were largely responsible for creating the minstrel show craze in Britain during the mid-1840s. The troupe included early blackface luminaries such as Charles White and

R. W. Pelham. Dumbolton was their manager. For an extensive record of U.S. entertainment exports during this same period, see Michael Leavitt, *Fifty Years in Theatrical Management* (New York: Broadway Publishing Co., 1913).

75. These essays were later revised, reordered, and published in book form as *Humbugs of the World* (New York: Carleton, 1865).

76. Barnum continued to wrestle with this dilemma through the end of his career. The most famous example took place in 1884, when his genuine white elephant, Toung Taloung, was denounced as a fake. Two documents from the controversy are reprinted in gallery 4 of this volume.

77. James Capen "Grizzly Bear" Adams was a California trapper who went into the circus business during the mid-1850s. In 1860, he relocated to New York and partnered with Barnum on "Grizzly Adams' California Menagerie."

78. When Barnum reprinted this essay as chapter 2 of *Humbugs of the World*, he added a lengthy critique of promoters who deface public sites (such as the Egyptian pyramids) for their own gain.

79. Richard Adams Locke's 1835 "Moon Hoax" was one of the major events in the history of the penny press. The hoax involved a long (but entirely bogus) account of life on the moon, printed on the front page of the *New York Sun*. The gimmick dramatically increased the fledgling paper's readership.

80. This criticism is somewhat surprising because Barnum employed a fortune teller at the American Museum for many years.

GALLERY 2
BARNUM'S PROMOTIONS

1. Barnum's best-known promotional ghost writer was Richard "Tody" Hamilton, who became a star puffer in his own right during the 1880s.

2. This anecdote originally appeared as part of Charles H. Day's weekly Sawdust column for the *Sporting and Theatrical Times* (Chicago and New York). It is reprinted in William L. Slout, ed., *Ink from a Circus Press Agent: An Anthology of Circus History from the Pen of Charles H. Day* (San Bernardino, Calif.: Borgo Press, 1995), 126–27. On the development of circus advertising,

see Fred Dahlinger Jr. and Stuart Thayer, *Badger State Showmen: A History of Wisconsin's Circus Heritage* (Baraboo, Wisc.: Circus World Museum, 1998); Janet Davis, *The Circus Age: Culture and Society under the American Big Top* (Chapel Hill: University of North Carolina Press, 2002).

3. For a helpful theoretical discussion of "publics," see Michael Warner, *Publics and Counterpublics* (New York: Zone Books, 2002). As we shall see in gallery 4, Barnum's puffery crystallized plenty of opposition, too.

4. The reference to the Boston Museum

owes to the fact that Barnum coproduced the Feejee Mermaid exhibition with Moses Kimball. During its first few seasons, the exhibit split time between Barnum's American Museum (in New York) and Kimball's Boston Museum. It also toured the South in 1843, but with far less success. In Charleston, South Carolina, for example, the local gentry launched a campaign in the papers to have the mermaid run out of town as a fraud. For analysis of this conflict, see Kenneth Greenberg, *Honor and Slavery* (Princeton: Princeton University Press, 1996), and James W. Cook, *The Arts of Deception: Playing with Fraud in the Age of Barnum* (Cambridge, Mass.: Harvard University Press, 2001), 107–17.

5. At this point, the text launches into a lengthy history of mermaids over many centuries.

6. This biographical sketch was published about halfway through Barnum's *European Correspondence*. It appeared as part of the *New York Atlas*'s long-running Portraits of the People series and was attributed to an unnamed friend of the showman. There is little doubt, however, that Barnum had a hand in the essay. He may have simply provided the *Atlas* editors with notes. Or perhaps he generated some of the text from England. But either way, many of the details on Barnum's early career (e.g., his previously undisclosed ownership of slaves during the late 1830s) are too intimate to have come from any other source. One begins to sense a second authorial voice towards the end of the essay, particularly in the section that takes Barnum to task for his practical joking. That final section was probably written by Barnum's friend and coeditor of the *Atlas,* William Cauldwell. Cauldwell went on to edit the *New York Mercury* and was centrally involved in publishing Barnum's *Ancient and Modern Humbugs of the World.*

7. The original pamphlet text is quite lengthy, covering twenty-four pages of small print.

8. This concluding review (beginning with "In strength, activity, and vivacity") was attributed to a Dr. J. V. C. Smith.

9. The following song is from a final section of the pamphlet, entitled "Songs, Scraps, Etc., sung by General Tom Thumb, at his Public Levees." Other selections include "Life on the Ocean Wave," "Old Dan Tucker," "I Should Like to Marry," "Lucy Long," "Come Sit Thee Down," "Dandy Jim," "General Tom Thumb's Farewell to England, and his Illustrious Patrons and Patronesses," "General Tom Thumb's Song," "General Tom Thumb," "Lines on Tom Thumb," "Then You'll Remember Me," and "Rosin the Beau." Almost half of the songs Stratton sang before British nobility came from the American minstrel stage.

10. Like other published guidebooks for Barnum's American Museum, *Sights and Wonders* is a lengthy, often soporific document. Dozens of paragraphs do little more than list multiple varieties of birds, fish, and fossils. The sections reprinted here focus on three issues: the museum's relation to its larger urban environment; Barnum's promotional strategies; and the museum's interior features.

11. This pamphlet also contains a lengthy section on the "Aztec Children."

12. John Greenwood Jr. was a close friend and confidante of Barnum. For many years he served as the American Museum's day-to-day manager.

13. Sylvester Bleeker, a longtime Barnum agent who managed the Tom Thumb Company's global tour, is credited as the author of this pamphlet. The text is divided into chapters on various tour stops. The following excerpt comes from the chapter on China.

14. This circus program was a general guide for the entire 1879 season, although it does mention one specific engagement, "two weeks only, commencing Saturday, April 12th" at the "American Institute Building, 63rd Street and 3rd Avenue."

GALLERY 3
BARNUM'S GALLERY OF WONDERS

1. Scholars have yet to examine the multiple ties–personal, aesthetic, professional–connecting these middle-class tastemakers. Another major figure in the same New York milieu was Mathew Brady, whose daguerreotype studio stood across the street from the American Museum. Brady produced souvenir portraits of most of Barnum's star performers during the 1850s and 1860s. On Currier and Ives, see Harry T. Peters, *Currier and Ives: Printmakers to the American People*, 2 vols. (Garden City, N.Y.: Doubleday, Doran, 1929–31); Jane Cooper Bland, *Currier and Ives: A Manual for Collectors* (Garden City, N.Y.: Doubleday, Doran, 1931); Peter C. Mazio, *The Democratic Art: An Exhibition on the History of Chromolithography in America, 1840–1900* (Boston: David R. Godine for the Amon Carter Museum of Western Art, 1979); Bernard F. Reilly Jr., *Currier and Ives: A Catalogue Raisonné* (Detroit: Gale Research, 1984); and Bryan F. LeBeau (Washington, D.C.: Smithsonian Institution Press, 2001). On the development of middle-class culture more generally, see Mary Ryan, *Cradle of the Middle Class: The Family in Oneida Country, New York, 1790–1865* (New York: Cambridge University Press, 1981); Karen Halttunen, *Confidence Men and Painted Women: A Study of Middle-Class Culture in America, 1830–1870* (New Haven: Yale University Press, 1984); Carroll Smith-Rosenberg, *Disorderly Conduct: Visions of Gender in Victorian America* (New York: Knopf, 1985); Stuart Blumin, *The Emergence of the Middle Class: Social Experience in the American City, 1760–1900* (New York: Cambridge University Press, 1989); John Kasson, *Rudeness and Civility: Manners in Nineteenth-Century Urban America* (New York: Hill and Wang, 1990); Richard Bushman, *The Refinement of America: Persons, Houses, Cities* (New York: Knopf, 1992); Joan Shelley Rubin, *The Making of Middlebrow Culture* (Chapel Hill: University of North Carolina Press, 1992); Burton J. Bledstein and Robert D. Johnston, eds., *The Middling Sorts: Explorations in the History of the American Middle Class* (New York: Routledge, 2001).

2. Nathaniel Currier's professional breakthrough was an 1840 lithograph of a steamboat fire for the *New York Sun*.

3. This number is based on the combined listings of Bland, *Currier and Ives: A Manual*, and Reilly, *Currier and Ives: A Catalogue Raisonné*. Currier and Ives also produced a few lithographs for Barnum that were not part of the Gallery of Wonders series. See, for example, Currier's *First Visit of Jenny Lind in America* (1850), reproduced in Philip B. Kunhardt Jr., Philip B. Kunhardt III, and Peter W. Kunhardt, *P. T. Barnum: America's Greatest Showman* (New York: Knopf, 1995), 97.

4. Plumb was a major figure in the early daguerreotype industry and maintained a gallery just a few blocks away from Barnum's museum. See Floyd Rinhart and Marion Rinhart, *The American Daguerreotype* (Athens: University of Georgia Press, 1981). At least three other lithographs in the Gallery of Wonders series (figures 13, 20, 25 in the present book) were similarly modeled after photographs. For reproductions of the photographic sources, see Kunhardt Jr. et al., *P. T. Barnum*, 112–13, 162.

5. Recent scholarship has gone a long way in exploring the ideological complexities of this cultural phenomenon. See Leslie Fiedler, *Freaks: Myths and Images of the Secret Self* (New York: Simon and Schuster, 1977); Robert Bogdan, *Freak Show: Presenting Human Oddities for Fun and Profit* (Chicago: University of Chicago Press, 1988); Ivan Karp and Steven Levine, eds., *Exhibiting Culture: Poetics and Politics of Museum Display* (Washington, D.C.: Smithsonian Institution Press, 1991); Susan Stewart, *On Longing: Narratives of the Miniature, the Gigantic, the Souvenir, the Collection* (Durham, N.C.: Duke University Press, 1993); Rosemarie Garland Thomson, ed., *Freakery: Cultural Spectacles of the Extraordinary Body* (New York: New York University Press, 1996); Bluford Adams, *E Pluribus Barnum: The Great Showman and the Making of U.S. Popular Culture* (Minneapolis: University of Minnesota Press, 1997); John Kuo Wei Tchen, *New York before Chinatown* (Balti-

more: Johns Hopkins University Press, 1999); James W. Cook, *The Arts of Deception: Playing with Fraud in the Age of Barnum* (Cambridge, Mass.: Harvard University Press, 2001); and Rachel Adams, *Sideshow U.S.A.* (Chicago: University of Chicago Press, 2001).

6. Surprisingly, this episode does not appear in any previous study of Barnum's career. For contemporary coverage of Tillman's rescue effort, see *Christian Recorder*, July 27, 1861; *Har-*

per's Weekly, August 3, 1861; *New York Times,* December 24 and 25, 1861; and William Wells Brown, *The Negro in the American Rebellion* (Boston: Lee and Shepard, 1867).

7. Reilly lists one other print with the same bilingual pattern: *The Wonderful Albino Family / La Maravilosa Familia Albi* (*Catalogue Raisonée,* #7311, pp. 756–57). A copy is now held by the Library of Congress: digital ID# cph 3b51176.

GALLERY 4
BARNUM'S PUBLIC RECEPTION

1. Neil Harris, *Humbug: The Art of P. T. Barnum* (Chicago: University of Chicago Press, 1973), 61.

2. I discuss this issue further in *The Arts of Deception: Playing with Fraud in the Age of Barnum* (Cambridge, Mass.: Harvard University Press, 2001), 1–29, 73–167.

3. Cornish edited two of the nation's earliest African-American newspapers: *Freedom's Journal* (1827–29) and the *Colored American* (1837–41). Douglass edited *The North Star* (1847–51) and *Frederick Douglass' Paper* (1851–59). Tanner was editor of the African Methodist Episcopal Church's *Christian Recorder* between 1867 and 1884.

4. For helpful discussion of consumer "knowingness" in a related context, see Peter Bailey, *Popular Culture and Performance in the Victorian City* (New York: Cambridge University Press, 1998), 128–50.

5. Roosevelt's criticism of the European avant-garde was provoked by the 1913 Armory Show in New York City.

6. Michael Walsh was a well-known Irish-American printer, editor, and politician. His weekly periodical, *The Subterranean,* operated in New York City for two years before a libel conviction forced Walsh out of business.

7. This article first appeared in the English satirical journal *Punch.*

8. This text comes from a review of Barnum's 1855 autobiography.

9. *The Drunkard,* William H. Smith's 1844 temperance drama, was among the best-known plays to appear at Barnum's Lecture Room Theater. Like much of the moralizing fare that Bar-

num featured during this period, the play had an earlier run at Moses Kimball's Boston Museum.

10. *Godey's Lady's Book* was the most popular women's magazine of the mid-nineteenth century. Featuring fiction, poetry, and advice columns, *Godey's* helped create the era's dominant ideals of feminine style and virtue.

11. Horatio Bateman, a Boston shoe merchant, operated one of the most successful "colored" baby shows that ran in parallel with Barnum's whites-only contests. On the relationship between these shows, see Bluford Adams, *E Pluribus Barnum: The Great Showman and the Making of U.S. Popular Culture* (Minneapolis: University of Minnesota Press, 1997), 97–111. Significantly, Barnum never put his name on Bateman's Boston enterprise, although Douglass's correspondent clearly suspected that the New York showman was behind it.

12. Eight more columns of text, listing the entire contents of the American Museum, follow here in the original.

13. The August 10, 1865, issue of *The Nation* contained a lengthy letter from Barnum responding to some of the criticisms in this piece.

14. Clemens is referring to Barnum's unsuccessful run for the U.S. Congress in 1867. Barnum did, however, serve multiple terms in the Connecticut state legislature between 1865 and 1880. He was also elected mayor of Bridgeport in 1875.

15. William Cameron Coup first worked with Barnum's Asiatic Caravan, Museum, and Menagerie during the early 1850s. In 1869, Coup became a partner with Dan Castello, a former

acrobat, clown, and animal trainer. A year later, Coup and Castello coaxed Barnum out of retirement, forming the largest circus company in American history, P. T. Barnum's Grand Traveling Museum, Menagerie, Caravan, and Circus. In 1872, the company became the first to travel by rail.

16. Barnum et al. were acquitted the next day. See the *Washington Post,* April 4 and 5, 1883.

17. The animal in question here was Barnum's rare white elephant, Toung Taloung. For much of the previous year, Barnum had devoted himself to securing the wonder and negotiating its transfer from Burma to Madison Square Garden. In this case, the novelty was indeed genuine. Right from the start, however, Barnum's control of the public reception was tenuous. Some critics denounced the idea of white elephants as pure fiction; others argued that the showman's stories of Burmese religious rituals represented a crass marketing gimmick; still others pointed to the disappointing color of the beast, which, by most accounts, was somewhere in the gray range. Barnum's rival, Adam Forepaugh, added insult to injury by introducing a brighter, whiter specimen named Light of Asia (which, in fact, was an ordinary circus elephant covered in plaster). For more on the controversy, see Harris, *Humbug,* 266–70; James W. Cook, "Humbug Universal: P. T. Barnum and Perils of Artful Deception," paper delivered at the 2000 American Studies Association Meeting, Detroit, Michigan, November 2000; and Janet Davis, *The Circus Age: Culture and Society under the American Big Top* (Chapel Hill: University of North Carolina Press, 2002), 252.

18. George Oscar Starr became a press agent for Barnum in 1878. Prior to the 1889 tour, the showman sent Starr to England as an acquisitions specialist.

Index

JAMES W. COOK is associate professor of history and
American culture at the University of Michigan.
He is the author of *The Arts of Deception:
Playing with Fraud in the Age of Barnum.*

The University of Illinois Press
is a founding member of the
Association of American University Presses.

———————————————————————

Composed in Berthold Walbaum
with Poster Bodoni and Gill Sans display
by Celia Shapland
for the University of Illinois Press
Designed by Copenhaver Cumpston
Manufactured by Sheridan Books, Inc.

UNIVERSITY OF ILLINOIS PRESS
1325 South Oak Street · Champaign, IL 61820-6903
www.press.uillinois.edu